PRAISE F

Save the .

T0248704

"[A] wry *Sex and the City*–style memoir . . . Engaging and disarmingly honest."
—*People*

"Doll herself is a funny, bright, complicated leading lady . . . Contemporary heroines are not necessarily brides; they are also the friends, colleagues, classmates of brides, and their stories do not want for depth just because they're not the ones wearing white. Doll's own story—a good one—lays out a disruptive new path."
—*The New York Times Book Review*

"Chronicled with the sharply wielded wit that presumably got [Doll] invited to so many weddings in the first place . . . [*Save the Date*] touches a cultural nerve, ultimately, because it summons, in unsparing detail, a cultural ritual as relentless as it is familiar."
—*Newsweek*

"A smart examination of just how weird weddings can be when put under the microscope. . . . The ultimate wedding party favor is a good story. Doll has several."
—*Time*

"A meditation on the marriage ceremony and on how, by bearing witness, we shape our perspectives on love, friendship, and commitment . . . Advice anyone seated at the singles table can take to heart."
—*Entertainment Weekly*

"Anyone who has ever witnessed a wedding will appreciate Jen Doll's wry pew-side musings."
—*Good Housekeeping*

"An endearingly funny memoir of the writer's vast experience watching other people get married—and the lessons she's learned about love, friendship, and herself."
—*O, The Oprah Magazine*

"To prepare yourself for the summer-wedding onslaught, grab Jen Doll's ingeniously subtitled new book." —GQ

"*Save the Date* is the kind of amusing and inventive memoir that's almost impossible to put down and ripe for sharing amongst friends (bring this baby to your next girls' brunch and watch your lady friends clamor to be the first to borrow it). It's breezy and quick and dead funny, but it also aims straight for the heart with the kind of wit and honesty anyone would want to cherish for many years to come." —Bustle

"Droll, charming . . . chock-full of hilarious observations . . . lively anecdotes . . . and lovely description." —Slate

"Hilarious." —Flavorwire

"Jen Doll knows all the ins and outs of attending and taking part in someone else's big day . . . for better or worse. . . . In [*Save the Date*] she shares some thoughtful (and funny) insights into dating relationships, marriage, and friendship." —PopSugar

"[*Save the Date*] offers witty and smart insights into modern wedding culture, while still having a good time with all the tomfoolery." —The Frisky

"A witty, easily devoured memoir, simultaneously personal and universal." —The Huffington Post

"The insightful, soothing literary balm you need when you're stuck at the destination beach wedding you've paid too much to attend." —The Daily Beast

"*Save the Date* is a hilarious, open-eyed account of one woman's life as a wedding guest. Doll chronicles the good, the bad, and the drunken with wit and insight into the state of modern marriage."

— J. Courtney Sullivan, author of *The Engagements* and *Maine*

"Reading *Save the Date* is like attending a wedding with the coolest plus-one ever. Jen Doll is witty, charming, and can see through all the BS of the wedding culture while still having a fun time with it."

—Drew Magary, author of *Someone Could Get Hurt* and *The Postmortal*

"Jen Doll's sharp, funny true tales of guesthood acknowledge— at last—that attending other people's weddings is a unique rite of passage in itself. *Save the Date* is a welcome companion."

—Wendy McClure, author of *The Wilder Life*

"Jen Doll addresses relationships, romance, weddings, and love with the sharp and intuitive eye of a psychotherapist, and the impeccable comic timing of, well, an impeccably good comedian. Not only that, she coins a phrase that is not only brilliant, but important: 'My unemployment jeans.' *Save the Date* is a self-examination of the single gal at its cleverest, funniest best."

—Sara Barron, author of *People Are Unappealing: Even Me*

"With humor and honesty . . . Doll offers a refreshing take on society's evolving ideas on marriage and the importance of knowing oneself."   —*Publishers Weekly*

"Doll is an engaging guide through the landscape of modern-day courtship and nuptials."   —*Booklist*

"A thoughtful meditation on the institution of marriage . . . A great book to pack for the plane ride to that friend's destination wedding . . . [a] fun rumination on love, marriage, and adult friendship."   —*Library Journal*

Save the Date

*The Occasional Mortifications
of a Serial Wedding Guest*

JEN DOLL

RIVERHEAD BOOKS

New York

Riverhead Books
An imprint of Penguin Random House LLC
375 Hudson Street
New York, New York 10014

Copyright © 2014 by Jen Doll
The Library of Congress has catalogued the Riverhead hardcover edition as follows:

Doll, Jen.
Save the date / Jen Doll.
p.   cm.
ISBN 978-1-59463-198-6
1. Marriage.   2. Weddings—Planning.   I. Title.
HQ519.D635   2014   2013037123
392.5—dc23

Printed in the United States of America
1   3   5   7   9   10   8   6   4   2

Riverhead hardcover edition: May 2014
Riverhead trade paperback edition: May 2015
Riverhead trade paperback ISBN: 978-1-59463-386-7

Book design by Gretchen Achilles

*Names and identifying characteristics have been changed to protect
the privacy of the individuals involved.*

Penguin is committed to publishing works of quality and integrity.
In that spirit, we are proud to offer this book to our readers;
however, the story, the experiences, and the words
are the author's alone.

For Mom and Dad, Brad and Scarlett,
and all the wedding guests

"Saw a wedding in the church. It was strange to see what
delight we married people have to see these poor fools
decoyed into our condition."

—SAMUEL PEPYS

"It is such a happiness when good people get together—
and they always do."

—JANE AUSTEN, *Emma*

Author's Note

✦

The stories that follow may not be absolutely chronological, nor the napkins that precise shade of blue, but the events and my emotions are presented honestly, as I remember experiencing them. That, along with a waitstaff that pours generously and returns regularly to refill your glass, is one of the main things you can hope for with regard to a wedding.

Contents

✦

1.

I Bought You
a KitchenAid

✦

Allow me to begin by saying, I am very, very happy for you. Allow me to begin by saying, Once upon a time there was a girl who met a boy, and they fell in love and wanted to be together forever, and she wore white, and he wore a tux, and they walked down an aisle strewn with rose petals into their bright, shining future. That girl was not me. Congratulations! Or is it best wishes? Here is your KitchenAid. Le Creuset Dutch oven. Kate Spade stemware. Crate&Barrel flatware. Highball glasses. Crystal paperweight shaped like a heart. Hundred-dollar gift card to that furniture store you like. "Informal pasta," whatever that is; you had it on your registry, so it *must* be good! Four tea towels, a stainless-steel garlic press, a "Love" coaster set, a pack of organic coffee filters, and a butter knife, because I didn't have a moment until just before this grand event to go online and buy you anything and that was all that was left. Your family sure is proactive.

How can you stand them? Oh, here is your bowl. Yes, I bought you a bowl. I realize it wasn't on your registry, but I got it for free when I bought the same bowl for myself. I guess that doesn't mean I bought it so much as acquired it, but, wait, I'm talking too much, aren't I? You look amazing! Cheers to the gorgeous couple! Yes, please, a refill would be excellent.

But let's backtrack.

Weddings.

Sometimes they come once a year and seem like a good excuse to go on a vacation to a predetermined destination, a place with built-in friends and a legitimate purpose and even a prepared schedule of activities, a wedding gift basket waiting for you in the hotel room, packed with granola bars and locally derived tchotchkes and miniature bottles of sunscreen. Sometimes they come like migrating birds or wolves, in flocks or packs. When you glance behind your shoulder, there's another one gaining ground, and you can't seem to stay ahead of them no matter what you do. They've got their eye on you. Sometimes it seems every weekend is a wedding. On the odd occasion, one weekend brings two, forcing the invited into a perilous decision-making scenario that has grave, long-lasting consequences: Which couple will be anointed friends forever, and which will descend slowly but surely into the status of "mere acquaintances," their big day having been forsaken? Intrepid guests who don't want to choose will go to both, driving for miles, taking red-eye flights, swapping out dresses and shoes and jewelry and handbags and itineraries as if actors in a play or models in a fashion show, which is a not entirely inaccurate depiction of a particular State of Wedding Guesthood. *This is just what's happening to us right now*, the wedding guest of a certain age will think, gasping for breath but shrugging it off, going along. *We've reached that stage in life. It's only temporary. This, too, will pass!* At some point, surely, the perpetual wedding dance will cease, and we will be able to sit back in the comfort of our wedding guest retirement and possibly even save a little money by not going to so many weddings. But while we're going to weddings, we should try to have fun at weddings. They only happen how many times a year? Well, we really have no other choice.

And oh, there is fun! There is plenty of fun. There's fun even before you get to the chapel or the reception hall or the rented suite of the fancy hotel or the country club or your best friend's parents' backyard. The weeks and months preceding each wedding will inevitably involve secondary parties—bachelorettes and bachelors and showers and engagement celebrations and whatever else is deemed necessary to get the crowd pumped for the headliner. Do not be fooled by these seemingly casual add-ons: They are the octopus tentacles of the ultimate party, stretching farther in all directions, part and parcel of an event that in most cases, when all is said and done, guests will have shelled out rather a lot of time and energy and cash to attend. We do this willingly, even joyfully, because not only are we often actually quite happy to be there but also this is an algorithm we've been brought up to believe in. Tit for wedding tat; eventually it will be our turn, too, and we'll get back everything we've given and possibly more. You go to my wedding; I'll go to yours. I'll buy you a heart-shaped waffle maker (in stainless steel, per your request); you'll eventually return the favor with an enameled stockpot in

Marseille blue. There's little time to consider whether this formula will resolve as promised, who's getting a better deal, or if we even want our turn in the wedding lineup of the ages—and if we do, how and when and why—because we're already on to the after-party! The fun never stops.

To a single woman, a lifetime of weddings can begin to seem like a nuptial-themed *Groundhog Day*; we guests behaving slightly differently each time within the same basic framework as we strive for the ending that will put a stop to the unremitting weddings, or at least to the way we've been methodically acting our way through them. The story of a serial wedding goer is rarely the impeccable scenario depicted in the brochures and magazines or promised by the wedding planner, nor does it align with the aspirations of a pushy mother of the bride, an entitled groom, or one of those so-called bridezillas (such an awful word). The dream-wedding-in-the-bubble, the "perfect day" meticulously constructed to suit the whims or long-held fantasies of the marrying couple or their kin, is all too easily punctured by wedding guests who don't share quite those same goals and aspirations. Or who get drunk and then decide they don't. A "perfect day" becomes an entirely unrealistic concept when you start to let in the riffraff, not least because "perfect" is a matter of opinion. There is no "perfect day." There is only the day upon which two people are married, for better or worse.

Sometimes those days are worse. Take, for example, the wedding in Connecticut where I lost my mind and my shoes, the latter quite literally. (Wedding Tip: Avoid nihilism; the aftermath is bleak.) But there are many shades of weddings, and wedding guesthood: The destination wedding in the Dominican Republic, the first wedding of a college friend, was attended with none of the cynicism of my later years and, indeed, with little baggage beyond a suitcase full of colorful bikinis, strappy sandals, and summery party dresses. My best friend's wedding in Nashville involved the unraveling of my own relationship set upon the foundation of hers. Another series of weddings meant the painful end to what had been a valued friendship. There was the courthouse ceremony of two very good friends, a strikingly modest affair compared to the exotic locations of my wedding-going past—and no less satisfying for it. In the future looms my brother's wedding, yet to be planned despite an engagement and the dwindling comments of my parents, who've gotten tired of asking when. There was the wedding of relative strangers, attended with a date offering all the promise of new love. Someday, maybe, there will be my own wedding. Or maybe there won't be.

The wedding isn't the thing; it's what comes after that's truly important, yet the wedding is our focus, the vehicle chosen to represent a couple's love and the guests' love for that couple. It's an established, functional transaction, but it's also a performance with only a certain level of truth to it, everyone well dressed and on their best behavior—or at least, that's the idea. It's supposed to mean more than it does, to be more than a party or a day. With all the implications and expectations riding on this single event, it should be no surprise that things occasionally go off course.

The wedding stories that follow are my own, but attending weddings and even occasionally making a jerk of oneself as a wedding guest are shared experiences. Indiscretions and accidents and even major missteps are bound to occur, particularly when you add in the free-flowing alcohol, the tremendous amount of social pressure for everything to be "perfect," and the guests—the uncontrollable, incorrigible, independent-minded guests. We come, we see, we do not always conquer. Then, quick as a flash, the wedding is over, leaving us with traces of what we have learned and what we steadfastly deny learning . . . until the inevitable next one, featuring a revised color scheme and costumes, different flowers, a varied assortment of fresh players, and possible new feelings, or the old ones brought forth again, almost as if it were the first time.

While one might assume a wedding is about *them*—the couple getting married—a wedding is about everyone. It's a means through which we guests can identify and reidentify our friends, our enemies, our lovers, and those we no longer love. Through it we see what we want, what we don't want, what we think we want, and sometimes, dangerously, that we have no idea what we want. Each wedding we attend, in whatever role we uphold, will highlight some aspect of our own lives, reflecting and reframing the way in which we look at ourselves. We do not go to weddings as blank slates. The event may be a happy one, but we are still whoever we are, beings comprising our past histories as well as our desired futures, when we show up to celebrate.

At the very first wedding I remember with any clarity, I was eight and my brother was five. We danced exuberantly around the tables and on the dance floor. The cake-cutting was as engrossing as any Disney movie. We learned to our great pleasure that a lift of one's fork to a glass would impel the bride and groom to kiss. What strange power that was! Love and this celebration of it seemed, frankly, wonderful, and it also seemed inevitable. But nearly thirty years later, neither of us is married, though I *have* been to more than twenty weddings.

Think of how many you have attended that you remember. Then think of how many you don't remember, exactly or completely, because you were a child or perhaps very, very drunk, but nonetheless there exists horrifying photographic evidence of your attendance—yep, there it is! Untag yourself now. Imagine how many you'll have been to by the end of a life long and well lived, out of duty, friendship, hope, love, jealousy, self-torture, guilt, desire for free food or drink, or some confusing potluck mix of emotions. Sometimes the emotions evolve and change and are created anew right there at the wedding. Consider all the roles you'll have played, from guest to sister to bridesmaid to maid of honor to friend to colleague to date to person who has no idea why she's been invited—nor why she's come—to the one who will hook up with the best man, no questions asked, so that the bride and groom can, as they put it, "live vicariously" through her. We smile and nod and agree and wear what we must wear and do what we should do (or we try, we really try) because it's their big day. It's a wedding.

Count the dresses worn, gifts given, plane tickets purchased, and hotel rooms rented; the boyfriends forced to tag along and split the cost, or the groups of girlfriends shacked up for those weird adult slumber parties based in economy, hotel vanities cluttered with makeup and hygienic accoutrements, a cot shoved into a corner, an additional roommate sneaked past the eyes of hotel management to save a few more dollars. Number the brave or irreverent times you've gone solo and paired up with a grooms-man or another wedding guest—and the other times, nights ended alone watching pay-per-view in an anonymous hotel room, the wastebasket next to the bed (just in case), or crumpled, tear-soaked tissues surrounding the pillow. Add up the bouquets held for brides, the bouquets caught, and the bouquets abandoned at our feet, each petal an unspoken accusation. Make a note of the dances danced, glasses of Champagne sipped, speeches delivered, goblets struck with the silver tines of forks held in fingers mani-cured, smiles forced, smiles honestly given, tears shed, friends and strangers embraced, hangovers and regrets treated the next morning. How many feelings have we had? *How many feelings.*

Like the weddings, the feelings never end. Sometimes we have all of them at just one outwardly simple—simple but *elegant*—nuptial occasion held at the quaintest of inns in rural Vermont, or at a tropical resort set in cliffs and surrounded by impossibly blue water in Jamaica, or at the tree-lined, leafy-lawned country clubs of the hometowns we haven't been back to since graduating from high school and aren't sure we ever want to return to again. The feelings can grow greater than the weddings themselves as they play out in heightened relief each time we again bear witness to a couple pairing off and heading down the aisle, leaving us alone, date or no date—and let's get this straight: Being part of a couple doesn't mean we're not alone. Couplehood can make us lonelier than ever, especially if we're in a certain kind of couple-hood, barely hanging on, sniping and snarking or not really talking, or at least not "communicating," making it through yet another wedding.

For many of us who are single, it's not that we're dying to be married. It's more complicated than that. We'd never get married *just to be married*. We're set on finding that right one, whoever and however that may be, if we're going to do this thing. And yet, there's a certain misty desire that filters through even the most perseverant of hearts at the sight of a marrying couple, neither of them any better than us individually but somehow greater as two, vowing to stay together forever. All of this hope and light and the expectant faces and eager congratulations thrust upon the moment make it something we think we want, that we've been brought up to want. It is something of a luxury to be able to feel ambivalent about weddings, and yet, it's hard to feel *truly* ambivalent about weddings, about the institution as well as the reality of marriage. Both macro and micro, in the fabric of life, weddings are a primary thread—which is yet another reason denying any adult the right to weave that thread into his or her life seems so blatantly cruel, small-minded, and wrong.

But given the choice to marry, if we *don't* marry, are we, in fact, missing out? Is there something wrong with us if we never go down that aisle in the white dress or the crisply pressed tux, adhering to those old-fashioned, still-resonating traditions with our loved ones on hand to watch and support and celebrate?

Or is there something wrong with us if we do?

That what a marriage is in practice is hardly the same as this brief flower-and-cake-and-love-studded moment, the wedding itself but a second in hoped-for years and years of life together, means that if we're part of a couple already and watching it unfold, we might begin to wonder if we made the right decision, if he or she is "the one" after all. As for those of us who remain unpaired, wanting love or the idea of love at the same time we're figuring out what exactly that means, or who we even are: Many of us believe deeply but unspokenly that the "final wedding"— the one that will mean the end of all of those single-person concerns and erratic, complicated ways we have of behaving at weddings—will be our own, the answer to so many lifelong questions. After that moment, the rest of our lives, our real lives, can finally begin.

Of course, it doesn't quite work that way. As it turns out, our real lives have been happening the whole time.

This is the story of a serial wedding goer. Thank you for having me. I'm sorry to anyone I've ever offended. I really did have a very nice time.

2.

Something Blue

✦

All the single ladies! All the single ladies! Single ladies, please come to the front of the dance floor!" The call reverberated through the room, causing the chandeliers to shake and the ice cubes to clink in our crystal water glasses. All of us so being roused were human women between the ages of twenty and thirty; all of us were living on our own, had been living on our own for years, in fact. All of us were gainfully employed, and some of us were aspiring for things more than gainful. We were also, yes, unmarried, though that's hardly all we were, and we'd tell you that, point-blank, if you were to ask.

We were at a country club on Cape Cod, surrounded by acres and acres of manicured, impossibly green golf course. But more than green, we were surrounded by blue: blooming blue hydrangeas the color of baby bonnets and Easter eggs, planted around the perimeter of the building and then some—out in the distance, amid all the green, you could see more blue. Farther out, the deepest shades of the sea met those of the cornflower horizon.

Inside the country club, the walls were lined in periwinkle, or maybe it was Wedgwood, a slightly lighter tint than the deep royal of the plush chair cushions upon which we perched, legs crossed at the ankles, ladylike, sipping Champagne. Still lighter were the pale blue linen napkins spread primly across our laps, and darkest of all was what pumped through the veins of so many around us, or so I had heard whispered, mouths covered by hand-kerchiefs held in the withered blue hands of some of the older women present. It would have been impolite to mention, so I didn't, but many of these blues appeared to be in fierce competition with one another.

It was late afternoon. The day had been hot and long, begin-ning on the beach, where we saw our friend marry her now-husband as the tide came in a few minutes too soon, or the wedding, more likely, had happened just a few minutes too late, despite careful timing based on the lunar schedule. For a moment midway through the ceremony, we were separated from the cou-ple and their minister, the three of them on a temporary reef while the rest of us watched from a narrowing peninsula. Many of us took off our shoes and moved our folding chairs; others chose to stand on top of those chairs, a precarious decision that ended wetly for a few. There was a brief pause while, some of us damp, others damper, we found our way to drier land and laughed and hushed one another and laughed some more at this sudden, unexpected lightness in the serious, formal moment. Quickly, before the tides moved farther, the vows were given and the cer-emony was over. The string quartet disappeared into the tall sand grass and up into the dunes with their cumbersome loads, the rest of us traipsing behind, happy to be headed indoors, on to the next portion of the wedding.

I was wearing a white dress. I know, I know. I was twenty-eight and had been fully versed in the etiquette—one is not supposed to wear a white dress to a wedding unless one is herself the bride—but my justification for the choice was that the dress was only white in the most basic of ways, as a canvas. On top of the white, at the neckline, the dress was embroidered with an array of flowers, purple and pink and yellow and red; notably absent, in this small case, was any blue. There was a wide purple sash that clasped around the waist, and though the majority of the full knee-length skirt was white, there was stitching around the hem to match the flowers that lined the top. The three thin straps that held the dress up over each shoulder were purple, the same hue as the belt and my kitten heels. I liked this dress, and I wanted to wear it. *So there*, I thought. This was not my first rodeo.

Inside the country club there was a plentiful spread of upper-crust fare, food like chilled shrimp and new potato salad, rare steak, pâté with grainy mustard and sour gherkins, and the tiniest, sweetest decorated cakes for dessert. The string quartet had repositioned themselves to provide blithe musical accompaniment to our eating and drinking. There was always so much wine at these things, but wine was something I associated with this friend in particular—the one who was now a Mrs.—and, in fact, with all of us. There were six of us here who were close. We'd gone to college together and had become inseparable during a semester in Italy, which itself was permeated with wine. At night during those spring-into-summer months we'd sit together at alfresco cafés, sipping countless vinos and smoking cigarettes badly as we chattered in the way of college-aged American women in foreign countries. Smoke billowed from our mouths, but our pleather pants, comfortingly tight, kept us in check as we reminisced about what we missed back home: our boyfriends, American cheese, our hairdressers' mastery of subtle blond highlights. More and more frequently, though, we spoke not of what we'd left behind, but of the future.

I was arguably the one closest to the bride. We'd dated brothers: hers the younger who went to our school, mine the one who'd graduated from another university a few years earlier and come to visit his sibling on the weekend we met. Once we'd dined out with the boys' parents, gossiping to each other in the ladies' room about the meticulous mother and avuncular father. There we'd confided our mutual surety that we were hated by them, even as, I think now, we each felt ourselves to be the one favored in the parents' eyes. We eventually broke up with the boys—me first, Ginny shortly thereafter; or at least, that's how I remember it. But she and I stayed together and grew closer. We graduated from college and at one point were nearly roommates. It was not to be. Neither, ultimately, was our friendship. This was the friend who chose marriage over me.

It sounds complicated, even illicit, but in one way it was actually very simple: Ginny and I were the best of friends until she chose a man whom I found I could not be friends with. She could not forgive me for that, and for what transpired because of it, no more than I could forgive her for choosing as she had. As I saw it, she'd done the unthinkable: marriage to someone who didn't treat her the way I felt she deserved to be treated; marriage, even, for the sake of being married. That she wouldn't acknowledge my concerns galled me further. I didn't understand how with this engagement she could pretend all was rosy and turn a blind eye to what, from my vantage point, still felt so unresolved. She thought that I didn't understand—that I refused to understand, perhaps—and should have supported her choice regardless; friends should have each other's backs, in romance as in everything else. Quite possibly, she was right. *Definitely* I should have done things differently. But by the point it became clear that our friendship would be the sacrificial lamb in all this, we'd gone too far down that road to turn back.

At her wedding, however, we were still okay. We were still friends. I may have had my doubts, but I was hiding them, I thought well. I had put on my dress and I would dance and celebrate and enjoy myself, and enjoy her, too, my friend who looked so beautiful and happy I could almost forget about those other things, information about her relationship I held in my mind but wasn't supposed to consider now: the bitter squabbles, the unkindnesses and misunderstandings and questionable truths. These are behaviors exhibited by nearly every couple in some way or another, but in her retellings they had made me wonder whether my friend might be making a terrible decision. Worse, it was a decision I worried she thought she had to make because she was on the verge of thirty, and he had asked, and would there be another chance again?

But this was hardly productive thinking. I was at a wedding!

This was a fresh start, the leap they were taking together, and he wanted it, and so did she. Would it kill me to embrace it? Your friends always tell you about the fights, about the problems in their relationships, far more so than they share the good stuff, I reminded myself. It wasn't as if he'd been physically abusive, or done anything illegal—the circumstances were far less black-and-white than that. Yet in some way that only made how to negotiate the situation more confusing. If it was purely that I thought she could do better, well, who was I to say? Who was I to tell them, or anyone, how they should live their lives, who they should date, who they should marry? It's not like I had things figured out, but she, by all appearances, had figured *this* out. She'd chosen him. Here we were, amid all the pomp and circumstance of that choice.

So I pretended to be happy, so happy my face felt like it would nearly split from all the happiness. Outside on the porch a boy who I suppose was really a man, with brown hair and too-intense eyes (I didn't need anyone to see through me to the truth), told me he liked my dress. He asked if I was single. I told him I was seeing someone, which was true, though he wasn't here with me. Awkwardly, the most recent person I had dated previously *was* here, with another woman. He was the man whom Ginny and her husband—*husband*, I had to get used to that—had introduced me to in the beginning, when it seemed like everything was shaping up to be great, when it seemed like we'd at the very least double-date our way into the blue, blue horizon. My feelings for this ex had by now dulled into near nothingness. The fact that he had brought a date who was wearing a tacky neon-green dress, a date who all of my friends told me I was *so much better than* (they were kind, my friends, even if they were liars), didn't thrill me with the satisfaction it might have months ago, when the breakup had been fresh and my feelings raw. The sadness in me was a different kind and not something that could be fixed with a man, whether it was getting attention from a new one or making an old one feel regret.

"Single ladies to the dance floor!" came the cry again, a masculine voice urging us forward. Couples parted, creating a narrow path for the responding train of unmarried women to parade through in their finery to that designated spot where they would be awarded the opportunity to grapple for what was far more than a clutch of secondhand flowers. But we single ladies no longer looked so fine, so sparkling or radiant as we had that morning. We were worn and tired, sweat beading down our necks, hair up in makeshift buns, sand between our toes and crunching unpleasantly in our shoes, which were wearing raw the backs of our heels. Our faces were red and shiny, and our mouths had the slackness of a full day of drinking. We should have been lying down in cool rooms elsewhere, dresses uncinched, the blinds drawn, glasses of icy, hydrating water next to us. But the wedding was not over. We knew what was next.

My friend Nora grabbed my arm and pulled me close. "Do we have to do this?" she whispered. "This is so embarrassing. Isn't it sort of, you know, sexist? I cannot believe bouquet tosses still happen in this day and age."

"Let's go hide out in the bathroom," I suggested. The bathroom was a nice place at this country club. I'd noticed it had supplies of deodorant and hair spray and hand lotion, as well as wipes for dabbing the day's perspiration from one's nose and cheeks and forehead. There were mints and packs of gum and miniature bottles of Listerine, too. It was better than being out here. We could probably even take a bottle of wine with us. But it was too late. We'd been herded along with the rest of them, and there was no way to hide or break rank without making a scene. I could see the bride's mother eyeing me. It seemed that she, if no one else, was keenly aware of how I really felt. So we proceeded in mincing little chain-gang steps as if we were all somehow attached at the ankle, a line of grown-up women marching forward in our brightly colored dresses, once smartly pressed, now limp from the doings of this long July day. There was Ginny, next to the band, facing us. Her new husband stood away from the crowd, watching her with an expression that I found inscrutable. The guy with the biggest instrument, the cello, I think, picked up the microphone and said with one of those comedic trills in his voice, as if to be followed by a *bah-dah-bum*: "It's time, ladieeeeees, the big moment you've all been waiting for—the bouquet toss!"

Nora and I glanced at each other, and I mouthed, *Hell, no*, because somehow we were positioned front and center, and then Ginny was closing her eyes and thrusting her two hands skyward. Her wedding-toned arms followed in a graceful arc, her triceps rippling with the slightest edge of defined-yet-ladylike muscle. Her diamond was glinting in the sun, and that photo-ready bouquet of ice-water-blue hydrangeas she'd picked from her mother's own garden was soaring up high. I closed my eyes, too, because I didn't know what else to do. There was a light thud, and then there was silence.

When I opened my eyes, there it was. The women had not moved. Not one of us had spoken or stepped across the invisible line that separated us from the bride. A few spots down, another guest gestured silently, *Pick it up! Pick it up!* but it's not like she was leaning in to grab it, either. Nora was frozen, halfway between laughter and tears, and I didn't dare look at Ginny or her mom, so instead, I did this: I stepped back. I stepped away from the bouquet, which had landed, a flat sack of impending floral decay, directly in front of my feet in their dainty purple shoes that had seemed comfortable so many hours ago. I tried to put as much space between those plucked flowers and myself as I could, without seeming to notice them at all. *Oh, I must be going now, I really need a drink refill, it's time to take my medication. What's that you say, we're at a wedding? Thank you so much, I don't even golf!* I feigned complete befuddlement and obliviousness because I simply could not pick up those flowers. I was physically incapable. It would break me. So I stood, shuffling infinitesimally backward, and the seconds seemed like hours.

I was saved from imminent social disgrace by our friend Mattie. Quick as heat lightning preceding the summer storm that would follow that evening, she rushed forward and stooped down and scooped up the bouquet, which she held aloft in her right arm, proud and tall, as if showing off an Olympic gold medal. She even managed a little hop in the air as she shouted, "I got it!"

Ginny beamed. The crowd went wild.

3.

Anything for a Story

✦

Here's a great irony for you: A wedding is something that signifies permanence, but itself is the very opposite of that. It's one day, one insanely orchestrated, improbably beautiful day, that most people hope they won't see fit to repeat in a lifetime with anyone else. And just as the bride and groom and the wedding planner or whoever is in charge do their very best to tell the single story they want to convey at a wedding—to reflect an enduring life state, to make the grand, high-concept, intricately planned moment represent "forever"—the guests, especially those who've been around the wedding block a few times, come with their own small and large dreams, goals, and even a certain number of meticulously plotted MacGyver-esque missions. We all have stories we want to tell, and stories we want to experience so we can tell them later, as we engage in the self-propelled mini-dramas, comedies, and occasional tragedies taking place across the wedding stage. We may not be the main plot, but we are a subplot, and a not unimportant one at that.

Save the Date

From one wedding, I vividly recall moshing sweatily on the dance floor to the Killers and, later, wandering around the after-party looking for the cute guy I'd seen at the reception and had just started to make promising conversation with when the band stopped playing and the bartenders ceased to refill my glass. (Weddings can have the worst timing!) The sweat dried on my bare arms, and later, my skin felt almost crunchy, smelling of salt and sun and eau de Chardonnay. I remember finding that guy and arranging to meet him at a bench outside the bar after I returned to my room for the Red Bull and vodka I had stashed in the mini-fridge. But by the time I got to the room, which I was sharing with a friend, I'd decided not to go back out after all. As she and I compared our own reflections on the evening, we occasionally guessed at the absent third perspective, the guy waiting alone on that bench. Of course, I don't know whether he showed up at the bench at all. Whatever happened to him that night is no more my tale than it is the story of the bride and groom.

At some deep midpoint down the wedding road—say, ten weddings in, in our late twenties or early thirties—we may even try our hand at creating our own stories, inventing dramas to keep things interesting and ourselves on our metallic sandal–clad toes. It's not that weddings are boring, but sometimes we want to bring a piece of ourselves to them that we don't get to put forth in our normal lives. The manufactured ecosystem is already primed for excitement. It's a quick and easy step to throw ourselves on the stage, too, trying out new roles, just to see. We become inherently unreliable narrators, unreliable characters, because we are each there in some way in our own interest and to continue the

21

storyline for which we have come, even as we're *ostensibly* there for our friend/this blessed event/to support the sanctity of marriage/for love/for fun/because we want cake. I suspect that even the most selfless among us can't help bringing it back home now and again, making the wedding in some small way just a teeny-tiny bit about ourselves. It's human nature, and human nature is often bared to its core at a wedding.

I was thirty-three years old and had been to more weddings than I could count on both hands by the time Lucy and David's invite came. I'd met Lucy at the ad agency that had hired us both in our first post-college jobs more than a decade before, and David through Lucy. She'd gone on to become a lawyer, and he was one, too, each of them as ambitious and driven professionally as they were personally unpretentious and laid-back. They'd met at a firm where they'd worked, and they'd become friends there. As they told it, he had a deep crush while she was preoccupied with someone else. Eventually he convinced her to go on a date, and then another, and at some point, the other guy was forgotten and David became the one.

Their wedding would be in June, in Jamaica, and they urged guests to stay for as long as they'd like; make a vacation of it! No longer was I a naive twentysomething with a sundress and a giant bottle of Coppertone traveling to see my first college friend do this crazy grown-up thing. I *was* a grown-up, at least by the standard definition, earning nearly $400 a day as managing editor at

OK!, a celebrity weekly magazine. And I hadn't left New York City in months. The photos on the resort's website depicted an island paradise with tiny villas scattered throughout rocky cliffs, tropical forests full of flowers and lush greenery, and suspension bridges dangling romantically over cerulean water. Plus, free yoga in the morning, open-air showers, fresh fish at the resort's three restaurants, coconut cocktails, sunsets, snorkeling, massages. The wedding itself would be a breeze: Throw on a dress. Walk a few steps to the designated area of the resort where the ceremony would take place in front of a sweeping ocean view. Watch. Celebrate. There were no kids under twelve allowed on the premises given the danger of their falling and injuring themselves on the jagged terrain—an oversight, then, that they *did* allow drunken thirtysomethings. Danger be damned, I was in.

In preparation for the trip, I bought a tropical-print cotton halter dress in sunbaked reds and purples, an emerald-green frock with a skirt full of ruffles, a bright gold silk minidress, and, for more casual outings, a pair of baggy jeans with numerous rips and tears—you know, the kind the quirky-cool retailer names "boyfriend jeans," the kind my mom would question my paying actual money for had she been there. I bought my ticket to Jamaica, reserved a hotel room for a full five nights and six days, and laid down my credit card for an array of trip-related goods and services—including the wedding present. And then one morning, approximately three weeks before I was scheduled for departure, I went to work and came home unemployed. I would go on to wear those ripped-up, baggy jeans for most of the summer, in the absence of a boyfriend or a job, dubbing them my "unemployment jeans."

My parents seemed perplexed that I'd take this rather dire career moment to jet off to Jamaica.

"Are you sure this is wise?" asked my dad.

"I've bought the tickets already," I explained, further rationalizing as only a city dweller can that I'd probably spend less money *off* the island of Manhattan and on another. "Either you have a lot of money and no time," I said sagely, "or time and no money."

My dad grunted, clearly unimpressed by my logic, and later that week a copy of Suze Orman's *The Courage to Be Rich* arrived in the mail. But, I thought, this trip could be exactly what I needed. It would give me a moment to reevaluate this weird professional time (in the sun) and figure out what I really wanted to do. There was something else, too, which I didn't tell my dad—something I'd discovered a few months before buying my ticket. This would be a wedding with a revenge subplot, if the nerdiest revenge subplot that had ever existed. Which meant I *had* to go. It was a story.

As a senior in high school, I had been the captain of my debate team in Decatur, Alabama. I did Lincoln-Douglas debate, which is a talky, moralistic kind of enterprise, values debate as opposed to the "policy" version, in which competitors appeared to just read things out as quickly as they could regardless of intelligibility. For L-D, each person wrote and argued an affirmative and a negative side, alternating through the course of the competition, on specific topics like "Is Assisted Suicide Ever Justified?" or "Should Prostitution Be Legalized?" I was pretty good, hence the captainship and the handful of silver platters, the L-D award of choice, stashed away in my closet at my parents' house. Senior year in the state finals I was up against a boy from Montgomery, Alabama, a prep-school kid with a fancy tie and too-large teeth who seemed all bluster and bravado. He was also two years younger than me. This was my win.

Yet I lost. I was shocked. How could this have happened? Clearly I was better. Clearly this had been fixed, to champion the younger boy from the private school in the state capital over the girl from the public school, the Yankee transplant residing in one of the northern-most of Deep South towns. This was sexism! Paternalism! This was unfair.

After my loss I shook hands with the boy, as we were forced to do, and I noted the smug, self-righteous smile on his face. He, too, thought he'd been better. The indignity of it all too much to bear, I turned away and didn't look back, went to college, got a job, led my life, got another job, went to weddings. But then I found out he'd be at this one. And then I got fired.

He was a friend of the groom. They'd gone to college together. He was single, like me. I'd long forgotten the topic of our debate, and my coming in second had lost any import or meaning in my actual life, but if I was going to face my onetime competitor while dateless at a wedding, you could be certain I'd find a way to win. I was jobless, spending my days writing blog posts for free on a site I had created about being unemployed. I *needed* a win.

In the dinners we had preceding the wedding, Lucy, who found it hilarious that two of her wedding guests had known each other in a way previous life, confessed all she knew about Boyd. That was his name, my high school debate nemesis: *Boyd*. He was, I inferred, still rather full of himself. He was a lawyer. A litigator, of course. He'd dated one girl for a while, but they'd broken up when she moved away. He had recently run a marathon. He was terribly conservative, Republican, at times a self-professed chauvinist. "Oh, you'll hate him," Lucy enthused. "You might even make out with him." I smiled and feigned indifference to what might happen. Then I went home and found that Boyd had friended me on Facebook. *Hahahahahahahaaaaa*, I thought, with imagined diabolical hand-wringing. I would be his wedding kryptonite.

I flew to Montego Bay one early Tuesday morning in June, and at the airport located a driver with an unmarked white van, as the bride and groom had advised, to take me to our spot on the island. Upon arrival I was greeted by the hotel staff and ushered to my small room, one of the cheapest available. It offered just one window, shadowed by an overhanging roof, and my bed was topped with a large mosquito net. Contrary to the photos, my outdoor shower seemed dark and bug-enticing rather than serene and brightly tropical. On the plus side, the refrigerator in the room was stocked with Red Stripe. I popped one open, plugged in my laptop—I'd blog once daily, I had vowed—and unpacked my island attire, changing into my swimsuit and a dress and sandals for my walk to the pool, where I'd been told the happy couple was waiting.

I was one of the first guests to arrive. Boyd was not expected until later in the week. Time to stake out the place and make arrangements as needed, I thought, marveling at how well Mission: Debate Tournament Revenge was working out already. I wasn't sure exactly what I'd do when I finally confronted Boyd—pummel him with coconuts until he admitted his win was unfair? Stage a winner-take-all Round Two debate? Employ the age-old technique of revenge by seduction?—but it seemed like being tan and relaxed, with supple arms from morning yoga, would help.

At the pool, I greeted Lucy and David with hugs and that universal destination-wedding croon of "How lucky are we? This is amazing!" before selecting my lounge chair and beginning the business of relaxing. Outside, everything was as expected: the sun hot, the water cool, the service pleasant, the couple thrilled to spend pre-wedding one-on-one time with someone who had virtually no (ostensible) demands, except to coexist in peace and harmony alongside them in their selected form of paradise. This was a brief lull before the rest of the guests and family arrived, and we all appreciated it for what it was. We stayed at the pool into the late afternoon and ate under the stars that night. In opportune moments, I surreptitiously dug further into the secrets of my wedding nemesis ("So, who at the wedding would you say is the most afraid of snakes?" "Are there any allergies I should know of?"). After dessert the couple went off, hand in hand, to the honeymoon villa, and I trudged back to my slightly damp room by myself and listened to the Kinks on repeat. "Strangers on this road we are/We are not two we are one" kept running through my head even after I shut down for the night. I pulled down the mosquito netting and closed my eyes.

By Thursday evening most of the guests had arrived, and we gathered to eat in the more casual of the restaurants on the premises. That's where I first saw him, my rival, my scourge. He looked about the same. Taller. Wearing a bigger belt. I would have recognized him anywhere at this resort, not least because I knew he'd be there. We were at opposite ends of a long table and so did not talk, but our eyes met, and when they did I would quickly look away, a theme repeated throughout the meal. After dinner, the crowds quickly dispersed into their separate groups, him with his friends, me with mine, and no commingling between. It was a slight disappointment. The next day, I kept scanning the pool deck, gazing laser-eyed and keen into the waves, thinking of what I might say in case he suddenly appeared. There was no sign of him, though, and I started to doubt my initial interpretation of his look, his Facebook friending of me. Maybe he didn't actually want to meet again at all. On the other hand, maybe I had to be patient.

The next night, at the rehearsal dinner, he and I were seated at separate tables. I was across from two friends: Natalie and her fiancé, Luke, who she'd later marry in Connecticut. To the left of me was my newly appointed Best Wedding Friend (BWF), a man named Fred. Fred had gotten to Jamaica early as well, and in the last few days together we'd found the easy harmony of destination-wedding friendship, with all the necessary confidences shared, jokes told, drinks drunk, and our separate lives communally affirmed. We were similar enough at the same time that we were suitably dissimilar: He was gay and stylish and, a matter of key importance, he'd never beaten me in a debate competition. He lived in New York, too, and we'd promised to hang out in the city. We probably meant it.

Fred had known Boyd from college, though they hadn't run in the same crowd. He'd been brought up to speed, of course, on my hankering for restitution of an ancient wrong. He leaned in and reported, "He's looking at you. Oh, oh, he's coming in for the kill . . ."

He was. Not for the kill, per se, but for something. It could be the kill. *What was the kill, anyway?* I turned to Fred to ask, but Boyd was already in earshot, loping toward us in khaki pants and a baby-blue golf shirt that, I wanted to mutter to Fred, only emphasized the lobster hue of his face. (Destination Wedding Tip: SPF.) He stopped, gave us a sort of leering half smile, and slapped my BWF on the back. Fred, who'd been sipping his drink, held back a cough. Boyd then turned to me. "Hello, Ms. Doll," he said, wasting no time pretending he didn't know exactly who I was. "I trust you've had a splendid evening?"

I nodded. "Highly splendid. The most splendid."

"We have something to discuss," he said. "Can I interest you in a nightcap back at my villa? As an added enticement, I have a bottle of Jamaica's finest. And cigarettes. And—"

My suave demeanor was toast, because despite all the plotting and planning, I'd never successfully figured out what I might say in this initial interaction. I was terrible at this, really. I would have sucked at espionage. I relied on the oldest trick in the book: postponement. "Oh, hey, there's Lucy. I have to talk to her," I mumbled, departing hastily and snagging a fresh glass of wine on my way to the bride, who was gazing dreamily out at the water and moonlit sky.

"Did I just see you talking to Boyd?" she asked, snapping to attention. She had always been an excellent multitasker.

"He invited me back to his villa," I told her. "For a nightcap. Who says 'nightcap'?"

"Boyd does. Also, he told David he got that villa on purpose just in case he needed 'extra room for guests.'" Lucy looked at me pointedly.

"What's he going to do, house the wedding band? He hasn't even spoken to me since he got here!" I said.

"Well, he just got here," was her response. "You should give him a chance."

"You think?" This was not the first time I'd been given this advice. There were plenty of paired-up couples in my life who seemed to see me as a hard-hearted ballbuster who never opened up, who refused to even *consider* anyone less than some idealized form of man. In truth, I knew that my heart, though deeply crusted on the outside with a protective layer of sarcasm and revenge schemes, was as welcomingly pliable as any of the hearts of the married twosomes I'd seen into wedlock. I might present a tough barrier, but it was a thin one, and once a man had found his way in, I was as accepting as anyone else, possibly more so, probably to a fault. I was starting to consider another truth: that I gave too many chances to people who didn't deserve them.

But with Boyd, we were suspended in the faux reality of the wedding. Whether I gave him a chance or not didn't really matter, not in terms of any permanent situation, not in terms of having to clean something up afterward. Not in terms of heartbreak. He'd made an offer, the most basic of overtures. I knew I could take it or leave it, and I knew that leaving an offer on the table, while occasionally advisable, is almost always the inferior basis for any sort of experience you might want to tell someone about later.

"So, are you going to go?" she asked. "You'll go. You always go."

"What's *that* supposed to mean?"

"It's a story," she said. "You'll do anything for a story."

I might have smiled—she knew me after all—but I kept it from getting out of control. I had a cover to protect. "I'm really happy for you," I said. "You and David are a great couple." I meant it. They clearly loved each other, and that was far better than any false impression of idealized couplehood, which, I'd come to realize, was a cruel form of deception to both those who wed and their guests. Lucy and David bantered and bickered and laughed and teased, but his expression when he looked at her, which he was doing right now, though she didn't appear to notice, was one of joy and amazement. *I am so lucky*, it seemed to say. For some reason, out of me came these words: "Not everyone gets this."

She smiled, that dreamy look crossing over her features again. "I know."

On the way back to our rooms, Fred and I decided we'd take a quick dip, because no matter how often you get to jump into a pool overlooking the ocean under the light of the moon, it's not enough. We traipsed through the resort, which was quiet but for the chirping of tiny tree frogs and the occasional rustlings of nocturnal creatures or other humans wandering back to their rooms. We emerged from a wooded patch to find ourselves not by the pool but in front of one of the expensive villas, an entity on its own. I'd seen the photos on the website: Underneath that thatched roof was an enormous four-poster bed surrounded by floor-to-ceiling windows so as to allow a guest to gaze out at the ocean while horizontal. Adirondack chairs were perched outside on the rocky patio surrounding the hut, which had its own personal climbing ladder for access to the water beyond the cliffs. Outside of this hut there was a man sitting and smoking in his Adirondack chair. We were all in shadows, but there was no doubt in my mind who it was, and soon we found the man knew exactly who we were, too. "Oh, hi," I heard, a familiar voice emerging through the dark over the crashing of the waves. "I was hoping to see at least one of you."

Fred gave me a look, squeezed my hand, and was gone. I picked my way along the rocks, trying my best not to trip in my heels, until I arrived at the empty chair next to Boyd. Brave through drinks, I looked at him, not letting my gaze waver when he stared back at me. In the dark his eyes resembled those of a raccoon interrupted while picking through the garbage. I realized he was waiting for my next move before he made his. "I was robbed," I said. "You do realize that."

He laughed. "Sit down." He gestured toward the nearest chair, but I waited a moment, gauging him; even, I thought, making him sweat. Of course, it was hot. He'd be sweating anyway, as evidenced by the splotch of perspiration that was currently working its way down my own back. More important than any sort of suspense or nervousness-making, though, was that from this vantage point, standing above him, I had room to consider. Who was this man? Not just the guy I'd put together from Facebook status updates and photos and Lucy's stories. Not just the boy I barely remembered from so many years ago, the young man I spent an hour standing next to, trying to convince a judge, who may or may not have been asleep, that my side of a hypothetical argument was best. Nor was he even some clear combination of the two, bound together by the indignation that silly incident had wrought. This person, while someone with whom I shared a strange, brief history, a specific moment in time, was largely a mystery. He was also more real than any of the options I'd considered up to this time. I must be the same for him, I thought. We were characters to each other, but we were not only that.

"Do you think people ever know people?" I asked, but before he had a chance to answer my seemingly random question, I eclipsed it with another. "I heard you dated Naomi Windham." She was a girl who'd been a sophomore at my high school when I was a senior. I'd also heard that the relationship had ended badly, but I kept that to myself.

"I did," he said, offering nothing more than a lengthy drag on his cigarette, which he then handed to me. "Want?"

I didn't smoke, but I took it. It seemed the thing to do, companionably, even if what I really wanted was another glass of wine. He noticed me glancing at the cup near his feet and heaved himself out of his reclined position. "I'll make you a drink," he said. "You really are the same, you know that?"

"You never even knew me," I managed, before breaking into a fit of coughing. He shook his head, went into his villa, turned on lights, poured something into a cup, and emerged again. I sat watching and wondering how I'd gotten into this, at the same time aware that to get out all I had to do was walk away.

I'd figured out by now that there are times in a person's life when she knows what will happen before it actually does. One might argue that this was such a time, that this had been in some ways predetermined, even before that debate competition fifteen years ago. That we would reunite at a wedding made our romantic interaction inevitable—because it was a wedding, because we were both single, because of our shared history, and because, practically speaking, it's better to try your hand at a seduction scheme than it is to pummel a wedding guest with coconuts. Just because.

There are other times when a person has no idea what will happen, but is pretty sure whatever it will be will be interesting, and so chooses to stick around and see. Lucy was right. Anything for a story.

I took the cup he handed me and drank.

The reception took place steps away from the spot where Lucy and David had, earlier that evening, said their vows before their collection of guests and the ocean. Boyd and I were seated next to each other at a table covered in a white linen tablecloth and scattered with bright flowers. He was wearing a pink collared shirt. I had on a blue silk dress, turquoise like the color of the pool under full sun, and a necklace of matching blue beads. My fair, freckled skin glowed with its own pinkish hue. In my week poolside I had managed to acquire some semblance of that much congratulated "bit of color" wan East Coasters traveling to beachy locales crave.

When I arrived, he was already there, and he smiled up at me as I set my clutch down at my place setting. "Well, hello, there," he said. This was the first time I'd seen him all day. The night before, we had sat outside and talked until the sun was rising and I was forced to sneak back to my room so that no one would see where I d spent the night. There had been one kiss, or two, possibly more? It had blurred around the edges in the end, but I'd pulled myself away and gone back to my room. I'd woken up excited, eager to see what would happen now. And now. And again, now.

With him staring at me in his preppy wedding clothes, his face sun-pink and shiny, I had no idea if what I'd felt the night before—a certain fondness for him, a camaraderie paired with that antagonistic jousting that could, in some situations, resemble a kind of sexual attraction—was even remotely real or just some sort of wedding-induced haze. After a brief intermission, the wedding play was coming to its last act. So what would it be? I grinned back at him. "Hello."

"You should get food," he said, looking down at his already full plate. I made my way to the buffet, where I was served coconut chicken, tilapia cooked in banana leaves, and a medley of greens grown locally. There was an ice sculpture adorning the table, two great swans, their necks entwined. I paused at it for a moment, considering the plantains below and watching water from the ice slowly drip onto the tablecloth. I wondered how long we had until the statue melted entirely, given the temperature, and why there was any need for an ice sculpture in Jamaica, anyway. It seemed an odd motif for a celebration of forever.

Interrupting these thoughts was a sharp cracking noise as one of the swan heads broke off and plummeted down. I gasped and involuntarily reached up to grab it in what may be the only truly athletic effort at hand-eye coordination I've ever made, at a wedding or otherwise. I succeeded, though the rest of the sculpture came crashing down soon after that. As the resort staff gathered to take care of the detritus, for a few long moments I was left standing, figuratively and literally frozen, a cold chiseled swan head in one hand and my plate in the other.

The crowd of guests had hushed, and someone punctured the silence, asking, "Are you okay?" I looked down at my plate, full of water and chunks of ice, the *Titanic* of wedding dinners, just before it was whisked away and I was offered a new one upon which was quickly served a replacement meal. I took it and returned to the table, where I showed everyone the remains of the ice ball. It was speedily whittling itself down to a chip. "You hate swans!" said Fred, adding to me alone, "You either have some serious wedding mojo or some serious *anti-wedding* mojo." I laughed nervously and set down the piece of ice, which melted into a damp smudge on the tablecloth and was gone.

The reception had begun. "To Lucy and David!" we shouted, lifting our glasses. Boyd caught my eye, winked ostentatiously, and raised his drink toward me.

Well after the pool had turned a dark, muted blue, the party continued. There was a makeshift tequila bar set up just before the cliffs began, and I stepped over to it in my high heels. They were silver and gold with an intricate crisscross weave on the tops. If worn too long, they would leave a contrasting pattern on the tops of my feet. I had worn them too long.

"Tequila shot?" asked the bartender, a jovial man in a short-sleeved, collared shirt and pastel bow tie. I nodded, holding out my hand to accept his offer. A pleasant burning sensation traveled down my throat and into my stomach as I drank. Boyd appeared next to me and requested his own shot. For some reason, I took this to mean I should have another. We clinked glasses for the second time that night, simultaneously put our drinks to our lips, and gulped.

That was a mistake. There was a queasy churning in the depths of my stomach, a roiling that I knew from experience would not end well. Without saying a word—there was no time—I stepped away from the bar and out onto the jagged terrain surrounding the resort, toward the ocean water, darker and more sinister than the contents of the pool, though its surface was smooth as glass. In the distance, music played under the cabana, where couples were still dancing. That would serve as a noise muffler, I hoped. I quickly, neatly vomited between a pair of jutting rocks, wiping my mouth with a wadded-up old tissue discovered in my clutch. I suddenly thought I knew the real reason they didn't allow children at the resort. It wouldn't be fitting. After all, you never knew when a wedding guest might have to puke and rally on the cliffs.

An hour or so later, as I was preparing to jump into the pool, fully clothed, with the remaining, still-standing guests, Boyd grabbed my arm and pulled me toward a quieter area, away from everyone else. "Let's go," he said, glancing back at the now-defunct tequila bar, and then beyond, where I'd made my clandestine trip earlier that night. "Let's go get your *toothbrush*, and then we'll go to my villa."

There are times when you're nearly struck by a collapsing ice swan but escape unharmed. There are times when you drink one too many tequila shots, but you fight back, and you win (or maybe you lose, but press on just the same). There are times when your wedding hookup has been predetermined since long before the wedding itself. And there are times when you'll do anything so you can later say you did, because when all is said and done, the party favor you'll take home with you is the story.

What can I say? I wanted to see what those premium villas were like inside.

I brushed my teeth and put on shorts and a T-shirt, then walked with him to his room, where we spent the night making out as I would have in high school on his fancy four-poster bed. Early the next morning, I crept back to my room and packed up my things, and without the need for a proper good-bye, we all flew back to our respective cities and homes. For the rest of that summer, I blogged and freelanced. Boyd and I Gchatted a few times, but soon stopped. The wedding, its characters, my tan, and eventually my layoff, too, faded, and I found myself with a boyfriend and another job. Even when we're not going to weddings, the stories of our lives continue to unfold.

I still don't know why the swans chose to collapse on me, or if the fact that they did has any importance or a greater cosmic intent. Ice in the tropics is a risky endeavor. It could have happened to anyone. Perhaps my timing was wrong or, better, just right. We all have things we want to experience, if only so we can share them later, and we bring these nascent yarns and hoped-for renderings with us wherever we go—most especially to weddings—in pursuit of an ending that suits our beginning, and if we're lucky, the middle, too.

4.

First Comes Love,
Then Comes Marriage

✦

The first wedding I remember attending was when I was eight years old. There had been weddings before, but they were events at which I was a tiny, monosyllabic figure, barely even a person, held by the hand or carried by a relative when I was included at all. I'd stumble upon pictures of these moments in my occasional perusals of the big family photo album, and my mom would notice and come over to point me out, reminding me of a me I didn't remember—*Oh, weren't you adorable in that bonnet and ruffled diaper; it matched the place settings! Here's a photo of you at three months old, sleeping through a wedding in Vegas!*

Sometimes I'd hear about weddings by keeping a sharp ear to the adult conversations percolating around the dinner table. These frequently had to do with couples my parents and their friends had helped usher off into "for better or worse," who were heading now, in later years, toward worse—and often divorce. But all stories, from the silly to the dramatic and even tragic, seemed to garner new import when linked to the main events of life, and one of the *main* main events of life, it became clear, was a wedding. A ruined cake was one thing; a ruined wedding cake was something very different. Weddings were just a bigger deal, inherently or because they helped us remember the important moments better, or both. Whose children were at which weddings was a time stamp of sorts: My cousin Vince, for instance, had been at my parents' ceremony as a little boy, which made him privy to something I'd never be able to experience. I was somewhat envious of that, and in awe of its strange permanence. Even after he grew up, to my family he would always exist as the adorable, suit-wearing toddler present at the church that day.

The most interesting bits of the wedding stories, though, had to do with me. Yes, it's narcissistic, but isn't it true? Information related to ourselves is almost *always* fascinating, no matter how mundane (my diapered presence at my uncle's wedding was hardly the showstopper of the day), especially when that information pertains to a previous version of the self that one must rely on others to define: *You wailed during the vows and Dad had to take you outside! You were left behind at a hotel with a babysitter, and when we got home you demanded to know why you'd never gotten to have your own wedding!* Or the anecdote my mom loved to tell, particularly when I got older and began to imbibe myself, of a teenaged me chastising, "You're drunk, Mom!" after she'd had a few too many glasses of Champagne at one celebration. Her response, which she delivered with a proud flourish in retellings, had been, "No shit." These details felt real, but the weddings of my childhood did not: They had to do with people I hadn't known; people who, in most cases, I would never know aside from the stories and the pictures. I wasn't all that concerned with how those people were getting along in their post-wedding lives, or that they weren't, and I was equally irrelevant to them, having not been old enough to truly count as a guest at their wedding. It's not like a two-year-old was going to eat surf and turf, or gift anyone a soup tureen. Even if I'd been there, as the photographic evidence indicated, it wasn't like I'd *really* been there.

By third and fourth grades, though, shifts were occurring, superficially and otherwise. I'd seen the magazines, watched the movies, become enthralled with the white dress and that formalized walk down the aisle, the dad-and-daughter dance, the special party everyone got to have at least once. We had a tape deck in the car, and sometimes, while riding shotgun, I used it to blast Pachelbel's Canon, a piece of music I enjoyed so much I was learning to play it on the piano. My dad, confused by my new penchant for high-decibel classical music, would ask me to please turn it down. I started to listen on my Walkman, where I could hear it as loud as I wanted, and on repeat, *so totally rockin'*. This was around the time that I planned my own double wedding with my best friend, our vows to be delivered on a trampoline, with refreshments of ice cream cake and lemonade. That we had no grooms (we were considering an array of rockers and boy celebs from our *Tiger Beat* and *Bop* magazines; I'd narrowed it down to a lucky two) didn't matter any more than the fact that a trampoline ceremony for four might present some problems—was there a trampoline that large to be found? How do you kiss without breaking each other's teeth, or noses?

When a distant relative's wedding was announced in the fall of third grade, I was ready. Attending a wedding when you're eight, when double digits are lurking around the corner, when you've started at least tentatively to look at boys and they've begun to look back at you, is hardly the same thing as attending a wedding when you're a baby clad in a ruffled diaper, being carried by an uncle. I'd remember this one. Maybe I'd even pick up some tips. This would be the beginning of *everything*.

I wore the outfit I'd later wear in my fourth-grade school picture. It was a department store dress version of a wedding cake, layers of lavender ruffles covered in a faux fondant of tiny white dots, with fabric tiers encircling my body from midcalf to waist, and then again at the sleeves. In a photo from this day, my hair, which hung past my collarbone, is brown and has a wave to it without the aid of styling products or a curling iron. My bangs, cut with the assistance of a piece of Scotch tape, are jagged across my forehead. My eyes are open wide, my eyebrows raised in an expression of expectant surprise. There is the early beginning of a smile on my face. I'm waiting for something exciting to happen, holding on to the table in front of me for balance. Next to me, my mother, slim with her dark hair cut in a bob and her striped dress paired with a long necklace, smiles prettily, and my five-year-old brother, to her right, gives a purposely dour stare to the camera from underneath his bowl-cut head of hair, his tie amusingly askew.

I assume my dad is on the other side of this photo.

Whose wedding was it? A family member, a far-flung cousin

or uncle or niece or aunt of my father, or a direct relation of my grandmother; it really didn't matter. What mattered most immediately was the ride to the wedding, a journey in the back of the navy-colored four-door Buick sedan with the velveteen seats we called "the Blue Buick." Then, of course, the wedding itself, but first the ride: This was a trip long enough that a grubby old car towel that usually resided on the floor had been placed on the backseat between me and my brother, Bradley, as a dividing line across which we were not allowed to tickle or pinch or pull hair. It would be several hours to our destination in Michigan, and I had a stack of books on my side of the towel. In those days, my mother's most frequent complaint was that my nose was always in a book (this complaint would continue for much of my car-riding life with my family), and she took this drive as an occasion to reiterate that I should really look out of the window, have a conversation, do something, *anything*, other than stare at printed words on pages. "Doesn't reading in the car make you nauseated?" she'd ask. For some reason, after that question, it always would.

I was in a nickname phase. I had taken to calling Bradley "Zook," short for "Bradzooka," the name I'd used previously until I'd bored of it. Hopelessly and hilariously a step behind us, Dad was still calling Brad "Bradzooka." I'd have to move on from Zook when he finally caught up, so I was keeping a list of options, "Bubsy Orlando," for some reason, at the top. Zook's wedding outfit was a dark gray suit, one tailored to his five-year-old proportions. The look was completed with a fresh haircut and a maroon tie—real, not a clip-on—atop a relatively crisp white button-down shirt. He might have been commuting from the Chicago suburb in which we lived to his office in the big city, a bright-eyed, bushy-tailed, dapper young businessman, minus the fact that he was a kid and he was toting around a stuffed monkey. We called this monkey Bobo. He was small enough to hide in a lady's purse, but since neither of us carried such a thing, my brother held him in his arms and sometimes transported him on his shoulder. It was of vital importance that we not lose track of Bobo. He was a willing subject for the photos we planned to take upon the first opportunity we had to sneak the camera away from our parents at the wedding. Plotting our camera takeover may have, in fact, been some of the reasoning behind our cease-fire across the Great Dividing Towel. Also, we'd learned that in crowds of grown-ups there was safety in kid numbers. Alliances were key.

Along with quiet plans sprung up in the backseat, on the ride to Michigan there was much talk of weddings. Getting married was something grown-ups did when they decided they wanted to be together forever, said my mom, who clarified that this was the wedding of the daughter of cousins of my father, of the niece of my grandmother. I paid only partial attention to this complicated relationship, noting that the woman getting married was Susan; the man she was marrying was Carl. These sounded to me like old-fashioned names. Susan and Carl must have been in their twenties or thirties, pretty much *ancient*. But there was another problem here, a bigger one, to tackle: Married grown-ups didn't always stay together, I interjected, citing my mom's own divorce, before she married my father, and also my uncle's. "By all counts," I said, quoting some stat I'd heard on TV or in school that indicated that remarried couples were more likely to split, "you and

Dad should be divorced by now, too." My mom sighed. "My nose isn't in a book," I said.

To divert us from such incendiary topics, my dad piped up. "Weddings are an excuse to have a big party and celebrate and bring all your friends and family together, kind of like a reunion," he offered. "They're what people do. It's what people do, especially before they have kids." He and my mom gave each other a look that I was not sure how to interpret, because, the thing was, my parents did not have a big party for their wedding. They'd wanted to get married on Thanksgiving, but the small brick chapel where they had the ceremony was holding church services then, so they did it on the following Saturday. My mom wore a lacy, lingerie-esque minidress with a V-neck and sheer, flowing bell sleeves, her legs clad in the nearly opaque flesh-colored panty hose of the sixties and tucked into thick-heeled, shiny shoes with square toes. It was November in Chicago, and in one photo she is jacketless and probably shivering. Her hair is long, jet-black, and curling in ring-lets that flow down her back. In a sepia-toned photo shot inside the church, my bespectacled dad is wearing a black suit and dark tie, looking serious but pleased, even smug, a large white flower in his lapel. My mom smiles with her lips parted, all big eyes and glow-ing skin. In another photo, they face each other in front of church candles, holding hands. You can see the impressive scope of my mother's hairdo and how the transparent sleeves of her dress draped just so. And in a picture taken from such a long way away you can't see any expression at all on their faces, they stand in the chapel doorway, underneath a bell, poised to walk into their new life as a married couple. Both of my grandmothers stand over to the side, leaning against the church in fur-trimmed coats, seemingly oblivious to their picture being taken.

After the ceremony, they all went to a restaurant, its name and type of cuisine and, most likely, the establishment itself lost to time, and then back to my grandmother's house, my mom had told me. There, they opened a few gifts—"I know you'll ask what they were, but I have no idea," she'd said. "The usual stuff a young couple gets." There's a picture of this part of the wedding, too, a wrapped gift topped with a bow on my mom's lap, my dad next to her on my grandmother's couch with his hands on his knees. In front of them is an array of other packages, and while she's smiling outright, he's got something of the expectant look I have in my photo from Susan and Carl's wedding, his eyebrows raised over the rims of his glasses and his lips curled up as if to smile.

It's a nice picture, but I was dismayed with this wedding story. It was all so terribly practical. There was no beading on an ornate, expensive, long white gown. There was no tux, no huge bouquet, no crowd of beaming guests, no rice-throwing like I'd seen in weddings on TV and in magazines. No adorable old car with tin cans tied to the back and "Just Married" written on the window. No giant pile of fancily wrapped gifts. Was my mom even carried over a threshold? It seemed unlikely, given the length of her dress and my parents' overall casual attitude toward this wedding. Her previous marriage had been to someone named Troy who was a cop and blond, two types of men I decided at a young age I disliked immensely. That this was her second time down the aisle is why, she said, the wedding was especially simple. True, it was my dad's first, but there was no sense in carrying on. There *was* a short notice in my grandparents' paper, featuring my mom's face and her maiden name, along with the salient details of the day. The headline: "Will Be Bride Saturday." It states that my uncle, my dad's brother, was the best man, and my aunt, my mother's youngest sister, was the maid of honor, but they are not pictured in any of the photos I've seen.

Far more interesting than their wedding and more frequently discussed in my family were two other tales: how my parents met, and how my dad proposed. The meeting story is especially great, because it is scandalous and occurred in a bar. My mom was meeting a man who had not yet arrived for a date, and my dad showed up and offered to buy her a drink. In my imagination this bar is one long, narrow tunnel, customers packed in side by side, with barely any standing room. The lights are dim and bathe the room in a faint reddish hue. There are candles situated about, and cigarettes, smoked throughout the place, allow for further pinpricks of light. My mom, twenty-four and very pretty, long-haired and olive-complexioned and thin, tells my future dad, who is a few years older and a bit of an engineering nerd in glasses and a short-sleeved button-down shirt, that unfortunately she's waiting for someone. It would be rude to accept a drink from him in these circumstances. My dad says, "Have a drink with me, anyway, while you wait," and so, not being the sort of person to pass up a free drink from a nice man, she does. I picture them sipping from glasses decorated with parasols and maraschino cherries, offering lights for each other's Lucky Strikes, their arms nearly touching at the bar. I imagine them laughing. My dad can be very funny.

When her date finally does show up some entirely unacceptable amount of time later, my parents-to-be have found themselves in deep conversation. They have more in common than was expected. There's chemistry. My dad has pulled out all the stops in the charm department, or the drinks are that good. My mom's erstwhile date stumbles up behind her, taps her on the shoulder rudely, and gestures toward a room at the back of the bar, ignoring my father. This other man says—and I imagine this in gutturals or a series of grunts, so Neanderthal-like is the depiction my parents have given me of him—"I be in da back." My mom nods politely; my dad looks at my mom; she stays put. He asks, "Do you need to go?" and she says, "I'm fine right where I am." I do not know this for a fact, but I am certain they ordered another round.

This story has a certain mythology to it, more so than the wedding tale. It's been repeated often in my family, as has the story of my dad's sort-of proposal at the top of a revolving restaurant in Chicago. He'd been broaching the topic of marriage, but my mother, freshly divorced, was not eager to give up her new single life and rush right back into the chapel. As they enjoyed the view and their drinks, my dad decided to take a new tact: brute interrogation. "Why won't you marry me?" he asked.

She brushed it off with a laugh, saying, "Oh, come on, not this again," which made him angry.

"Why are you laughing?" he said. *"Why won't you marry me? Why won't you marry me?"* My dad is not someone who gets angry and yells very often, but the result this time ended up being his desired one, even if the engagement story was not.

She stopped laughing and offered her own counterproposal, not thinking he'd agree: "If you buy me a diamond wedding band, I'll marry you."

"Okay, let's go shopping," he said.

"Okay," she responded. This to me is the mysterious power of an engagement. Getting someone to stop laughing at you and say okay, diamond wedding band or not.

Susan and Carl's ceremony was unexpectedly boring. In my pieced-together recollections, I was next to my brother in a church pew, with Bobo between us. We alternately stood up and sat down along with the other people in the room—some hundred of them, mostly grown-ups, but a few kids here and there—when it appeared that we were supposed to stand up and sit down. There was a lot of talking, but it was all up at the front of the church, and it was difficult to keep up. If we tried really hard we could pick out every couple of words, and we could follow along, sort of, as the minister gestured one way or another, as the rings were exchanged, as each party played his or her role. My mom kept hushing us, even though we weren't talking, and craning her neck farther toward the front in an effort to hear. I wished I'd brought a book. Then and now, it's annoying to be at a wedding when you can't understand what's happening.

There were, however, two good parts: first, when the wedding party began to stream down the aisle, the ladies smiling and wearing matching dresses and carrying flowers, clutching the arms of the men, who wore tuxes and more serious expressions.

They filed carefully into place at the front of the church to impressively swelling organ music, and then there was an expectant hush. Everyone stood, and out came the bride from behind the two big doors. She was wearing a big, white, poufy dress with a long white veil, the kind of dress that, unlike my mom's in her wedding photo, *did* look like what I'd seen on TV and in movies and magazines. There was a communal intake of breath followed by a responsive utterance from the crowd: *The bride! Isn't she beautiful!* It was as if someone sainted or magical had fallen into our midst, and so we stopped and stared, reacting almost involuntarily. We couldn't tear ourselves away from the sight. Some women in the crowd dabbed at their eyes with Kleenex.

Susan took the arm of the older man standing next to her—her dad, my mom whispered—and they walked slowly, grandly down the aisle, which had moments before been strewn with white petals by a little girl I was jealous had gotten to play such an important role in this performance, essentially by making a mess. After the bride got to the front things became dull again, nobody really enunciating properly and lots of shuffling and rustling in the pews, until another key moment when it appeared we were nearing the end. The minister cleared his throat and everyone leaned in with renewed vigor to catch the last bit. "I now pronounce you man and wife," he said, and nodded his head with a certain grave definitiveness. "You may kiss the bride." This was the second good part of the wedding. Carl lifted Susan's veil, and she looked at him intently, and he laid a smooch on her that had my brother and me nearly falling out of our pew in hysterical laughter. "*Shhhhhh,*" my mom reprimanded, frowning at us.

My dad suppressed a smile. Buoyed by the renewed fun, my brother and I made increasingly grotesque kissy faces at each other, and at Bobo, until we'd exited the church.

It was when we walked into the hall where the reception was being held that I realized *this* was the meat and potatoes of the event. This was what we were here for. Round tables draped in white, flower arrangements centered in the middle of each, were stationed around a large, temporary dance floor made of collapsible parquet flooring. It was as I envisioned an Academy Awards dinner, famous people clustered about at tables, supping on chicken and lobster as they politely congratulated one another on their successes. In this case, though, there was no gold statuette, no clapping for a win other than the win of the bride in snagging her husband, or the husband in landing his bride. In the years to follow, this marriage would end, but that hardly mattered at the moment, and though it might have been predicted given the divorce rate I'd mentioned to my parents earlier, no one at my table appeared to have such thoughts on his or her mind. If they did, they didn't speak them.

Certainly, my attention was on far more basic things. We ate. Like most wedding food, it was nothing to write home about, but it served its purpose. We frolicked around the room. We met other kids, journeying in packs, friending easily and discarding those friends as they were rounded up in stages to go home. Zook ran around blowing out candles placed on tables until my mother, who'd surreptitiously removed the film from the camera, passed it to us. We continued to do laps around the room, around the dance floor, snapping pictures of everyone we could find, plus some with Bobo for good measure. We got our fifteen minutes of fame, being videotaped by a man with a camcorder who asked us to "Say a few words" for the bride and groom. Zook, budding comedian, looked back at the camera and without a hitch said, "A few words," not even cracking a smile. I danced, with my dad, with my mom, with my brother, with my grandmother, who was there with her boyfriend, Henry, and even with strangers, a whirling, swirling vision in my tiered-ruffle dress. Shyly, I danced with the tall, handsome groom.

I also watched the adults, seemingly at ease in this habitat, the women in fancy dresses, the men in suits and ties. They sipped from glasses and shook hands with one another and kissed one another on the cheeks, and sometimes a man would clap the groom on the back and offer congratulations, or a woman would hold the bride in an embrace and whisper in her ear. On the dance floor, the adults paired off in twos and clutched each other, moving slowly, back and forth, forth and back, to the sway-worthy stylings of the wedding band. At tables they'd sit and clang silverware against their wineglasses, then pick up the wineglasses to drain them and instantly receive refills from the waiters always hovering nearby. We dashed our forks against our own glasses, which held juice, not wine, and watched the bride and groom kiss. Mad with power, we did it again and again, until my mother took the forks away from us and set them out of reach.

Somewhere in the midst of all of this, I paused and had my photo taken next to the couple's three-tiered, ornately frosted white wedding cake, both of us positioned in front of a brick wall. The cake does resemble my dress. Its tiers reach up in the distance, over my head, defying gravity. The very top of it is cut off in the image, but it appears to be decorated with branches or foliage of some sort. I have that half smile again. I'm sleepy, on the down side of a sugar rush, and altogether self-satisfied. I am *owning* this wedding. My looks may read eight-year-old girl with a party dress and a mullet, but there's something deep in my lightly dazed expression that says, "Hell, yeah." It's a wedding.

It got late, and we grew tired, nodding off to sleep in our chairs. We were gathered by my parents and my grandmother and returned to the little motel where we were staying for the night, the boys—Dad, Zook, and Henry—in one room; my mom, grandma, and me in the other, right next door. We all clustered into one room at first, though, to rehash the gossip of the wedding and to talk about plans for the next day. That's when Henry announced that he wanted to marry our grandma, and Zook and I, suddenly awake again, began to jump up and down on the bed, shouting, "Hooray! Another wedding!" Weddings were *fun.*

Henry and my grandma would never actually marry, and the next wedding I would attend as a bona fide guest wouldn't be until I was in my twenties. My grandmother, though she was proposed to several times throughout her life and engaged more than once, would only be a wife to one man, my dad's dad, my grandfather, who died before I was born. Following his death, a man with the wonderful, austere name of Hamilton Booth had proposed to her, and she'd accepted, but he'd died of a heart attack before they could marry. She took the engagement ring he'd given her and used its diamond, along with diamonds from other rings she owned, to create a new "cocktail ring," as my mom called it. At one point, I thought it might be my own engagement ring. It has been mistaken for such, even though I wear it on the fourth finger of my right hand. Usually it's my only jewelry.

As for Henry, he may have been swept away in his own wedding euphoria, but I'm sure he did love and want to marry my grandmother. It was, after all, simply what was done among a certain generation. If there was love, or something that looked like it, why wouldn't there be a wedding? But there were younger generations to contend with. That night, after my brother and I had stopped jumping on the bed and been tucked in and fallen asleep, my grandmother told my mother that she didn't know why he'd brought that up again. He'd asked her before, and the reason they couldn't marry was because Henry's son's wife was in a stew about who would inherit what if the two were to wed. It was too much to contend with, and though everyone else in the family loved my grandmother, she refused to be brought into that drama in order to become a Mrs. again. That wasn't something she needed. Though it was never made legal, their relationship continued until Henry died, a handful of years later. My grandmother outlived him and died, well loved but single, at the age of ninety.

While my mother and grandmother spoke, I was adrift on thoughts of weddings, that big party all of us would eventually get to have, dancing forever in ruffles, the power of a fork to a glass to make grown-ups kiss, adults who hugged you and told you they couldn't believe how big you'd gotten, cake and more cake, and getting lifted into the air by the most famous man at the party, the one in the tuxedo, on the dance floor. I couldn't wait for the next one. Someday, I'd meet a boy, too.

5.

Homecoming

✦

It was November in Alabama, and while it was not yet cold, not *Northern* cold, it was solidly sweater weather, a fall crispness and hint of oncoming winter in the air. The leaves remaining on the trees surrounding the Burning Tree Country Club, where the wedding reception would be held, were, I presumed, the colors the club had been named for. Orange and gold and crimson and yellow and burnt sienna, they were as reminiscent of college football and high school homecomings as they were of nature. They dripped onto driveways and draped across the crusty yellow-brown winter yards of nearby houses in a languid fashion that belied the inherent drama of seasonal change. A fall wedding holds a different sort of beauty than the June standard.

Leaves were all over the yard at Marjorie's house as well, where we were staying for the wedding of our high school friend Claire. This was the reason we had traveled from our respective towns back to the place where Marjorie and I had grown up, and the reason Brian, Marjorie's boyfriend, was there, too, making me something of a third wheel. Earlier that day her mother had taken a photo of the three of us—daughter, daughter's boyfriend, daughter's best friend—with the glorious fall color behind us. In that picture, I'm wearing a long-sleeved gray T-shirt with an orange star in the middle, very nearly the costume of a Dr. Seuss character, and smiling with the sun in my eyes. I was twenty-five, and it was the first time I'd been back in years.

The night before the wedding, Marjorie's parents had long since gone to bed, but she and Brian and I remained in the kitchen, drinking and talking. I reached into the ice maker, the one I knew so well from high school—it still looked and worked exactly the same, I marveled, as if we'd never left—cupped a few fresh cubes, and replenished what had melted into my Jack and Diet Coke.

"I wonder if Nathaniel's in town," I said. Nathaniel had been my high school boyfriend. Before I'd left for college, I'd broken up with him, and he'd eventually moved farther south to a slightly bigger city. I had no idea where he was now, if he was single, if he lived here. If he would be at the wedding.

"Probably," said Marjorie. "No one ever leaves."

"You guys left," pointed out Brian, taking a swig of bourbon.

"Well, my parents moved," I said. "And it's not like I'm really from here. I was bound to leave." Marjorie shook her head. It bugged her when I acted as if I were free from what it meant to have lived here for the formative years of my life. I backtracked. "I mean, in fairness, we've been talking about getting out of here since ninth grade."

"And we did," said Marjorie. "But that doesn't mean it's not a part of us."

I changed the subject. "Last I heard, Nathaniel was in Birmingham. He's probably married. Maybe he's got kids." I found myself hoping that was not the case. "Can you imagine getting married here?"

"Don't let my parents hear you," said Marjorie. "Once that idea gets into their heads, it's over." She checked the clock and smoothly poured the watery remains of her drink into the sink. "We should probably go to bed. It's late, and tomorrow's going to be later."

My family moved around a lot: Texas, South Carolina, Illinois, South Carolina again, another place in South Carolina, another stint in Illinois. When I was in fifth grade, we moved to a midsize town in northern Alabama named Decatur. We'd stayed there for eight years, until I graduated from high school—the longest amount of time I'd lived in one place in my life up to that point—and then, as I headed to college in the Northeast, my parents would move yet again. With all that moving around it was hard to pinpoint what place I belonged to, exactly, and what I could claim in return, so I learned to choose intriguing vagueness rather than specificity. If you gave the place a name, you had to deal with the repercussions. Nowhere felt right enough to want as my own, not only for what it was but also for what it reflected of me, forever. I didn't have an accent. My parents were Yankees. I could be from anywhere.

So "we moved around a lot" was what I would say when the inevitable question was asked. "Military brat?" would often be the follow-up, and I'd shake my head and give a second routinized response: "My dad's an engineer . . . not the kind that drives trains," which for a number of years seemed a vital clarification. If the person asking actually cared, I might explain further, listing the various cities and the whens and hows and whys. Usually, though, "we moved around a lot" was enough to satisfy the fleeting interest of strangers who were just asking to be polite, the geographically based version of the "How are you?"/"Fine" exchange that could be broadly deciphered as, "We are both acknowledging that we are living humans on this earth; okay, carry on, thanks."

Anyway, it was true, we moved around a lot. By the time I was six, my mom bragged to her friends, I'd lived in six different houses. And when I left for the first day of kindergarten in my new town in a suburb of Chicago, Illinois, I walked through the door not of a house but of our Winnebago motor home, which was parked in the driveway of the mustard-yellow two-story abode my parents had purchased but not yet had time to move us into. Something in this peripatetic existence appealed to my mom and dad, who'd, respectively, grown up in the same neighborhoods of Chicago and northern Michigan their entire lives. We were hardly roving vagabonds or wandering hippies, though. Dad was a chemical engineer who stayed with the same company for his entire career, responsibly putting in for promotions that might allow our family to venture to new soil. I think they liked the idea that however bourgeois we might be, we were attached to no place for so long we'd become stuck. We had packed up and left home before and could always leave again. Home was where you made it; the home you could take with you wherever you went was your family.

As a kid, however, I didn't want to make a place home. I wanted it to *be* home, an entity I could rely on and even start to take for granted. Instead, the excitement of every new house was tempered with the knowledge that we could move again in a matter of months, through no decision of my own. Perhaps it was because of this that I was shy around strangers, preferring to make my brother—a handy, built-in companion who didn't mind being instructed and would talk to anyone—order our root beers at the mini-mart or ask the bowling alley attendant for change to play an arcade game.

My parents persisted in urging me to speak up and not be afraid to say what I wanted, and by the time I reached fifth grade in that same Illinois suburb where I'd gone to kindergarten, an epic stay for us, I was starting to come into my own. I had just won a fierce electoral battle for treasurer of my class against a male opponent who'd run his campaign on the assertion that girls should not be in charge of money. That I'd beaten him soundly was progress for women, but progress, especially, for me. And then it happened: Shortly after we celebrated that win, my dad came home and told us we'd be moving to a new town in an entirely new state. It's rare that a bookish fifth-grade girl with glasses wants an adventure that doesn't come in the pages of one of her beloved books, but that's what it would be, I was told. An adventure. Second-grade Brad relished the idea, but I was not so thrilled. It hardly mattered what I thought. It was not my choice.

We packed up and moved to another two-story house, this

one gray with giant decorative columns and a large, willowy tree in the front, an attached three-car garage to the side, a deck in the back, and a big backyard with grass and trees and even an enclosed hot tub. It was located in a neighborhood within walking distance from my new school. By all appearances, it was a very nice place.

The disasters began nearly immediately.

The first problem was my new teacher. I'd never had a teacher who didn't like me and whom I didn't adore in return. After all, I played school for fun and kept lists of must-read biographies and wrote letters to the president in my spare time (to my great disappointment, he never answered). My fifth-grade teacher in Illinois had been young, with curly, golden hair and an infectious laugh. But in Alabama, Mrs. Pilcher had clawlike hands tipped by pointy coral nails, and a Southern accent so deep I had trouble understanding her. A pouf of colorless hair sat on top of her head, and her powdered, papery skin sagged around her eyes and chin and elbows. She frowned a lot, which made everything seem to sag further. I was not her dream at all; instead, I seemed a special affront to her sensibilities: an interloper in an already full class and, worse, a misfit who hailed from a place she didn't much like. Before we moved I had never heard of the War of the Northern Aggression, but I learned quickly that the Civil War was called something different in this state where battle reenactments were held on weekends, and where, in those reenactments, the South won.

I muddled along. Then came the Ma'am Incident. Mrs. Pilcher was standing at the front of the room, a piece of chalk in her crooked fingers, scrawling on the board. She asked a question. I raised my hand and answered. I do not know what that question was, nor what I responded, but I know what happened next.

"What did you say?" she asked.

I repeated my answer.

"What did you say?" she said again.

I turned red. Could she be hard of hearing, like my grandma? Was she confused? "Uh," I stammered, and slowly repeated my answer again, louder. Her frown cut deeper into her face. I squirmed in my desk. The class laughed, uncomfortably.

"Jennifer," she said, waving her hand with the chalk still in it, her fingers gnarled like those of witches. "In my classroom when you address the teacher, you say 'ma'am.' Yes, ma'am. No, ma'am. This is the answer, ma'am. Do you understand?"

The class stared at me. Some of them were still laughing; others looked plainly horrified. "Yes," I said. It came out in a whisper, and she jabbed her chalk at me, accusingly. *"Ma'am."*

I hadn't even known *ma'am* was a word, much less something I needed to say in school, and when I went home, I explained what had happened and cried. My mom called the teacher to tell her I was not intentionally rude; we were simply from another part of the country. I don't know that that helped.

The next humiliation came at the hands of my own classmates. People were pantsing one another on the playground; it was a phase, and I was desperately afraid it would happen to me. I thought about it when I put on my clothes in the morning. If the underwear I picked for the day was going to be seen by twenty kids, it better not have something embarrassing on it, like cartoon characters or hearts and stars. Better stick with solids, preferably in dark colors, and definitely, definitely make sure there were no holes or raggedy spots. The pantsings were generally done by the popular girls, who probably picked the game up from the popular boys, who may have done it to one another congenially for a day before moving on to playing dodgeball. With the girls it was less game and more psychological torture, a form of bullying that escaped being called that because, *ha ha, wasn't it hilarious?* No one got hurt; it was kids being kids! When the teacher sent us out for recess in the afternoon, the most awful part of the day (*she* got to stay inside), I clutched my hideously uncool pants, which had been fine, even hip, in Illinois—stonewashed jeans or Z. Cavariccis—tightly to my waist, wary of other girls, dressed in matching brightly colored outfits with brand names like Benetton and Esprit, getting too close. When it did happen, I was prepared. Oversized Coke-bottle lenses can come in handy. I saw my attackers reflected before they pounced and held tight enough that my high-waisted bottoms did not give. The other me, the Illinois me who had never struggled to keep her pants up on a playground, felt a long way away.

The adjustment to the South wasn't so hard for the other members of my family. My dad, who'd received a raise and promotion in his move to this new town, had a whole set of coworkers who had to treat him well since he was the boss. As for Brad, from the moment we arrived he had a host of new friends, including some who lived just doors away. His afternoons were spent running through the streets, playing in the creek, and terrorizing the nearby cul-de-sac in the way of prepubescent boys, more mischief than malevolence. There was a bunch of second-grade girls who wanted to marry him, he'd complain. My mom was more like me, ill at ease in this strange land of buffets and sweet tea and neighbors who said "Bless her heart" when they really meant "What an ass," though she at least had the safety net of being the boss's wife. No one would dare pull down her pants on a playground or make her say *ma'am*; she'd get all sugar and Southern hospitality, at least to her face. Meanwhile, behind her back, her use of multicolored Christmas lights instead of the neighborhood-approved white-only ones caused a stir for several seasons among certain ladies of the town. Those who were too young to know better were more upfront with their opinions. Mom volunteered for a field trip with Brad's second-grade class, and one of the boys, hearing her thick Chicago accent, asked my brother what planet she was from. We might as well have been from Mars.

In a departure from historical precedent, we stayed put, and as always, I adjusted. By the end of elementary school, my report card would read "excellent" for my courteousness and respect for authority. The years kept passing, and it became home, if not the home I might have chosen. Along with when to say *ma'am*, I learned what to wear, how to say *y'all*, and who to be friends with. I met Marjorie in seventh grade. By eighth grade we were hanging out in the elementary school playground where I'd nearly gotten pantsed, experimenting with smoking cigarettes. By ninth we'd graduated to wine coolers and loitering in the parking lot of that school at night, in the cars of boys who could drive. Her family lived in a rambling, multi-winged brick-red house with neat white shutters and matching trim, perched on the top of a hill near the edge of town. Its kitchen was warm and well lit and usually smelled of fresh-baked, delicious food homemade by her mom, who for a while had run a catering business. Marjorie and I shared crushes on senior boys whose girlfriends were the girls we dreamed of growing up to be. We joined the same clubs, running for different offices. We sat next to each other in our classes and passed notes in plain view of our teachers, our allegiance to each other, not them. We rushed for the same high school sorority—an association of girls intended to prep us for the real thing in college—and when those parties and formals started happening, we would ask boys who were inseparable twosomes like us to go as our dates.

Around that time I took to wearing my mom's engagement ring, the one that her ex-husband had given her, an emerald-cut diamond that looked like what I imagined an engagement ring should be. Given what I knew of my mom's marital history, it may have been odd that I chose this ring as my preferred accessory, but somehow its wearing seemed an important thing to practice. Plus, it was a diamond, and from what I had heard, diamonds should be seen, not hidden away in jewelry boxes and forgotten. For some reason my mom let me appropriate it, and because it fit there, I wore the ring on the fourth finger of my left hand, not knowing there was any presumed marital karma in that decision. I worked for a while in a grocery store in town, and people would see it and ask if I was married, and I'd give them dirty looks because I was still in high school. *Marriage?* I was far too young for marriage or, for that matter, even a permanent declaration of love. I'd only just gotten my driver's license, for heaven's sake.

That didn't mean romance wasn't something I longed for. As sophomores, Marjorie and I had noticed two senior guys who did a funny thing in our yearbook. In all the photos in which they appeared, they were always the tallest boys, and they tilted their heads and gave knowing, goofy looks to the camera, gesticulating with pointed fingers at each other. One of them had loose, floppy skater hair, an overgrown brunet bowl cut. He became my new crush, but he had graduated from high school, and there was little chance of my ever meeting him. Until, suddenly, there was. He was staying in town and going to community college. Over the summer before junior year, I was in a car with a friend one day. We went by his house, and she pointed it out, a landmark: "That's where Nathaniel lives."

"Oh," I said, nonchalant, but after that day, I drove by again and again. Sometimes I was alone, sometimes I had friends with me, sometimes I was in another friend's car. It was a shortcut on the way to a drugstore, I reasoned; this was entirely acceptable behavior, not creepy *at all*.

He was rarely outside, though, and the little blue house sat quietly and low on its haunches, unassuming. Sometimes his Volkswagen Golf would be parked in the carport, and I'd think, *He must be home*, and try to imagine what he might be doing. All of the drive-bys did not go unnoticed. Sooner or later it got back to him that there was a high school girl with long brown hair who wouldn't stop driving by his house. We met, awkwardly. We met again, less so. And then we were a couple. It had all been so simple, but for the gas money and, later, the breakup. As the conclusion to my senior year approached, I tried to tell him we needed to end things. He couldn't understand why, and I couldn't, really, either, only that I knew it was something that I had to do. I needed to go on to the next stage of my life on my own, without him. It didn't make sense—*How do you love someone so much, and then abruptly change how you feel?*—but it was the only thing that made sense.

On graduation night at a party in a cornfield I kissed another boy, and though it meant nothing, it was freeing. I was done, I told Nathaniel, it was over. He did not take it well, nor did my own family, to whom he was very nearly one of us. "How could you?" I remember my brother saying. "Oh, Jennifer," my mom had groaned. My dad had been silently disappointed, feeling sorry for the nice young man he'd gotten to know. Of course, they'd forgiven me, and in the years that passed, it seemed that Nathaniel had, too. He'd sent postcards, and word would occasionally come about his whereabouts from friends. I was glad he was doing well, glad in the way that you can be glad for someone you used to know while also feeling that pang of *What if*. What if I'd done things differently, where might I be now? You can't go back, and it wasn't that I wanted to. But a person couldn't help wondering.

Like romantic relationships, high school friendships don't always make it through college separations, but Marjorie's and mine did. We'd made a commitment, promising each other that after we graduated from our respective universities we'd move to New York City. We'd rent an apartment together and be successful career women and have the best lives ever, although Marjorie planned to stay for a few years only, after which she'd move back to the South, get married, and start a family. I planned to stay as long as I felt like. I had a feeling New York could be my new home, the permanent home I'd been looking for. I needed one, because my dad's job had taken my parents to London the summer I graduated, and then to Singapore and Indonesia, farther and farther away from that Alabama town in which I'd spent eight years.

Marjorie and I did what we said we'd do: We moved to New York, and we got a place on the Upper East Side with another high school friend, Violet. It was a three-bedroom apartment insomuch as there were three bedrooms side by side, with thin walls between them and their doors connected to a narrow communal living space. Not one but two brothels were busted in the building in the time we lived there, and at one point, a cop knocked on our door, thinking one of those apartments was ours. Marjorie let him in and insisted, "We're not prostitutes!" and he nodded and said, "Three girls living together? Sure." We didn't know if we should be horribly offended or proud of ourselves. It was awesome, this grown-up life. Mostly.

Together, we got our first and second jobs and learned the ropes of our newly adopted city. We had bad dates and hookups and breakups, got dumped and dumped others, dealt with boys who called repeatedly and those who never spoke to us again after the first or sixth night. We even stayed friends through the one time a man peed in our refrigerator. Then, just like she'd warned us she would, Marjorie moved back to the South, to Nashville, a few hours from our hometown—close enough, not too close—but not before she met Brian. From the beginning there was a seriousness to their relationship, and it threw me for a loop. That you could identify the person with whom you wanted to make a life, nail it down, and do it, seemed so inexplicable, so incredibly slippery. Did you just know? Did you close your eyes and turn and point and hope for the best? Perhaps choosing had the power of making that choice the one you wanted. The only person in my life who seemed remotely worth choosing, in retrospect, was Nathaniel, and yet that didn't feel right, either. If it was true that someone was better than no one, what was the deadline for picking that person? *Why did no one tell you this stuff?*

With Marjorie leaving town for good, and Violet enrolling in an out-of-state graduate program, our three-person unit was broken. There was nothing keeping me in New York, so I decided to make some changes. Like my parents, I would move, if only to prove for certain that New York was the place I wanted to be. I chose Boston, where a close college friend was living, and where, when I visited, things had seemed rather pleasant. Though once I got there I began to strategize my move back nearly immediately, just knowing I could get up and start a life somewhere else was confidence-inspiring. My excessively mobile parents had been on to something after all.

In the midst of plotting my return to New York, the invitation came. Claire, a fellow high school sorority sister, was marrying a man from Louisiana. They'd gone on a date to a concert, and that had been it. We didn't know much about him, and I hadn't kept in close touch with her, either, in the years since we'd graduated, but this was a milestone. It seemed important to be there, as much for ourselves as for her.

Marjorie called me. "I think we should go," she said. "Fly to Nashville, and we'll drive down together. We'll stay with my parents. Brian will come, too."

I imagined my old house, the trees in the front yard, the parties we'd thrown back in high school. I could see the football stadium, the old make-out parking lot, the gas station where we'd bought Marlboro Reds and Boone's Farm. I pictured the country club, where we'd thrown so many formals, and now the adult version that comes after. I didn't know what I might find—baldness, weight gain, station wagons, babies?—but it was guaranteed to be at the very least interesting, worth the several hundred dollars I couldn't afford on a plane ticket to delve again into my youth. And it was about looking forward, too. This was where so many things had happened. It might be time to consider what those things meant about who I was now, and who and where I wanted to be.

"I'm in," I told Marjorie. "Can we do a drive-by of my old house?"

"Of course."

I wore a wrap dress from J.Crew, small paisley patterns on black, paired with a wrist bangle and some cheap, blingy earrings. This was one of the few wedding-appropriate dresses I owned, though I'd frequently worn it to work, too. We spritzed and powdered and lipsticked and mascaraed and rolled our hair, sipping from little cups of booze, flagrantly breaking Marjorie's mom's No Drinks Upstairs rule. After a final check in the mirror, we grabbed our clutches and headed downstairs. Brian was waiting on the couch, watching a football game with Marjorie's dad, who was reclining in his La-Z-Boy.

"Oh, you look so beautiful and grown-up," said Marjorie's mom. "I might cry!"

Marjorie's dad tore his eyes from the TV. "Lookin' good!" he said, giving a thumbs-up before a touchdown pulled him back in. I glanced at my friend. We did look beautiful and grown-up. As we should. We were on our way to see someone we'd known in high school get married.

The majority of weddings I've been to in my lifetime have not been in churches, but this one was, a church with a choir and organ music and people seated neatly in mahogany pews. We filed in, the group of us in East Coast black. In contrast, the bridesmaids were dressed in a peachy, poufy pink satin, the color of a bride's blush. The Southern ladies wore bright floral dresses while the men leaned toward navy and khaki, with preppy, colorful ties. Scriptures and stained glass filled the room, and there was a pastor in front of a cross. Before him were hands clasped in a promise, and after that came the pronunciation of man and wife. Violet, a bridesmaid, stood at the front of the room, holding a bouquet of flowers against the bouquet of material formed by the voluminous folds of her dress. I remember a feeling of surprise when the minister uttered a line about a woman's role being to honor and obey her husband, though I've been told since that was another wedding entirely. That's the trouble with weddings. As real as they feel in the moment, the memories, blurred by what you drank and how late you stayed up and how many people you spoke to or saw, but most of all by what you brought to the wedding yourself, can end up pretty cloudy. My recollections of this one are particularly so, it having been more than a decade ago, and attended by someone who in certain ways was more different from the person I am now than even the eight-year-old girl was.

We arrived at the country club and made our way to a banquet room where silver buffet trays were lined up on tables covered in starched white tablecloths, Sterno burners underneath to keep things hot. The scent in the air was heavy hors d'oeuvres—melt-in-your-mouth fatty things, like baked brie and cheese straws and fried chicken fingers and Swedish meatballs. There they were, being carried about on plates, fragrant little gravy vehicles. There was no fear of butter here. Food was supposed to taste good. The walls were dark and woody, and the room felt akin to being in a high-end cave, or some wealthy person's basement outfitted with all the bells and whistles so that if you didn't want to, you'd never have to leave. The open bar was just opening. In the excitement of getting ready for the wedding, we'd barely eaten. I realized I was hungry and got in line.

"Jennifer Doll," I heard, and there was Nathaniel's old best friend, Buddy, grinning at me and shoveling meatballs onto his plate. I had liked him a lot, until, in typical rumor-mill high school form, another friend had revealed he'd mocked my relationship with Nathaniel, saying he doubted we'd even kissed, much less "done it," and that poor Nathaniel probably had blue balls worse than anyone in the whole damn town. That statement had brought more mortification to me than if someone had said the opposite. To be prudish, or to be considered that way, had made me feel I was forever uncool, the Coke-bottle-lens-wearing girl nearly getting pantsed in the playground all over again. There was also the fact that his statement wasn't entirely false. Nathaniel and I had kissed, but we hadn't slept together. I guess by the point we might have gotten around to it, I was already preparing myself for the future.

We know this from class reunions, but it's true at weddings, too: Just because you get older doesn't mean you're different inside. Feelings long past can pop right back up again when you're confronted with something that wounded the previous you, especially when you revisit high school feeling only marginally confident about your adulthood. At twenty-five, I was sure of very little. Yet my former classmates were getting married. It was hard not to think about where I measured up, and I was afraid that when it came down to it, I hadn't done much at all, not in my eyes, and not in anyone else's, either. I desperately wanted to be something beyond misfit fifth-grade Jennifer, or high-school-debate-captain Jennifer, or throwing-parties-when-her-parents-were-out-of-town-and-getting-grounded sophomore Jennifer. Or Nathaniel's-girlfriend Jennifer. And I was, I was! I was an adult, I had a job, I had a new town and an old town, too, I reassured myself. I had nothing to be afraid of. Also, Buddy might have information.

"Hey, you," I said. "It's been a while."

He swallowed a meatball and nodded. "Sure has. How's life?"

"Great!" I said. "I moved to Boston, but I'm probably headed back to New York soon. I don't know if you knew I was living in New York? Boston is great, too! Busy, you know, working, going out a lot . . ." As I rambled, I looked around the room. "How's stuff here? Have you seen Nathaniel lately?" My ex didn't seem to be in attendance.

Buddy followed my eyes and inspected the crowd as well. "Last I heard he was living in Birmingham, dating some girl."

"Oh," I said.

"It's Decatur, you know," he continued. "Same old, same old. Claire getting married, though, wow. I guess we're old, huh?" He seemed slightly dazed as he turned back to his meatballs. It appeared I wasn't the only one confronting strange feelings about growing up.

Moments later, Marjorie and Brian were at my side, ushering me to a table, sharing gossip. Weddings and babies, but also rehab stints, failing parents, even a divorce or two. Houses had been bought, companies founded. Jobs had been won and jobs had been lost. I didn't see anyone who was suddenly bald and fat and driving a station wagon, just lives being lived, here like everywhere. "There they are!" someone shouted, and we all turned to applaud the bride and groom, headed out among their guests following their post-wedding photography session. "He seems nice," said Marjorie. "She looks gorgeous. Oh, they're so happy!"

I caught sight of Jesse, another high school friend. He was the one who'd kept me most reliably informed about my ex over the years. He waved and walked over. "Well, hello there, stranger," he said. When I'd broken up with Nathaniel, Jesse had not been happy with me, but he hadn't stopped talking to me or even, like my brother, yelled at me for being a jerk. He wasn't judgmental. He had stayed in our hometown after graduating. His family was here, and I suspected he had never planned to leave, not permanently.

"Hi, Jesse," I said, getting up to give him a hug.

"Mind if I sit?" he asked, gesturing to the place next to mine.

This wasn't a mere hello. He had news. I moved my bag to make room.

"So, I have to tell you something about Nathaniel," he began.

"I just saw Buddy," I said. I stopped eating and took a sip of wine. Everyone else at the table appeared deep in their own conversations. I swallowed. "He hadn't seen him, though. What is it? Is he okay?"

"Nathaniel is *married*," said Jesse. "To a redhead! Get this: They eloped to Hawaii."

"Hawaii? Eloped?" This information did not compute. The Nathaniel I had expected, if not here, would be at home, watching TV from the couch of his little room at the back of the house, his Golf parked in the carport, its tape deck cued up to his favorite Hüsker Dü song. My Nathaniel, a lei around his neck, hula-ing into the sunset, cavorting in impossibly blue waves with *a redhead*?

"As you can imagine, his mother was not happy with the elopement," he said. "Anyway, his wife sort of looks like Little Debbie!" As Jesse began to laugh, I tried to conjure the all-American cartoon girl on the box of snack cakes, an image I hadn't thought of since high school. I couldn't picture her, and I couldn't picture her as Nathaniel's wife. But more than that, despite myself, what I felt was a strange kind of pride. Eloping to Hawaii has oomph. That's the kind of thing I'd hope a future husband of mine would have the nerve to do, too. *He must really love her*, I thought.

"I think he's really happy," said Jesse.

We were interrupted by another friend from high school, a girl who'd been a cheerleader, who'd had the sort of popularity I'd once fruitlessly dreamed of attaining considering my lack of coordination and mud-brown hair. "How are you?" she said, grabbing my arm and squeezing. "Oh, my God, you look great. What are you up to now? Are you still living in New York?"

"*You* look great," I said. "You look exactly the same! Um, I moved to Boston for a while, but I'm in the process of moving back to New York. I miss it, you know?"

"Totally." She might not have known what I was talking about, but I got the distinct impression that she really did want to hear about my life and how it might compare and contrast with her own.

Later that night, I found myself sitting at the country club bar next to Buddy. I'd had many drinks and, despite my best intentions, not enough Swedish meatballs. Things were winding down, but there was still that particular sort of tingly wedding electricity in the air. It's a neutral energy that can so easily veer one way or the other. You can end the night in joyful tears over the shared beauty and love in this place, among these people in this moving marital moment. Or you can see fit to annihilate everything in your path. You will regret the latter, and you may even know that to be true as you persist in doing what you're doing, but sometimes you can't help yourself. As much as you try to stay with the light, there are certain weddings that take you into the dark.

Buddy and I were talking or, more accurately, flirting. He'd always dated another of our friends, the artistic one with the great clothes, and I'd been with Nathaniel. Of course, Nathaniel was married now, I reminded myself. It seemed like the friendship between the two men had lapsed as well. All bets were off. I poured on the charm, talking Buddy's ear off, bragging about how much fun grown-up life was in the big city. He seemed impressed, so I went a step further, wanting to rehash and resolve old wounds. "You know," I said, "you really shouldn't have talked about my lack of a sex life to everyone in high school."

"*You never talked* in high school," he answered. "You never said a word. We were all just wondering who you were."

"That's funny," I said. "'Cause I was wondering that, too."

"Well, shit, girl. We were in high school. Who wasn't?" He motioned to the bartender for another drink.

Marjorie, suddenly at my side, interrupted. "Claire's dad is cutting everyone off," she said. "We should go."

At this wedding, I listened, and we did.

On the way home, they told me later, I slid from side to side in the backseat of the car. I might as well have been on a roller coaster, involuntarily tilting back and forth, my whole body enjoying the ride. I sang along loudly to "Drift Away" and "Take It to the Limit," alternating lyrics, as Marjorie and Brian laughed at my tuneless renditions. But it was a wedding, I thought, too deep in my own mind to explain; this was exactly what you were supposed to do at a wedding. *Take it to the limit. Drift away.*

I woke up from a dream that I was in a dark cave permeated with a strange red light, and when I was able to pry one eye open realized I was facedown on one of the twin beds in Marjorie's childhood bedroom. The pulsating numbers of a clock positioned next to me made for the crimson glow seeping into my subconscious. It was later than I'd intended to sleep. I touched my face. I hadn't washed off my eye makeup or even taken off the dress I'd worn the night before. My shoes and bag were strewn across the room. Phone, check, next to my bag. What about my friends? Where were Brian and Marjorie? Had I lost them, through misplacement or, worse, offense? I heard laughter from the next room, her brother's bedroom, which he'd vacated for college and where they were staying for this visit home. I pulled myself up into a sitting position, my hair a tangled mess around my face. My makeup, I was sure, was smeared down my cheeks. But I was here, and they were there, and nothing had happened. Nothing had happened. I was both relieved and disappointed. I shifted to the edge of the bed, and the clock fell to the floor with a loud thud.

They heard. "Jennifer! Are you awake?"

"Glahhhhhrrr," I responded, seriously considering putting my head right back down on the pillow.

"We need to get going if you want to see your old house!" shouted an altogether too-chipper Marjorie. "Mom's made breakfast. Some food will do you good!" I heard the clomping of their footsteps as they headed down the stairs, the clanking of silverware, bustling morning kitchen sounds. It sounded like home. It smelled like home, too, a home I remembered.

For special events and holidays while we were in high school, Marjorie's mom had made an egg, sausage, and cheese casserole, the sort of Southern food hospitable Southern ladies like to cook and serve. My mom would never make or consume such a thing, and surely it's because of that that I loved it. It reminded me of growing up in this town, of the friends I'd made and their families, of who I was when I got here and who I was when I left. It made me think about the person I still had left to become. If family was the home you took with you, hometowns could also be families, no matter how distant they grew or whether you returned to them or not. Marjorie was right. This place was as much a part of me as Nathaniel was, as much as any of the shared history among all of us was. That didn't mean it was the only part. But the next time I was asked *Where are you from?*, I might just answer *Alabama* and leave it at that.

"Jen!" yelled Marjorie again. "C'mon, it's getting cold!"

My old house looked almost exactly as it had when my family had lived in it: same gray paint, same trees, same Gothic columns, same three-car garage I'd parked in once I got my driver's license, and even the same mailbox with its perky little flag. Across the street, there was the same sidewalk I'd taken every morning to get to the elementary school. It was all so familiar, like looking at an old photograph, and yet, as we slowed to a crawl and I stared long and hard at my former home from the window of Marjorie's car, I could feel it wasn't the same at all.

6.

It's the Journey,

Not the Destination

✦

One weekday morning in the winter of 2010, I emerged from the subway to find I had a voice mail from my parents. Calls from them at odd times would always send a current of fear through me. We usually talked on weekends and in the afternoon or early evening. Why would they be calling me now? As I listened to the message, my anxiety level spun skyward. It was my dad, saying words no one ever wants to hear: something about Mom, a "brain bleed," and the emergency room. I called him back immediately.

"Hello, Jennifer," he said, maintaining his trademark fatherly calm even in the face of inconceivable news. "I'm at the hospital. Mom woke up in the middle of the night and couldn't move. I called 911 for an ambulance, and we rushed her to the ER."

I was stunned into silence. The last time I'd spoken to them, a week before, they'd regaled me with tales of upcoming biking and kayak trips and dinner plans with friends. There had been no clue of anything wrong. My dad had been making his famed beer-can chicken; my mother had been relaxing outside on the patio with her martini, enjoying the balmy Florida night. "Oh my God," I whispered, trying not to cry.

"She's with the doctors now. They say she has dual hematomas, with bleeding on both sides of her brain. She's going in for surgery within the hour."

A flood of questions began as I tried to find some way to make sense of this news. Information. Information always helps. "Does Brad know?" I asked. "Should we fly down? What's going to happen? I don't understand, *how* did this happen?"

"I'm calling Bradley next," he said. "I'll know more in a few hours. Stay by your phone, and I'll call you as soon as she's out of surgery."

"But do they think she's going to be okay? She's not—"

"Oh—the surgeon needs to talk to me," he said. "I'll call you back."

The kitchen is the comma in the middle of my parents' house, itself punctuated in the center with an island, a sturdy block of granite-topped wood. It's here that my mother chops, cuts, mixes, tells my dad he's not chopping or cutting or mixing properly, and instructs the family in the art of candle-lighting, wine-opening, table-setting, vinaigrette-making, pasta-shell-stuffing, relationship-maintaining, and, most of all, in the dark magic of keeping up one's own side of a conversation even if no one *else* has anything interesting to say. The kitchen itself is airy Florida architecture: tall ceilings, gold-yellow walls, polished cabinetry, countertops with black-and-gray marbling, and numerous windows to let in the sun, which almost always shines. The room is form as well as function, and the objects within it adhere to that mantra. My mother adheres to that mantra. My mother is a benevolent dictator, usually, and her throne is the kitchen.

She would not consider this in any way sexist. This is just the way it is. She's chosen it, and if you do wrong in her domain—where there is no KitchenAid, but recipes are filed neatly in a brown wooden box I've known since childhood and shelves are stacked with spices arranged to her particular needs and tastes, *labels facing front!*—you will be exiled. She moves easily from thing to thing, stirring a pot, tasting the soup and pronouncing it delicious, moving leftovers to a smaller container and fitting the old one neatly into the dishwasher. All of it is under her control, and she smiles as she shares again how Brad, as a child, told her she looked like a "microwave mom" but she sure didn't cook like one. She is secure in this, in her cooking ability, her mom ability, her wifehood, herself, just as she is in the martini my father mixes each night at six p.m. and she drinks, with a glassful of ice next to it to add as needed. "Cocktail hour," my dad will say, though when Brad and I are home it goes on for much of the night. My dad makes my mom her drink, and then he pours his own, and if we are there, too, he asks what we'd like and serves it. He always makes my mom her drink first, but that day in the winter of 2010 we were not there, and it was the first of many in which no drinks were made at all.

Save the Date

. . .

There's one wedding that most of us never get to attend, and yet it's one that impacts us in the most fundamental of ways. That, of course, is the wedding of our own parents. Yes, I'd seen the photos and heard the stories of that day, but I wanted to delve deeper into the fabric of my mom and dad's relationship. Beyond how they met or wed, why did they choose each other? What were the parameters of marriage for the time in which they met? How did they view their own union as well as the overall institution, and how do they see those things now? What did they think about the relationships of their own parents, or even their grandparents?

I talked to them individually about these and other questions, and the conversations that ensued were some of the most revealing discussions we'd ever had. Just as we all have wedding stories, each family has its own intricately woven marital anthropology. There are amazing discoveries to be found with some digging. My dad told me of one of his first memories of his grandparents, who, when he was a little boy in the 1940s, drove him in their Ford V-8 out to a plot of land they owned in the country for a picnic. "I remember pasture land and trees and country," he said. "They were walking hand in hand. It was a very nice day, and a nice, loving type of relationship they seemed to have."

My parents were married in 1969, at a time when having a wedding by a certain age came as pretty much a given. My dad explains it frankly: "That was just what people did." There was no question in his mind as to whether he should marry or not. He went to college, he got a job, he had a car and an apartment. At twenty-eight, he'd accrued all the right things for the next stages in life—marriage and then starting a family. This was how it worked. As for choosing whom he'd marry, "it was a searching-out process," he said. "You look around and see who might be a good match. You don't want to get stuck with baggage, an anchor, someone with beliefs you don't share. You want to know what their families are like." That's not all that different from how people approach finding a partner today, though of course the hows, whens, and even ifs as related to the searching-out process have changed.

So, why my mom in particular? "We had fun together," he said. "We liked going out, having dinner, having a few drinks. We would get together with our other friends and do things . . ."

Compare that to the tale of my mother's grandparents' road to marriage. Great-Grandpa had lived in a boardinghouse, and the woman who ran it had a niece back in the old country. "Whoever would pay her passage from Italy could have her as a bride," my mom recounted. He did, and they married and had four children, though it was said they never got along. "They must have gotten along sometimes!" said my mom.

Marriages today are expected to be about far more than getting along. We want more than the marriage certificate. We want that other thing, too, the thing we can't put a finger on, though we know it's passionate, romantic, soulful, cosmic, fulfilling, and individualized to our own couplehood, so somehow utterly unique. As for how we obtain it, the messages are confusing and often contradictory: We'll know it when we see it; we can't force it; we have to put ourselves out there and go after it; timing is crucial; it never comes when we're looking for it; we just haven't found the right person yet; if we don't know what it is, we'll never find it.

"Wait, what about love?" I asked my dad about his courtship of my mom.

"Oh, of course there was love," he said, as if surprised by the question. "Love and romance and all that. I guess you'd say that clinched it."

When she was a young girl, my mother was introduced to the boy who would become her first husband. As they grew up, they started to date. He was a marine, and they wrote letters to each other while he was away. When he came back, she'd graduated from high school, and he proposed. She got married at nineteen, at a time when most of her girlfriends were married and some of them were already having kids. My mom's desire to wed had been practical, too, not only because it was what was expected, but also because her parents fought "like cats and dogs," and she wanted to get out of the house. "It was 1964. I didn't go to college," she told me. "If there was money for anyone to go to college after high school, it would be for my brother. As a woman, you were meant to be a housewife. At times, I thought, it would have been great if I had a couple girlfriends to live with—like you did after college—and work. But girls typically got married, or they ended up spinsters, or they lived at home with their parents and took care of them."

My mom's first marriage lasted five years. They had not been able to have children, and when her husband brought up the topic of divorce, that had been part of his reason for why: "Well, we don't have kids." Divorce had *not* been in her plan. Though it was becoming more common, it wasn't "what people did." My mom did want children, and she also wanted to understand why her husband no longer thought their marriage was worth having. "Things were not the greatest, but I didn't think they were bad," she explained to me. He refused to go to counseling, and the relationship continued to dissolve. "I got to the point where I told him, 'If this is what you want, do it, but I'm not going anywhere,'" she said. She stayed in the house, and he left, taking the car. Soon afterward, he served her with divorce papers.

As a newly single woman, suddenly her whole life was different. She had a job and, with the help of an attorney, got the car back. She sold the house and rented an apartment, where she lived on her own—though her mother was worried enough about that to insist she put "M." on the mailbox instead of "Ms." A few weeks after her divorce was final, she met my dad. They started dating, but given what had happened with her first marriage, she wasn't eager to jump right back into another. She took a trip to Hawaii with her sister, and they met men and partied and flirted and had what sounds like an utterly fabulous time. When she got back, my dad, who thought the vacation would help her get singlehood out of her system, kept doggedly returning to the topic of marriage. This was to her dismay. "I said, 'I'm really not ready for this. We get along, why should we ruin things?'" she recalled.

Of course, she did eventually say yes. Flash forward to that pivotal scene at the top of the revolving restaurant in Chicago and his repeat query, "Why won't you marry me?" When I asked her what had made her change her mind, she quipped, "Because he bought me a diamond wedding band, and I couldn't get out of it!" In truth it was more romantic and also more pragmatic than that. She might not have wanted to marry again immediately, but she had the keen sense that she shouldn't give him up. "I thought he was the right one," she said. "He seemed to be a steady person who had a lot of good values, and we spent some time talking about what we wanted out of life." Considering her fertility history, she thought it was only fair to tell my dad that she might not be able to have kids. He was not concerned that she'd been married previously, and he wasn't concerned about this, either. "Oh, *we'll* have kids," he assured her. Her agreement to marry him came approximately six months after their first meeting. The wedding followed shortly thereafter. Seven years later, so did I.

The marital takeaway could be seen as such: Just find a decent person with good values, someone with whom you get along, can communicate, and most of all, want essentially the same things out of life. (Prior to this discussion, of course, you must be able to express what those things are.) He asks and you say yes, even if at first you balk, or laugh, or request a diamond wedding band. Or maybe *you* ask, and he agrees. The years go by. You manage through the inevitable trials and enjoy the anticipated happinesses, and you emerge to find yourself still together, going on your forty-fifth wedding anniversary.

It sounds blissful, and maybe a little bit basic, but in reality it's never quite so easy. That kind of perseverance, and the initial leaping-off point, too, can seem even more difficult when getting married is not the only path we might take, or "just what people do." A lot of what we think we want, and are allowed to want, has changed. The marriage question is so complex for many of us today precisely because of the increasingly open-minded world in which we have been lucky enough to be brought up. In many cases, we have as many options as our parents dreamed of giving us. But as what we want becomes less codified and the paths we might take divide and multiply, the risk of choosing wrong can grow scarier than the risk of not choosing at all—especially when we don't *have* to choose.

The commonsense searching for a partner my father described doesn't seem like quite enough. We can have so much more, or so much less. We all know of healthy, supportive marriages, and we know of bad ones, too. If we knew, *really* knew, how to make sure we'd have the former and not the latter, maybe the decision to marry would be easy. *But how do you know you know? What if you think you know, and then you're wrong?* It's never easy.

My parents divided their roles in their marriage pretty traditionally. Though my mother worked when she met my dad and for several years after they married, when she had children she transitioned to being a full-time mom, staying at home and taking care of my brother and me. As long as I can remember, she went to the gym regularly, played racquetball, and volunteered for charity organizations, as well as maintaining a close group of friends and a most un-momlike sense of humor. I recall a day in what must have been a series of many that my brother and I were home from school, perhaps due to snow. Mom went to the garage, ostensibly to get something, but more important, to get a short respite from us. Brad followed her to the garage and knocked on the door. "Mom!" he yelled. "MomMomMommmmmmm!"

She opened the door. "I'm not your mother," she said to her dumbfounded son. "I look like her. I talk like her. But I'm not her. She'll be back in a little bit." She shut the door and, I'd guess, laughed hysterically while Brad circled back to me, his eyes wide, to share the story.

My dad, on the other hand, was the man who didn't have to stay home with the kids, taking garage breaks as needed. He was the breadwinner, a sometimes workaholic. He was the "fun dad" on weekends; Mom was the disciplinarian, the one you didn't dare cross. And, mostly, that worked for them.

Sometimes it didn't. "There were times when I thought he was spending too much time at work, and I wanted him to spend time with not only me but also you and Bradley," my mom said. "I'd go to the school and other husbands were there, and I'd tell him, 'You're missing these times.'"

Later, when Brad and I were in college, Dad spent more and more time at work in increasingly important management positions. I remember a family vacation in Turkey one summer when it seemed like their marriage was on the thinnest of ice, melting under our feet. "I was playing the career role more than the husband role, and Mom felt neglected. And maybe she was, because my mind was elsewhere," he says of that moment in their relationship. I remember a time after that, when they first moved to Florida and were coping with taking care of my ailing grandmother; how hard that was, not just for them as individuals but for them together. They stuck through both of those crisis points, and others, including some I surely don't even know about.

As my dad told me, "Marriage is a process. It's the journey, not the destination."

My parents have provided an enduring example of how to be with someone through the bad and good of a marriage, and why it's worth it to do so. Their relationship, like anyone's, has had its ups and downs, but it felt enough like an accepted, comfortable reality that I could take it for granted, so much so that as a kid I'd deliver those bratty censures to my mother for having the audacity to have had a first husband. As I grew up I came to know friends whose parents were separated and divorced, whose moms or dads had remarried, who had extended families with step-brothers or sisters or both. There were all these different ways of living, I realized, and many of them worked, and some did not. One truly bad iteration was the couple who stayed together and took their unhappy marriage out on their kids. It occurred to me that even though my mom and dad weren't exactly the Cleavers (thank God), I'd had it pretty good.

Yes, we've had it good, my brother and I. Yet we haven't married. We can wait as long as we like to walk down the aisle and as long as our bodies will let us to have children, if we decide to do either of those things at all. While we may be judged by a few people, prolonged singlehood is by no means the social end it once would have been. In fact, waiting to marry, for some at least, has clear benefits, allowing men and women to finish college and establish careers, thereby gaining maturity and building a stronger foundation for later together-lives. There is a class divide to note, though. Highly educated women who choose to wed later in life tend to have happier marriages and fewer divorces (they are, it's said, the most married group of women in America), but they do pretty well on their own as singles, too. Single women who are poor and less educated, on the other hand, often benefit greatly from marriage in earlier adulthood, particularly if they have children. And, of course, everyone benefits from a relationship that is good and stable. But whether people need to be married to have "goodness" and "stability" is another discussion. It's worth noting, too, that views of marriage are different around the world. In Scandinavian countries like Sweden and Norway, for example, cohabitation and marriage have become largely interchangeable, albeit with a twist: Those cohabitation arrangements are often the more lasting unions.

My own lack of a wedding up to this time comes with an array of possible reasons, among them, well, no one has ever (seriously) proposed. But I think there's more to deciding to marry than having someone ask and responding with a yes. Maybe I just haven't "met the right person," and maybe that's partly my own doing. I believe we directly or indirectly set up the situations that lead to marriage for ourselves, and thus far in life, I have not actively pursued it as a goal. I live in New York City, surrounded by people my age and older who are frequently unmarried and younger people who almost always are. The social and financial reality that means I don't *have* to marry is surely a factor in my singleness, as are what may be impossibly high standards for what I want marriage to be like if I do. Timing, too, has been important. I have not reached that moment in a relationship in which I've really, truly wanted someone to propose, nor that moment in which I would propose to someone else. While it would be difficult to convince me that I should have married any of my past boyfriends—hindsight being twenty-twenty, of course—there's also the fact that the focus of my life up to this point has simply not been marrying and starting a family.

At the same time, I don't want to cancel out those options, either.

We all have our priorities. I look at my friends and see two groups: the women who have married and had children, and the women who have found themselves, after years of work, at the top or nearing the top of their professions. Both groups have happiness, I think; both are indisputably admirable for what they've achieved, but there's a rare person in the mix who has managed to do it all, that itself not without its own sort of compromise. After all, that's what life is so frequently about: choosing one thing and in that choice foregoing the other. Even if we believe that "having it all" is the wrong goal—who can fit "it all" in a studio apartment that doesn't even hold a queen bed?—we still don't want to narrow the field so that things we might find we want someday, if not now, are crossed off the list and become impossible. For some of us, it may be that the *option* of having it all is far more important than actually obtaining it. We don't want to regret any choices made or not made, but in our daily, busy lives, our most immediate focus is often not marriage and children and what we hope for in the far-off but ever-approaching future. Tasks like getting a raise, a better job, and a great apartment are feasible to accomplish with some effort and in a certain accessible time frame, while goals like "being in love" or "finding the right one" at "the right time" feel capricious and very hard to achieve in any strategic, structured manner. So maybe it's not surprising that we often devote ourselves to the former.

It's taken me much of my adult life to feel confident enough to admit that whether it's a marriage, a long-term relationship, or even a short-term one, I do want love, the kind that is practical and makes sense, as my dad describes, but at the same time, all corniness acknowledged, knocks me off my feet. And even now, confessing that feels dangerous. If I need someone else in order to be happy or fulfilled, am I the stereotype, or somehow a bad feminist? Can I be a strong, independent, self-assured woman and also say I'd like a boyfriend, and maybe even a husband, someone to care for who also cares for me, forever-and-ever-amen? But if I don't say it, will it ever happen? Will that mysterious "right one at the right time" ever arise?

For women, marriage has traditionally meant greater limitations than it has for the men we choose, particularly with regard to life options beyond the family unit. Of course, throughout history, women have faced an array of greater external limitations compared to men. Getting married, as it was in my mom's day, was one of the few ways to start life away from one's parents. That's no longer true, but even now women face gender-based marital challenges ranging from finding work-life balance to determining how to share household responsibilities and child care, responsibilities that still frequently fall squarely on female shoulders. I am proud of my parents for their marriage, but the model that worked for them, in which my mom was the homemaker while my dad surged forward in his work, would not be sustainable for me. I want my own career, and I want my partner to have his, too, whatever that may be, and I want each of us to respect and value and relate to the other's choices, professionally and personally. It is for reasons of the past, present, and future that I am wary of the marital institution in principle and reality, to the extent that I would never, past the age of eight, blithely plan a double wedding on a trampoline.

Being single can also seem like the ultimate act of self-reliance, and a not entirely dishonorable one, considering the divorce rate. Conversely, the choice to pair up with someone else for an entire life can look a wee bit terrifying. Yet of all the reasons to marry, the honest desire to take that leap of faith and extend beyond the self and into a state of two—to ask someone to be there always and be answered with a yes; I'll take a chance on you, if you'll take a chance on me—is the most compelling to me. The active selection of that mutual compact (with or without an accompanying wedding) is an impressive one, which doesn't mean it's not scary, or risky, or that it doesn't have the potential to end badly. A proposal made without an awareness of the risks, though, is only the most shallow sort of proposal. A leap of faith requires leaping with faith, not blindness or blissful ignorance.

In fairness, it can be hard to tell the difference.

When Hurricane Sandy hit the East Coast, a man I was dating was visiting me in New York City, and afterward, my mom told me, "I was so glad he was there, so you weren't alone." That may be the closest she's ever come to telling me she wishes

I'd get married. Had I not been seeing anyone, she never would have said this, and I would have been fine, if a bit lonely, on my own, or I would have gone to stay with my brother, or with friends. And in truth, I was glad he was there, too. The flip side of that alone coin, though, is how utterly dreadful, how one hundred and ten times worse it would be to find yourself trapped in a tiny apartment with someone you can't stand for the duration of a massive storm. Weathering out the hurricane of life means you have to find, and choose, the right companion. I feel glad my parents get that. They've never tried to guilt me into being with someone I'd never share beef jerky or my last bottle of hurricane water with, much less my life.

One of the questions I asked them was, "Do you think people today lose anything by not getting married?" I was probing to see if they thought I'd miss anything if I remained single forever. I wanted to know if they were worried about me, if they thought I was doing something wrong, and if they felt there was something wrong with me. I also wanted to know what they felt they'd gained over the years, and what they might have lost if they hadn't followed in the course they had.

"It doesn't worry me that you're single," said my dad (thanks, Dad). "People don't marry today, in some cases, because they don't have to. They do what they do because they can. In my day, living together without being married was something only show-biz people might do." He was concerned, though, about missing out on the benefits of and the ability to compromise, "the rough-and-tumble of fitting in together," as he put it, if people don't marry. "You have to bend and fit in and adjust as you go through it. I guess at this point I'm full of bumps and Mom's full of bumps, but we're full of bumps together. If you did get married," he said, "it would be a learning experience."

I am sure he is right.

My mom had a slightly different take, about collective memory and the importance of keeping people around to remind you of who you once were. "Your dad and I can sit down and talk about things we did twenty or thirty years ago, things we still have jokes about. You don't get to have that history or connection or the memories if you're just meeting and dating and meeting and dating," she told me. "And the memories of the good times can help you get through the rough spots."

The day of my mom's brain surgery I sat with my phone next to me, ringer on, waiting and trying to work but unable to complete a single task. I spoke to my brother, and we consoled each other. "You know how she is," he said, "she'll be astounding the doctors with her superhuman recovery in no time."

"Yes," I agreed. "Of course she will." We hoped, we hoped.

Finally, Dad called to tell us she was out of surgery, but she wasn't awake yet, and wouldn't be for a while. They were keeping her in a medically induced coma as her brain healed to prevent any further damage to it.

That did not ease my mind much. "Do they think she'll be okay, though?" I ventured, not sure if I wanted to know the truth. "Her brain is . . . fine?"

"Apparently the bleeding was from old wounds," he explained, which wasn't really an answer but was a kind of reassurance, if we chose to see it that way. The previous autumn, they'd gone on a bike tour of New Zealand, and she'd taken a hard fall that cracked her helmet. While bruised, she thought she was fine. She wasn't. She'd been walking around with the hematomas for months, and they'd healed, and then they'd opened up again, the results of which had sent her to the emergency room. But she'd been *walking around with bleeding in her brain for months*, and during all that, her only complaints had been that she felt more tired than usual and her head hurt now and then. "So, you know your mom," he said with a raspy laugh. "She's not going to let *this* stop her."

Brad and I flew down. Daily, the three of us would visit Mom in the hospital. We'd stand by her bedside and look at all the tubes going into her body, her chapped lips, the bruises on her arms from blood taken, the cap on her head to prevent her stitches from becoming infected. We'd look at her and my dad would hold her hand and say, "We need you back, Marilou. We need you back." I'd try to will her eyes to open through the force of my own, and Brad and I would both talk to her. We'd tell her things that were happening outside in the world, though we barely knew what those things were because our world had shrunk to this hospital, this bed in this hospital, the person in this bed and the people who needed her to come back as soon as possible. *She* had always been the conversationalist of the family. We'd go home and sit in her too-quiet kitchen trying to eat some of the casserole dishes that kind neighbors and friends had brought over. We'd talk about what was happening or, more often, fall into an emotionally exhausted silence. The next day we'd wake up and do it again.

There was a wonderful nurse at this hospital who would sit with my dad and tell him it was going to be okay, that she knew my mom was a fighter, and that she would wake up and be herself again, she knew it. "Your dad is trying so hard to be strong for everyone," she said to me once, when it was just the two of us in the room. "It's good you kids are here. You can help him get through this. You'll get through this together."

Finally, the call came. My dad emerged from his office at the house grinning. "Mom is awake!" he announced. "She's talking! She's out of it, but she's awake!" We started to breathe, then. Our world had not collapsed in on itself permanently, though our fingers would remain tightly crossed in the weeks that followed. When we arrived at her room, we were privy to a disturbing sight: My mom was indeed awake, her paper gown in disarray, the hair they'd left her after shaving her head for surgery stringy around her neck. She was awake, and she was shouting at a hospital employee who was proffering a tub of fruit-on-the-bottom Dannon yogurt. She only liked Greek yogurt. "I'm not going to eat that!" she was saying. "It tastes like crap! Take it away. *Blech!*"

"Um, the medicine will make her a little . . . loopy for a while," a nurse cautioned.

"We'll bring you some good stuff from home," Brad assured Mom. "The kind you like."

"You better!" she warned. "Who are you!?"

"It's Brad," he said.

"Oh. Oh, hi, Brad."

"Mom's back!" he said, and we all stood around her, smiling so hard our faces hurt. It was the best thing we'd seen in days.

Later, my dad told me that what had gotten him through the surgery and recovery was "grim determination." He had no other choice, he just had to do it.

And so had she when, years earlier, he'd had heart surgery to combat what turned out to be significant blockages. After his operation, the doctor came out and motioned to my mother. "I want you to come with me," he told her.

"I thought, that's not good," she remembered. "We went into this room with all these monitors, and he showed me what he'd done, and said, 'He has to come back again. I couldn't do it all in one procedure.' I was leaving the hospital, and that's when it hit me. *Shit, I'm not ready to be a widow.*" They got through that, too, with grim determination and some dark comedy. In sick sense of humor and in health.

On the phone recently with my mom—who, as predicted, recovered with flying colors from her brain surgery, astounding the doctors, impressing friends and family—I asked, "Do you have a favorite memory from your marriage?" She had one at the ready, though it wasn't what I expected.

"It was my ten-year high school reunion," she told me. "All these people were there who knew I had been married and divorced, and that I had this new husband. I say to your dad, 'I want you to really be nice, not that you wouldn't, but please watch what you say.' We get there and are having a drink, and he starts to say something, I can't even remember what, some joke. I turn to him and say, 'You told me you'd behave,' and he goes, 'What are you telling me? I haven't said *fuck* once.' The whole table cracked up, and we all had a great time . . . until my girlfriend threw up all over the table."

I laughed, and she got quiet for a minute. "There's another one, too."

"What?"

"I was thinking about the time we went to Rome. It was our anniversary, and I had always wanted to go to Italy," she said. "One night we went out for dinner at one of those places where people come around and sing at the table. I'm a little bit uncomfortable with that, but it was pretty. They asked, what did we want to hear? And your dad tells them 'Al Di La.'"

"From *Rome Adventure*! Your favorite."

"They start singing, and I just start crying, and these guys are all looking at each other, thinking, *Do we sing so badly that she's crying?* Your dad waves them off, and I say, 'I'm sorry, I don't know what happened. Did I embarrass you?' and your dad, I could have strangled him, says, 'After all these years, it's nice to know you have a heart.'

"I hate to say it, because everyone says it," she added, "but you've got to have a sense of humor. If you were married to someone with no sense of humor, Jesus." There's a muffled yelling in the background. "Oh, hang on for a minute, you're so impatient," I hear her say, and then my dad's voice: "I put up with a lot!" to which my mom retorts, "You just wait for the next ten years!"

"What's going on?" I asked.

"I better go," she said. "It's cocktail hour, and your dad's made me a martini, and he thinks I should be drinking it."

7.

Greetings from Love Camp, Wish You Were Here

✦

The flight was bumpy, and I was nervous. All those years of air travel to the increasingly far-flung parts of the world where my parents had moved for my dad's job—London, Singapore, Indonesia—had resulted in an unexpected effect. As the hours I spent on planes accrued into triple digits, my level of nervousness on each flight ratcheted up as well. This wasn't rational, but that didn't change the facts: Any bump or lift or sway of the plane beyond the regular course, any hint of turbulence or shift in the way things felt or sounded, and I'd be clutching the armrests and gritting my teeth, engaging in some clandestine praying (regardless of how I felt about religion when my feet were planted on the ground), and generally promising to be a better person no matter what, just keep this plane in the air, please, please, please.

This particular flight was to a wedding in the Dominican

Republic, two hours and change from Miami, kid stuff. I had this. Or so I thought. Then came another bump, followed by a sharp jerk to the right. I clutched my armrest tighter, accidentally also grasping the hand of my seatmate, a blond girl who'd grown up with Caitlin, the bride, in Florida. Her name was Leigh. I'd met her at the bachelorette party, and even before that, when a bunch of us had stayed with Caitlin at her parent's house in Boca Raton for a couple of days before heading down to Key West for spring break sophomore year. Elsewhere on the plane, which was filled with wedding guests per the bride and groom's instructions, people stood up, out of their seats, in the aisles, chatting as if they had nary a care in the world. They were making me even more nervous. We were in a metal capsule hurtling through the air some thirty thousand feet above ground. *Oh, God, I don't want to look.*

"Pretend it's a bumpy road," said Leigh, who had inconspicuously moved her hand away from my sweaty grasp.

"Huh?"

"Someone told me that once. Turbulence on a plane is basically just like being in a car on a bumpy road," she said.

"Is it really?" I asked.

She shrugged. "I don't know. But it's made me feel better about flying ever since. Just imagine you're driving on a gravel road. It's no big deal; you've done *that* tons of times."

The plane jolted in the air again, and I loosened my fingers around the armrest slightly, but I kept my seat belt buckled low and tight across the waist, the way we'd been instructed by the flight attendant, for the remainder of the flight. No need to tempt fate.

A destination wedding! We're having a destination wedding, and we want you to be there!" It was a pronouncement as close to a gift that a post-grad with an entry-level salary and under-developed budgeting skills can receive. This would be a built-in vacation I'd *have* to take, to a destination I wouldn't otherwise think to visit or even be able to afford. As for affording, that was a stretch, but as luck would have it, Caitlin's dad would be discreetly subsidizing our stay in an elegant beachside resort known for its golf course and fine amenities. Sure, I had to buy a plane ticket, a dress, and another dress, and there would be eating and drinking and the price tags attached, but I justified those in my mind easily. You had to eat wherever you were, and wasn't the rest what credit cards were for? (Wedding Tip: Not exactly.) Anyway, this wasn't just any wedding. It was a *destination*.

At this point in my midtwenties, I was enamored with the concept. Why *wouldn't* you sequester all of your closest friends and your family members away to a place free from the stresses and obligations and distractions of day-to-day life, to a location where everyone could focus on the bride and groom and their love and promising future for days on end? A destination wedding seemed the best way, the only way, to do this marriage thing. I'd seen the movies. There would surely be some cute boys, whether they were wedding guests or not.

. . .

Caitlin and I had been next-door neighbors in our assigned dorm freshman year. I liked her immediately. She was tall and blond and from Florida—not the so-called Redneck Riviera where I'd vacationed in high school, but high-end, sophisticated Florida. Boca. She had a worldly air that I admired. She *knew* things, about dating and guys and how the world worked, about fashion and drinking and social situations. She'd come to college with at least one suitable fake ID, and well-placed connections for backups. I, on the other hand, had to doctor my actual driver's license with a pen. The bouncer at the off-campus bar known for its liberal carding policy took one look at my questionable artistry, said, "You can do better than this," and let me in anyway. "We've got to get you a *real* fake," Caitlin whispered to me once we were safely inside, and within several weeks we had.

Everyone loved her, and I felt lucky she loved me back.

When we graduated, she was offered a grown-up professional job with a grown-up professional sort of company, the kind at which a person wore smart suits and shiny, pointy, business-lady shoes. She moved to Boston and started her life there. I moved to New York. While Boston was close enough for visits, I mourned the separation and wished she'd change her mind and join the rest of us new Manhattanites. Oh, the adventures we would have! But it was not to be, because it was in Boston that Caitlin met Cash, the man who would become her husband.

They'd gone on a date to a Rolling Stones concert. Cash, who was several years older, was a die-hard fan. He was from New

Hampshire, and in the times I'd hung out with him, he appeared to want to get every last drop of enjoyment from life that he could. Despite his small-town roots, he was not staid or boring or conventional, and what Caitlin offered in sophistication and social graces, he put forth in optimistic energy, entrepreneurialism, and a boisterous sense of humor. The two of them wanted to travel, to see things, to have adventures, and to live a good and most of all interesting life. It made sense that this effort would be better with a teammate. The engagement seemed fast; she was just twenty-five. But both sets of their parents had married young, too. When it was right it was right, was what they said. No reason to hold off on starting your life with that person, once you found him.

I still had not even an inkling of the sort of person I'd want to marry, nor of the sort of person who'd want to marry me, much less how to find him. Moreover, I had no concept of what *being* married might feel like and when I might be ready to do it. I was just learning to pay bills on time and that my credit card limit was not "extra savings" in the bank. My relationships, insomuch as they could be called that, usually involved men who liked me but for whom I felt nothing, or at least not enough—or the opposite, me the awkward girl with a crush on someone who wasn't interested beyond a couple of dates or casual makeout sessions. I didn't feel jealous of Caitlin; I was more proud, and a little bit in awe. She had always been a step ahead of the rest of us, a girl who liked to get things done. She had direction, and for her, this marriage was an obvious next step in an adult life.

In that way the marriage was traditional, but that didn't mean there was anything wrong with it. In fact, this was one of those weddings at which no one had doubts, at least not doubts that I heard or saw expressed in any way. No one was afraid the couple wouldn't make it, that they were faking it, or that they were doing it for the wrong reasons. It may have been one of the most emotionally pure weddings I've ever been to, possibly due to the relative youth of the bride and groom. The thing about marrying older is that the so-called baggage can't help starting to pile on, our relationship experiences accruing like so many beads on a vintage bridal gown. This is not to say that people should get married early in life to avoid complications—we are all ready, if we're ready, at different times, and many factors go into that readiness—but simply that this particular union seemed remarkably complication-free for very organic reasons. No one would have protested, save a few guys from college who were still carrying torches for Caitlin, and they hadn't been invited. Everyone, from the parents of the bride and groom on down, just seemed so darn happy. It was infectious.

Cash had a close-knit crew of guy friends he'd grown up with in New Hampshire. They had funny nicknames, like Pickles and Rowdy, Scarface and Cobra. Caitlin had her own group, Leigh and other girls with whom she'd attended her private Florida high school. (They had very normal, decent, ladylike names.) These were the women she was closest to, along with her fresh-man-year roommate, Emily, and me, the three of us having gone on from our initial meeting to live together until we graduated. We'd all come to celebrate their union, as had her dad's golf buddies, old family friends, and extended family. It was a small number of people, fewer than fifty in all. Many were friends to begin with, and any who didn't know one another already would by the end of the trip.

Destination weddings are like camp, love camp, in that way. Guests are brought together for a reason that ties everyone there. In this safe place you find yourself more open to new friendships than you ever are in regular life, and you make them quickly, in whatever time frame has been allotted. Bound by all this happiness and goodwill, particularly when it stretches over several days and nights, you can't help wanting to snatch some of it for yourself. A mini-society built on love and togetherness is born, with collaborative activities and even shared morals and a certain kind of politics and government. You promise foreverness when you leave. You cry, you hug, you exchange contact information. And then, oddly, because the promises were sincere, only sometimes do you ever actually talk to any of these new friends again. Out of sight, out of mind, and anyway, outside of a wedding atmosphere, can you really reclaim the joy brought by an impromptu limbo tournament in the discoteca, the mother of the bride lifting her skirt to compete, or the sheer euphoria of driving around in a golf cart stolen from the resort, a wild and reckless rampage as hotel security closes in?

As with Las Vegas's famous refrain, sometimes those pristine wedding memories are better left where they've been formed, untouched and unchanged. Leave them alone and leave them precious, like the moment captured in the keepsake photo right before everyone jumped in the pool and ruined their silk dresses and tuxedos with all that chlorine. What you felt then, in that second, was real. What happens at love camp stays at love camp.

The plane landed safely. Everyone clapped.

The bride and groom had arranged a bus to the resort, and we departed from the airport in a big, convivial cluster, talking faster and louder as we passed scenic spots and photograph-ready vistas. Emily and I had been separated on the flight, but we reunited on the bus and began to make plans for our impending arrival at the resort: room, pool, room, bar, room, dinner. We were here. We were here! When we disembarked, members of the hotel staff placed tropical cocktails festooned with colorful straws and tiny drink umbrellas in our hands and greeted us warmly. "Welcome to your vacation home," they said, shaking our hands and smiling. "Much happiness for the wedding!" The sun was a glowing, unblemished orb. There wasn't a cloud in the sky.

Emily and I were sharing a room, to which we were delivered via golf carts. It was better appointed than anywhere I'd resided in my adult life. After testing the mattresses of each of the two giant beds and gazing at all the luxury we'd been bestowed, we hung up our dresses and opened the bamboo shades to allow a view of the patio outside our room and the pink and red and yellow flowers beyond. We were in a kind of heaven, one that we weren't sure how we'd gotten so lucky as to arrive at. Just by being friends with our friend? It seemed such an easy thing, and the rewards were so great.

Later, I wrote in my diary: "The wedding was amazing, more amazing, almost like a soap opera, but a positive one where everyone gets along and loves each other, with no evil person or babies born out of wedlock. It is a beautiful piece of unreality." That's the thing about a destination wedding, though any wedding has this aspect to some extent. They are unrealities, even if what they are meant to showcase and support is something that's very real. No one can live his or her life like it's a destination wedding, though while we are there, it's everyone's prerogative to try. Of course, it's not like you even have to try when it's eighty degrees and sunny and there's a swim-up pool bar within walking distance. It just happens.

That's where we went first. We put on our swimsuits and lathered up with the appropriate numbers of SPF and headed to the pool. Already an array of pasty wedding guests in freshly purchased bikinis and swim trunks surrounded the horizontal sliver of blue water. That's another thing about destination weddings. The group of guests can often by sheer numbers pretty much take over whatever location they've been bequeathed, and usually they do. We did. We swam, we talked, we drank, we hung out en masse. We commandeered the golf carts the resort employees used for delivering room service, clean towels, and delicately scented hibiscus soaps, and we drove them around late at night, drunk from gaiety as much as from booze.

The days blurred marvelously with unchanging weather as

we repeated the same basic non-duties over the course of our stay. Wake to the sun, breakfast on the restaurant deck overlooking the lush golf course. The grueling choice between fruit and pancakes or sausage and eggs. (Wedding Tip: Have it all!) The pool, or sometimes the beach, a snack or lunch, time to read or take a nap in the sun. Later, dinner and drinks and hanging out, at the discoteca or elsewhere. If we were lucky, Caitlin and Cash would join us for drinks or to eat or to lounge at the pool and would be treated like celebrities by their worshipful fans. But the bulk of our time was spent with other guests, because the couple was kept busy with family and the final arrangements for the ceremony, which would happen on the beach the day before we would all depart the resort. We'd heard the bride and groom would be delivered to their sandy, ocean-adjacent nuptial spot via horse and carriage like a princess and her prince, their kingdom awaiting, its citizens watching with bated breath. With the wedding our stay would come to an end. It was all happening too fast. We wanted the fairy tale to go on forever.

During all of this, friendships and even romantic relationships were being stoked. Lots of mild flirting was going on everywhere, thanks to potent quantities of translucent blue water, brightly colored daiquiris, vitamin D, and the overall vibe of honest, earnest emotion. At love camp, there's a captive audience for the affections of anyone who might be feeling anything, and it's hard not to *feel* at a wedding. That's a big part of why you're there.

Our time at the resort had saturated us in a new sort of

confidence, both in ourselves and in the sense that romance, despite what we might have known of it back at home, was possible and even likely. I remember hearing Caitlin's dad mention his daughter's friends to another of the wedding guests, an older man, and suddenly I realized he was talking about Emily and me. He described us as "beautiful and smart," and I felt honored, eager to embody those words. Here at love camp, I thought I might really *be* beautiful and smart, which were not two things I often felt so fully at the same time.

I was getting a refill at the bar, and Pickles sidled up next to me. "Hello, hello," he said. This wedding wasn't our first meeting. There had been a party thrown by Cash's family up in New Hampshire to celebrate the upcoming big event, and there we'd bantered pleasantly, but we hadn't spent any time alone together. He was older, Cash's age, with red hair, plentiful freckles, and a big laugh. He had a job in sales and traveled extensively for work. Cash had told me Pickles was starting to feel the loneliness of "life on the road" and was seeking a "suitable lady" to make his world feel complete. We'd been amused by the corny drama of that sentiment, which seemed to indicate that Cash's momentum to marry had made an impression on his friends. I was flattered, too, at any indication that a suitable lady could be me. Pickles didn't live in my town and wasn't the sort of guy I saw myself having a relationship with, partly because of the long distance, and partly because his nickname was Pickles. I hadn't figured out what that meant, though I guessed it might not be good. But he was nice, and very funny, and he was paying me a lot of attention. Half the wedding-relationship battle—and this may be true of any relationship regardless of weddings—is finding a person who gives you attention in the degrees you want and expect it (and, on the opposite side of that, learning to be okay with it when that occasionally does not happen).

He said, "Let me buy you a drink at the next bar."

"Oh, are we going somewhere else after this?" I asked. We were at a destination high in the cliffs, with striking aerial views. It was off the resort, and we'd been bused there. This dinner, and our return to the resort, had been the only plan for the night on the itinerary. But there was always more that could be done.

"The after-party plan is to go to the discoteca," he said. "Cobra and I drove our golf carts over here. Bets are being placed now for our race back." He glanced at his friends, who were deep in their own conversations. "You should ride back with me."

"I can't believe you guys stole the golf carts from the resort," I said. "Hotel security is probably looking for you as we speak."

He grinned at me. "Bad boys are hot, right?"

"As for your offer of a beverage," I said, "I think Cash's dad has the guests' drinks on his tab tonight. Which means that your kind gesture is suddenly somewhat less impressive."

He let loose with his laugh, and it echoed out over the ravine, a message right back to us. "Do you think I'd offer otherwise?"

I didn't ride with him to the discoteca, but Emily and I watched them from the windows of the bus as we shuttled back to the hotel. They were a couple of idiots, racing on sandy roads as fast as those little machines could take them, hooting and hollering the whole time, and though Cobra won, Pickles was never too far behind. We went to the discoteca, and if he didn't buy me a drink, he at least delivered several to me, and that was enough. "Want to dance?" he asked, and I got up and we moved around to ridiculous songs like "Achy Breaky Heart" and "Mambo No. 5," played with gusto by the resort DJ. There may have been a limbo, though it remains mercifully undocumented. When the bar closed, Cobra and Pickles drove Emily and me back to our room in the stolen golf carts. Both of us shared a private moment with our respective wedding liaisons before we reconvened. We collapsed on our beds, which had been decorated with towel swans, two on each with entwined necks forming the shape of a heart, romantic and silly, just like our evening.

"Do you like him?" we asked each other at the same time. "I don't know," came our in-sync answer.

"He's nice!" I said.

"He's funny!" said Emily.

"Caitlin will think it's hilarious if we hook up with Cash's friends at her wedding." I was basing this on the rom-com and wedding-movie fare I'd seen in my lifetime, but it certainly seemed true. Emily agreed.

"Isn't that sort of, I don't know, what we're supposed to do?" she asked. "Half the point of a wedding is for the great stories you tell the bride afterward. And all brides and grooms want to think that their love inspires others. Making out with a friend of the groom when you're friends with the bride is a rite of passage."

"It's the American dream," I said. "So, did you kiss Cobra? Is there a great love welling up inside of you? Is this a monumental occasion, after which your whole life will be different?" I threw a towel swan at her. "Do you want to *marrrrry* him?"

"Yes, obviously," said Emily. "I desperately want to marry him. In fact, it's all I've ever wanted, and I'm only just figuring that out now. What about you? Can you find the inner strength to settle down with a man known publicly as Pickles?"

"We could have a double wedding," I suggested. "But I'll have you know that my future husband's real name is Doug."

"Of course it is. Should I even ask: Why *Pickles*?"

"Not unless you know, Why *Cobra*?"

"He's saving that for our wedding night," she said, and we both burst out laughing.

My head on my plush pillow, I closed my eyes and fell asleep, thinking about love and like and the many strange permutations of each that could exist in this fine world in which we lived.

The wedding day dawned fresh and sunny and gorgeous, scented with exotic flowers and coconut suntan lotion, just like all the rest. I was feeling more and more heartsick that we'd have to leave our happy little created society, and it wasn't just about departing this place. I'd also have to leave the person I was here. I could barely remember life back home—pushing papers around in a cubicle, late to meetings again and getting scolded, the shadows of a bar and the glow of the cab ride home afterward as I fumbled through my wallet for cash, and how the mornings could feel purposeless and bleak—but I'd have to return to it. I hoped some of the self I'd found here would come back with me and even stay a while.

We were hungover that morning, but in paradise a moment outside or a quick dip could cure such ills easily, as could eggs and sausage, so we sat in the open air and ate, immersed our bodies in the cool waters of the pool, and then began to get ready for the wedding. I put on a clingy dress of varying shades of pink, from pale to deep fuchsia, with flowers patterned across it and one thin strap over the shoulder. I slipped on sandals, though we'd be barefoot on the beach. We made our way to the appointed spot to wait for the bride and groom to arrive, like real royalty— each in a horse-drawn carriage—and when they did we took picture after picture before following them, Pied Piper style, to the sand. There they stood before us, in front of the blue-green water, facing each other, their officiant off to the side. While he had a key role in this event, he was not who we were there to see.

The bride's gown was white with an overlay of lace and beading, and her blond hair was slicked back and tucked into an elegant bun topped by her long veil, which fell below her waist. Pinned over one ear was a huge pink flower, an accompaniment to the yellow and pink blossoms she held in her bouquet. At the bottom edge of the veil, in red glitter puffy paint, she had written "I ♥ Cash." He had on a dark suit, a yellow boutonniere pinned to his lapel, and underneath his jacket and his white button-down, he had her name tattooed on his arm in a heart. We'd seen it at the pool. That was love.

It was difficult to hear their vows over the crashing of the waves, but there was no question about the pronouncement of them as husband and wife, because right afterward, they shared one of those majestic cinematic kisses, him clasping her face in his hands. A photo of the moment remains on her Facebook page. Though it's more than a decade old now, a glance at it takes me right back to the occasion, with its upswing of emotion and the transformative, palpable joy we felt for this new official duo. Though it might not arrive in this exact form or shape, I felt sure that the mutual love and attraction wrapped in a promise of forever we were there to witness was something I wanted, too. Just as it had at the wedding when I was eight, its appearance someday, somehow, in the far-distant future, seemed indisputable.

That night we celebrated, all of us together for one last party. Pickles was by my side as we made the most of our final day of love camp. At the end of the evening, when the bar shut down and the music stopped, Emily and Cobra disappeared, and Pickles and I went to my room. We were wedding-exhausted, and I wanted to lie down. Fully clothed and demure, we both got into my bed, and he gave me a back rub as I fell asleep. It felt less a feature of a new romance than something a husband might do, after a long, hard day, for a wife, or vice versa. When I woke the next morning, he was gone, and Emily was sleeping alone in the other bed. I threw a pillow at her and she groaned, opening one eye.

"Morning, sunshine," she said.

"Morning," I repeated. "Ready for one last breakfast?"

"Mmmm," she said. "Always."

The flight home that afternoon may have had some turbulence, but Emily and I, sitting next to each other, slept through most of it, suddenly so tired from the past days that we couldn't keep our eyes open. In and out of consciousness I wasn't scared at all, but even when I woke up and the plane experienced some "gravelly road," I didn't worry. I thought of Leigh, and I smiled. Toward the end of the flight, just before we began our approach into Miami, I opened my eyes and there was Pickles, standing in the aisle. He was holding his business card, to which he'd added his personal e-mail address in a looping red scrawl. "I wanted to give you my contact information," he said. "I really hope we'll stay in touch."

I took the card, perusing the AOL e-mail address he'd wanted me to have. I felt goofy and awkward and, at the same time, triumphant. I'd met a boy at a wedding, just like I'd always thought I would. The little girl dream had come true. These things did happen, even if they didn't happen exactly the way they do in the movies.

"It gets lonely on the road," he said, and I suppressed a giggle. "Seriously, e-mail me. I'll be traveling to the East Coast again soon."

"Okay," I said, and I did, for a while. We sent messages back and forth for a few months, and he sent me a bouquet of flowers, multicolored long-stemmed roses, but soon enough the spell of love camp was broken, and we went our separate ways. I kept the business card, though. It's in a box full of photos and birthday greetings and notes from people I have cared for. These may be things no longer relevant in any current way to my life, but they are worth holding on to, nonetheless.

8.

I Think I'm Having
a Reaction

✦

We'd been in the rental car for twenty minutes and we were already fighting. We were on the West Side Highway, and he was asking me to figure out the directions, to just look at the map and tell him which exit we had to take; he needed it now or we were going to miss it. I was searching and not finding it. I wasn't so good with maps, I was explaining. I hadn't driven a car in years; what did he expect? He was too busy freaking out to hear what I was saying. Of course, he knew everything I was telling him already. We'd been dating for a year.

The truth was, I'd been pretty sure he hadn't wanted to go to this wedding at all. He was doing it to be a good guy, a good sport, and while I appreciated the effort, I would have appreciated it *more* if he'd truly been happy to be there with me. I'd packed my strapless J.Crew bridesmaid dress along with shoes, a pair of jeans, a couple of sundresses, and some layering sweaters—the nights were bound to get cold in rural Vermont, even in the summertime—knowing that the glimmer of excitement, of going-to-a-weddingness, that I felt was not something he shared. But he'd come anyway. He really didn't have a choice. He was my boyfriend.

Three years after Caitlin married Cash came the wedding of Emily, the second in our college roommate threesome to head down the aisle. Emily and I were still close, though we lived in different states now. We talked at least monthly on the phone, we e-mailed regularly, and we'd even traveled to our respective towns to visit each other. I'd met her soon-to-be husband, Mark, and I liked him. Their wedding made for a reunion of sorts: Caitlin and Cash would be there, and I'd bring Jason, my boyfriend, and the now-coupled college friends would be back together again, like old times but better.

There was more to it than that, though. At weddings, feelings are amplified beyond the norm, good or bad. When you add someone you're dating to the mix, especially someone who's not exactly new but who hasn't been around long enough to be considered "old," either, questions and concerns about your relationship are thrown into high relief as you compare yourselves with other couples present and, of course, with the bride and groom.

After the initial car drama, the right roads were taken and we calmed down and found a kind of symbiosis. The anticipatory wedding vibe I'd initially felt slowly seeped into the car and us both, I think, helped along by the sunny summer day and near-empty highways, the rhythmic turning of the rental car's wheels, and the music on our favorite CDs. It was just the two of us, with no decisions to make, driving. We arrived at our destination in the early afternoon, pulling onto a dirt road surrounded by trees that led to a colonial-looking inn set on rolling green hills. Emily ran out to meet us, wearing a floral shirt with a sweater over it, her dark hair pulled back in a ponytail, her skin lightly tanned and makeup-free. She looked just like the eighteen-year-old girl I'd introduced myself to that first day of freshman year in college. "I'm so excited you're here," she said, hugging us both. "We're going to have the best time!"

Emily had met Mark in their post-graduate premed program. She had a personal connection to medicine, having been diagnosed with a severe peanut allergy as a child. "I touched a peanut as a baby," she had told me, "and I broke out in hives." Since then, peanuts were the enemy, to be avoided at all costs. There had inevitably been incidents, when she accidentally bit into a peanut granola bar in high school and had to be rushed to the ER, for instance. Nearly everyone knows at least one person with a food allergy today (check your labels carefully!), but she was the first I'd met who had such an extreme reaction to the otherwise banal nut. She'd shown me how to administer an EpiPen: You pressed it into her outer thigh and, I inferred from her instructions, hoped for the best. I prayed I'd never be in the position of having to ham-fistedly attempt to save my friend's life.

This allergy was her only health issue, though, and she didn't let it get in the way of her physical or mental ambitions. She ran marathons and did a stint on the crew team, along with serving as a member of the group of student EMTs. She came to college wanting to be a doctor, but transferred to the business school after wrestling with organic chemistry. We graduated, and she worked for several years in finance in New York City before deciding to return to her first love and go to med school. She had to finish her premed classes before applying, and that's how she met Mark. As the older members of their program, they studied together and became friends outside of class, too. That connection led to more.

While I'd seen her date in college, and I'd heard much about her high school boyfriend, the guy she for a time thought she'd end up with, she sounded different talking about Mark. He was the smartest person she knew, she said, as if worried she couldn't match his intellect. His other qualities ran like a list of all the right check boxes in a man: He was handsome, athletic, a book lover, intelligent and easygoing, close to his family but not *too* close, and something of a do-gooder, like she was. He was also a vegetarian, though this part was concerning. He was someone for whom peanut butter was a staple. She was anxious, but not just about the peanuts. I detected the early fear that comes from meeting someone great, someone different from all those who have come before, and feeling afraid he might not return the affection. That was not a concern I'd seen in her previously. "Of course he likes you," I'd say. "How could he not?"

Soon it became clear that her worries were foundless, and anxiety gave way to planning. For med school, they applied to and got into Dartmouth together. They moved into a big, drafty house near campus that had more rooms than furniture, but their minds were on far more important matters than interior design or even heat, and both of them were happy that way, tossing another quilt on the bed, focusing on the future. After med school would come residencies; that they would be married at some point between those two stages became a foregone conclusion.

The invitation came. The wedding would take place at a quaint old inn in Vermont the summer after they graduated, the ceremony to be held outside in the afternoon sun, the reception under a tent just steps away. Wedge sandals were suggested, as heels would puncture the thin skin of the lawn and push through the soil. As a bridesmaid, along with Caitlin and Emily's younger sister, Rachel, I would don a reasonably priced pale blue dress with a seersucker pattern from J.Crew that seemed ripe for rewearing. I was twenty-eight, and, for the first time in my wedding-going career, I had a date, an actual boyfriend to be my plus-one. This would be our first—of, if all went well, many—together.

He and I had met in Pleasantville, New York, at Reader's Digest, where we'd both been hired to work on a test magazine for an online auction site. Like many such endeavors, the project never really got off the ground. After a few months of work, for which we first commuted from Manhattan to Westchester by train and later hitched rides with a semi-narcoleptic colleague who had borrowed a purple Dodge Neon dubbed "the Grape Ape" from a friend, the whole idea was killed. At least we'd been paid, which was more than some of our friends, toiling in other publishing pursuits, could say. But the most important thing that came out of that job was meeting Jason.

At first, I didn't think much about him. He was tall and very thin, with pale blond hair that he kept closely shaved, all the better as I still harbored a vague grudge against blond men on account of my mother's first husband. He had vivid blue eyes, which he considered his best feature, and usually wore periwinkle shirts and sweaters to highlight them. He was from the Midwest and had just moved to New York, to an apartment in the East Village, after completing a graduate program in journalism. Smart and industrious, he was, like many a twentysomething transplant to the city, eager to launch a successful professional career for himself.

I had been freelancing for Reader's Digest prior to this assignment, on projects that required taking the company's previously published book content and refurbishing it into magazine form. It was by no means scintillating work, but I'd just moved back from Boston and was happy to have a job related to words, even if it did involve a weird backward Metro-North commute, and a lot of cutting and pasting text about, say, vitamins. Quickly, I learned how things worked in that strange, cavernous place, which looked more like a college campus than the office of a global publishing company and often felt eerily vacant. Once the team was amassed for the test magazine, I'd see Jason on my train, and sometimes we'd sit together and talk, or not talk and just listen to our respective music. One day someone took Jason's spot in the long row next to me, and as he waved and walked past in search of an open seat, I acknowledged I was just a little bit disappointed. I decided I'd do my best to get to know him better, this quiet, funny guy who shared my interests in stories and writing and producing good content. He had at least one vice that I knew of:

He was an unabashed smoker, which helped boost his cred from "your average nice guy" into "ever so slightly bad," and that was appealing, too.

I don't think he even thought about liking me, though, until the project was over. One night I invited him to come along with a group of my friends to a bar in the East Village. It was near his apartment, so he couldn't say no. The hours passed and the evening turned into just the two of us. It became too late for me to go home, or so I said (a total lie: It's never too late to go home in New York City), and he offered his couch. Sleeping in his apartment that night felt right, even if I was on the couch. The next day, realizing I'd forgotten something, I went back, and that's when we finally kissed. "Was this supposed to happen last night?" he asked. Finally, he was catching on.

By the time we went to Emily's wedding we were an established couple. We'd told each other "I love you" and meant it. That said, we still lacked a certain confidence in our collaborative decision-making skills. We'd attempt to go out to eat, and no restaurant would be good enough. We lived in New York City, land of one million options, but I think both of us were deeply afraid of deciding on something the other didn't like. The burden of that—the possibility of making the wrong choice and then having to deal with the repercussions—was paralyzing, so we'd stay in and eat grilled cheese instead. He was, it must be said, very good at making grilled cheese. For a while that seemed perfectly fine, even desirable: a guy who would cook the most delicious grilled cheese sandwiches, and the feeling of comfort and safety and togetherness that brought.

We both knew that a cozy relationship confined to the walls of an apartment was not enough, though, cheese or no cheese. What did it mean if we seemed, when out in the world, so glaringly incompatible? A couple should be able to adapt in different situations and, I thought, have fun doing so. Yet we disagreed on such basics as what we even considered fun. He preferred to stay in and enjoy the creature comforts of home; when socializing, he tended to keep to a small group of friends. I liked to dress up and throw myself into the city, to go out and let whatever would transpire do so—the more, the merrier. But opposites attract! Or not. We'd find out. This wedding meant, possibly perilously, that we were taking our show on the road.

We headed to our room, complete with its gift basket of Vermont-inspired items, homemade jam and honey and (peanut-free) granola bars. Across the hall from us were Caitlin and Cash, no longer newlyweds but full-fledged happily marrieds, who, I feared, put us to shame with their vibrant show of love. We were quieter and less overt about how we felt about each other. Did we love each other less than they did? This wasn't a competition, I kept reminding myself. Jason was someone I could trust, my best friend, the person I turned to if things were good or if they were bad. He was my ally. Relationships were work, that's what everyone said. Annoyingly, what no one explained was how much work was the right amount.

We unpacked, hanging things that needed to unwrinkle, and then went downstairs to sit on the pretty white porch and look out onto the lush grass and talk with our friends, who, of course, were really my friends, not his. But they welcomed him, and he made an effort in return.

"Oh, so, you guys," said Emily. "The big thing is, we're going to have pie at the wedding, instead of cake."

"Pie?" asked Caitlin. "Really? Why pie?"

"I love pie! The wedding planner did not understand *at all*, but she got on board, eventually. Pecan and strawberry rhubarb. Doesn't that seem more Vermont?" Emily looked at us expectantly. Who here was an unimaginative cake person, and who appreciated the beauty and simplicity of pie?

"Pie is better," I agreed, and Jason nodded.

"We love pie," he said, putting his arm around me. It was the most coupled I felt that day, and it felt good.

Emily had a wedding planner. Caitlin had used one, too. Neither of theirs had been high-strung, reality-TV types, bustling around with clipboards and cell phones, yelling about bling and making bouquets pop, though. Instead they were unassuming women who stood at the edge of things, or completely hidden from view, and directed the setup of tents and chairs, told the bridesmaids to walk when it was time to walk, and subtly tried to ensure that things would run on time. The wedding planner was supposed to make things easy, so Emily could focus on her friends and family and not on the nitty-gritty details of the wedding itself. Emily didn't care much about the nitty-gritty, anyway. She wanted the day to be enjoyable for everyone, but she and Mark were both too pragmatic and easygoing to devote much time to worrying about the color of the napkins or whether there was a salad fork in the proper place at each table setting. Their casualness worked out well for us bridesmaids. I had only to wear the dress (which I would, in fact, wear again), to walk down the aisle with the bouquet in my hands, and to have the requisite number of photos taken as part of the bridal party. Oh, and to smile. Easy as pie.

The first night we stayed up and had drinks together in the lounge downstairs at the inn. Many of Emily's friends from high school were there, dates in tow. Emily had something to say about each of them, whispering in my ear, "He's sweet, but not very intellectual . . . She's always bossing him around, but he likes it, that's the way they work . . . She thinks he'll propose within the year . . . They're trying for kid number one already . . . Has it really been three years since we were in the Dominican for Caitlin's wedding? They seem like they're doing great!" and so on. Part of me wondered what she'd say about me and Jason. The other part didn't want to know what that same lens cast upon everyone else's relationships might reveal if turned upon mine. He and I hadn't slept together in a while—perhaps another symptom of our overall lack of confidence—and I doubted this would change in our hotel room in Vermont, the thin walls such that we could hear conversations in the next room.

I was right. When we went to bed he fell asleep quickly, and I stayed up, listening to Caitlin and Cash laugh across the hall, wondering if there was something wrong with us, something that couldn't be made right. My greatest fear was that our relationship was a charade, the two of us attempting to go through the motions of what was expected, but not really knowing how, or whether we even should. I wanted to be happy. I wanted to be in love. Yet at this wedding what I found myself feeling most of all was confused, hopping back and forth between joy and sadness, excitement and worry, optimism and defeat. I was more settled than I had ever been, and yet I was anything but that. Maybe this was just how weddings were, especially when you brought a date along, I thought. Everything felt larger than life, but there were real-life questions that still needed answers.

The inn was known for its proximity to a store famous for blown glass, made on the premises. They had tours, we learned from our wedding packet, and there was a restaurant there that Emily vouched for. So the next day we went, partly also to buy the couple a wedding gift, oblivious to the fact that everyone at the wedding who hadn't already purchased a present would likely have the same idea. The food at the restaurant was, as promised, good, and there were picture-perfect views of the nearby water-falls. We shared chocolate cake for dessert, alternating bites. Afterward we took a tour, watching a guy with a long metal tube and heat-resistant gloves turn a shapeless blob of molten glass into something beautiful, and then we walked through the aisles and aisles of items for sale in the adjacent shop. In the end, though, we couldn't decide what to buy. "I'll find them something in New York," I told Jason, and I did: vintage wineglasses in a shade of green I knew Emily loved, which I found in a shop near my apartment some months after the wedding. I signed the card from both of us.

. . .

We returned to the inn in the early afternoon and began to get ready for the wedding. I left Jason to shower and made my way with my dress and shoes and makeup bag to the suite in the next wing where we were to prep for the event with the bride. Emily was already there, standing in her white slip, her hair in curlers, being advised by the stylist she'd hired to do our hair and makeup. We primped and were pinned and polished, and as the sun streamed in from the windows, the pale blue of our gowns against the white lace of the bride's created a dreamy, enchanted effect in this room full of ladies. We all felt beautiful, but more than beautiful, we had been transformed. With the help of bobby pins and hair spray and lipstick and our pretty dresses, we had shape-shifted from regular girls into bridesmaids.

It was time to walk down the aisle, a narrow grass-covered path surrounded by white folding chairs some yards away from the tent where the reception would take place. A few paces back from Caitlin, I strode out onto the lawn, clutching my bouquet of wildflowers carefully against my waist with both hands. I had not been a bridesmaid before, and I took it seriously, biting my lip slightly to make sure I didn't laugh or cry. Despite the wedge warning, I'd worn heels, and they did sink into the lawn as mentioned, but I got through my brief journey without mishap and stood between Caitlin and Rachel, watching the ceremony from the bridesmaid vantage point that also allowed a view of the other guests. When Emily and Mark stood in front of us and promised the minister and the crowd of eagerly watching witnesses that they'd love and honor each other forever, I couldn't keep tears from welling in my eyes. The couple kissed, and I looked out at Jason in the audience. He was sitting alone in his suit and tie, diligently taking photos of me and my friends, and seeing this effort—an attempt to be a part of things without really having to be a part of things—again brought forth a complicated combination of pleasure and heartache. When he caught me looking at him, he smiled and pointed the camera in my direction. I smiled back.

The crowd descended on the bride and groom, hugging and kissing and back-slapping and congratulating, while in the background the lawn chairs were picked up and toted away. It was that in-between time, after the ceremony but before the reception begins in earnest, and Jason came over and slipped his arm around me. "You looked so serious," he said. "I thought you might cry."

"I almost did, a little," I admitted. "It was so nice, wasn't it?" He nodded. I remembered he'd once told me he wanted to get married in his own backyard, and I'd argued that the guy didn't get to just decide everything. As a wedding, this had probably not been too far off from what he imagined for himself. That felt like a kind of decision-making connection between the two of us, and I hugged him. "Ready for some pecan pie?" I asked.

"Mmm-hmm," he said.

He took my arm and we headed over to the tent, where hors d'oeuvres were being set out next to the bar. There were circular tables covered in pink tablecloths interspersed throughout the space. The band was setting up to play on the stage above the dance floor. Emily's little brother, a teenager in his own band, would be joining them for the first set. When he set foot onstage, the crowd began to cheer. Emily took to the dance floor with her dad, and Mark joined them with his mom. They swirled about elegantly at first before letting loose, legs and arms flailing, good and properly getting down.

The next hour, and the one after, seemed to go by in seconds. Wedding time is different, after all, than regular time. We mingled with other guests at our table and on the dance floor, catching up with those we knew and making conversation with those we didn't. As a bridesmaid, I was part of it, this thing. People stopped me to say they'd heard about me, Emily's college friend. They hoped everything was going well for me in New York, and what a pleasant day we were having! It was so wonderful that the weather had held. I'd looked lovely up there, during the ceremony. Had I nearly cried? They certainly had! Oh, was that my boyfriend? What a nice young man. He was, he was.

We helped ourselves to food and replenished our drinks, and then repeated. I convinced Jason to get up and dance, which was not an insubstantial win, and as we swayed in time to the music, the sun slowly set. Nearby, Emily's mom and dad were dancing, too, and beyond them were Caitlin and Cash. We were surrounded by couples, and for a moment, we all seemed perfectly aligned, artfully poised in the scene before the scene. It was an unsustainable note, but it was a glorious one. I have a photo of Jason and me from that day, our cheeks pressed together. His eyes are very blue and match my dress. He is holding my hand, and we look happy.

We sat down again, and it seemed to strike everyone at once that the bride was gone. We had not seen her in quite a while, in fact. Had anyone? Her groom was gone, too. While at most weddings a disappearance by the newlywed couple wouldn't necessarily be cause for alarm, this felt different. It was too early for the party to be over. We hadn't had dessert yet. The pie, they hadn't even brought out the pie. There was a cluster of people talking near one of the tents, and her dad was in that group. They looked serious. I left Jason at our table and made my way over. "Where's Emily?" I asked. "Is something going on?"

"The pie," said her dad, who put his hand on my shoulder, consoling and calm.

"The pie?" I asked. "What do you mean, the pie?"

"They were setting out the pecan pie," he continued. "She took a bite and had an allergic reaction. She's upstairs with Mark. We've called an ambulance."

"The pie had *peanuts* in it?" I said, flabbergasted. I knew Emily could not have failed to explain her allergy. It was the first thing she said to anyone who was offering her food. The wedding planner had to know, the wedding planner whose job it was to take care of things so Emily could have fun. I remembered my EpiPen training, and I ran upstairs, joining Emily's sister Rachel in the doorway to the room where we'd all gotten ready earlier that day. Inside, Emily was sitting quietly on a love seat with her new husband, who had administered the epinephrine. The yellow case that contained the injection lay discarded on a side table. He was checking her vital signs. "The ambulance will be here soon," he said, glancing at his watch. "How are you holding up, Em?"

Emily nodded, confirming she was okay, but Rachel and I were both near tears anyway. "What happened?" we asked. "How could this *happen?*"

Emily spoke slowly, wearily. She'd said this before. "There were peanuts in the crust of the pecan pie. I ate a tiny, tiny piece before realizing. I knew it immediately and told Mark. Don't worry, Mark knows what to do."

Rachel and I looked at each other, worried anyway. "Thank God they're both doctors!" I whispered, trying not to cry.

"Thank God she married him!" said Rachel. We clung to each other, staring at the couple on their love seat, and broke down in sobs like complete and total idiots. Everything is amplified at a wedding, feelings good and bad, and it may be that we were only doing our part to add to the emotional panoply at this event. We had to let our reaction to what had happened be known, to let it out somehow. It all felt so unfair. *Not peanuts, not on her wedding day.* Mark and Emily allowed us a moment before interrupting. This was their day, not ours, and they hardly needed two hysterical bridesmaids to make matters more dramatic than they already were.

"Look, you guys should go back to the party," he said. "The ambulance is on the way, and, seriously, everything's under control. Emily will be fine."

"I don't want you to miss anything," she added diplomatically, and Mark nodded, keeping a firm grasp on her hand and an eye on her pulse, too.

"It will be okay," he assured us again.

Emily's dad appeared with two burly EMTs. As she was being

helped downstairs, she yelled back at us, still enthusiastic despite the circumstances, "You have to tell me everything that happens!"

We returned to the party. It seemed the only thing to do, the one thing we could give the bride in this moment. But the mood had changed. While we danced and ate and drank, conversations would not start or end without understanding looks, hugs, and hushed side conversations: "Is she back yet?" . . . "God, I hope she's okay" . . . "I can't believe this happened at her wedding" . . . "Seriously, who puts peanuts in a pecan pie?" . . . "I would sue the shit out of that wedding planner."

The wedding planner could not be found. I imagined she had fled as far as she could possibly go, maybe even to Canada, knowing she'd have to show her face at some point, but not able to do it, not now. Out of respect for the bride, for a while most of us avoided the pecan pie, but it was left out and eventually it was gone, consumed by those who weren't allergic to peanuts. Hours later, after the band had stopped playing, the tent had been taken down, and the lawn behind the inn had grown hushed and dewy, bearing little trace of all that had happened earlier that day, Emily returned from the hospital. Most of us had changed into casual clothes, and Jason had already excused himself for bed, but I had stayed up, waiting to see my friend back to the inn on her wedding night, unable to sleep until I had. Her dad had ordered pizzas for everyone, and we snacked and chatted idly and hoped she'd walk in soon.

Mark was right, we needn't have worried. She was fine but tired, dazed from the epinephrine and her time in the ambulance and at the ER. It had been a long day. The couple came in together, him helping her across the threshold and into the room where we were gathered. When we saw them we broke into a round of applause. She managed to stay awake for an hour or two before going to bed, and at one point, she and I found ourselves alone in a conversation. She laughed as she told me of the sensation they'd made at the ER, her in her white wedding dress, Mark in his tux. "That's how you get service," she said. Mark joined us and was laughing, too, but when I asked what they were going to do about the mistake that had been made, he got as angry as I'd ever seen him. "We told that wedding planner over and over again that Emily's allergic to peanuts," he said. "We have it in writing. She could have died!"

"On my wedding day," said Emily, shaking her head. And then came the question we'd all been asking the entire night: "Who puts peanuts in pecan pie, anyway?"

The next day, Mark, Emily, and her dad were called to a meeting with an extremely nervous inn manager. The wedding planner was there, too, standing in the background, circles under her eyes, wringing her hands. She offered to quit. "That's not necessary," they said. The inn manager offered not to charge for the pies. "Really?" said Mark. "That's your gesture? You're not going to charge us for a *dessert that could have killed my wife?*"

In the end, I was told, the prices of the pies and a Champagne toast were struck from the bill. As doctors, with concerns about malpractice insurance long drilled into their heads, Mark and

Emily were not inclined to sue. As newlyweds, they just wanted to get on with the business of being married. But the very next morning, as Jason and I were having breakfast in the inn before we began the drive back to New York City, I noticed a big bowl of peanut butter with a spoon tucked in it, set out among the inoffensive array of cereal and fruit and coffee for guests to consume with their English muffins and toast.

"Are you kidding me?" I said.

"Oh, Jesus," said Jason. "Quick, let's get rid of it." We returned the peanut butter to the kitchen and asked the staff not to put it out again while the bride was still a guest there.

A year later, Mark and Emily received a card from the inn inviting them back with an anniversary discount of 10 percent. They did not return.

9.

Forever and Never

⋆✦

A little over a year had passed since Emily's wedding when
Marjorie and Brian announced they'd be taking their turn
down the aisle. I was still living in New York, still freelancing
in publishing, and still dating Jason. We were twenty-nine, and it
felt like it was time to start considering important things, like
whether this was the relationship we wanted forever and what
our next steps might be. I hadn't told my friends—admitting it
out loud seemed tantamount to relationship failure—but I was
deeply conflicted. Jason was my best friend, the most important
person in my life, and I couldn't see my future clearly without
him. Yet more and more I found myself thinking that if I *really*
chose him, for always, and he chose me, we'd be missing out on
something else, someone who would be better for each of us, and
the better, if abstract, life we'd have with that other person.

The news of Marjorie's engagement was hardly a surprise.
We'd been expecting it for years, and so had she. After finish-

ing grad school in Maryland, Brian had moved to Nashville to be with her. In my eyes, they were taking things slowly and reasonably, though later I learned that this time long distance had not been without frustrations. Marjorie was impatient to get things moving; Brian was hung up on finding the perfect book about proposing before he considered popping the question outside the confines of a page. They lived in separate apartments for a year before moving in together, into an actual house. Three years after we'd converged on my onetime hometown for Claire's wedding, I went to visit them and slept on a queen-sized blow-up mattress in their den. We barbecued outside on the deck in the heat of the Nashville summer and drank cold beers from the icebox outside. They coexisted in an adult fashion of which I had been envious, with cars and jobs with health benefits and dinners they'd planned ahead of time and cooked together while drinking martinis. It looked natural for them, though I didn't know if it ever would be for me, with Jason or without him.

Shortly after the proposal, Marjorie called to ask if I would be her maid of honor. I said yes and immediately went out and bought a couple of wedding-planning books to mail to her. This was the first and only such request I'd ever received (it still is), and I took it seriously. I would help in whatever way I could, I promised. Of course, I didn't live in the same town and might not be the right person to coordinate the shower or bachelorette, or to get in touch with vendors or do whatever my duties might be—*what might my duties be, exactly?*—but I would be there and take care of as much as possible. I wouldn't miss it for the world. Maid of honor: This was a big deal.

Plans for the wedding began to take shape. The ceremony would be at the couple's church in Nashville, the reception at the top of a building downtown offering panoramic views of the city. Marjorie, caught between the desires of her parents and future in-laws, and further challenged by the need to keep costs down, decided on a modest reception that she hoped would satisfy all. There would be beer and wine instead of a full bar, and filling snacks instead of a sit-down dinner. That meant crab cakes for Brian, a nod to Maryland; mini ham and turkey sandwiches for Marjorie, an homage to Southern banquet food; and a huge smoked salmon, lox without the bagels, to represent New York, where they'd met. I was invited with not just a plus-one, but with a date whose name came on the card, in calligraphy, right next to mine: *Jen and Jason*. We accepted with pleasure. *We* wouldn't miss it for the world.

A month or so before the wedding, a high school friend who lived in Nashville now, too, threw a shower for Marjorie. The New York–based bridesmaid team, which consisted of our former roommate, Violet, Marjorie's college friend Kate, and me, flew down for the weekend to don our most ladylike frocks and sit and watch Marjorie open her gifts while sipping sweet tea and eating dainty little cakes. I wore a purple dress I'd bought at Ann Taylor Loft. It had beige polka dots all over it and a sash around the waist and, I thought, looked precisely like what a nice, wholesome maid-of-honor-type girl would wear to a wedding shower in the South. I dutifully took photos and recorded the gifts and names of their givers in a small pink notebook, until Marjorie's mother, noting my unfortunate psycho-killer handwriting, took that duty over for me. I drank punch and ate finger sandwiches and mostly got over my latent horror of showers—is there anything worse than having to feign enthrallment over a bunch of brownie tins?—for one day. Violet and Kate and I had gone in together on our gift, which I did want to see Marjorie open. It was a large Le Creuset Dutch oven from Williams-Sonoma that I hoped would be a valuable contribution to the couple's future in dining together. It was the prettiest shade of yellow-green and would look great in their kitchen. "Yay!" she said, opening the package and tossing the ribbons and paper to the side, where they were quickly collected by another party guest to make the rehearsal bouquet. "Thank you, ladies!"

Along with attending the shower, we three bridesmaids were there to help tie up any loose wedding ends. Issue Number One involved our wardrobes for the occasion. After searching all over Nashville for a gown, Marjorie had gone to visit her parents in Alabama and found a dress she loved at a David's Bridal, that mass-market retailer that is both fearsome and functional, providing moderately priced, variously designed satin creations to the wedding-having public. Shipped to her in Nashville, the dress's tea-length skirt, Marjorie's rebel wink at tradition, had become a mess of wrinkles and uneven hems. While any issues were supposed to be referred to the store of purchase, the location where she'd bought it was nearly two hours away. That, combined with the matter of bridesmaid attire—we'd wanted to select our outfits together—meant a trip to her local David's Bridal.

I had never been to a David's Bridal. I think Marjorie was the only one who had, and she was the only one who was properly prepared. It's a vast behemoth, with storefronts all over the country. This one was situated somewhere on the edge of town, far enough away from the city proper to lend it the geographical span required to house the hundreds or thousands of dresses it contained. Inside, among the rows and rows of endless white, mostly white, but also hunter green and taxicab yellow, rosy pink and royal purple, and blue—so many blues—and red and puce and even mahogany fabric, underneath dizzying fluorescent lighting, were sample dresses that could be tried and fitted and purchased. They were in similar fashions but different colors, or similar colors but different fashions, and somewhere in this massive array of hanging clothing you might find the one you had dreamed of, if you looked hard enough and long enough, if you put your mind to it and really, really tried.

Weaving through the racks of material were women who seemed as if they might be twins, triplets, quintuplets, or possibly clones. They were small of stature, with pins in their pincerlike, lipsticked mouths and their reddish-brownish-blondish hair cut short for practical reasons. These were the wedding-dress matrons who, I had heard tell, would usher an unwitting girl into the giant dressing room at the back of the store and, within seconds, have her pinned up, tucked in, and matched with this gown or that one. They'd prop her on a platform facing a semicircle of full-length mirrors so she could see the front, back, and sides of her look, and they'd coo and sigh and, most of all, sell the dress. Then they'd start with the add-ons: a veil, the proper underwear and panty hose, the bridesmaids' dresses, the garter, a wedding purse (Why? Why not?) and on and on and on. You could spend your life buying things for your wedding, buying more and more things with money that would never see the satin-lined insides of your wedding purse. These women were pros. They took no prisoners.

One such lady saw us as we entered the store, the four of us girls, dazed and clearly out of our element. The lights were blinding; the air felt thin. All the white, shiny dresses in the room loomed before us like ghosts of brides past. "Hi," she said brightly. "Can I help you?"

We'd planned ahead that we would avoid revealing the whole truth about Marjorie's dress, since technically it was supposed to go to another store, and we didn't have time to be told no. Marjorie started. "I brought my wedding dress in," she said. "They were supposed to steam it, but it's a wreck."

"I'll take a look at that," said the woman, pursing her lips to keep nonexistent pins steady. She glanced at the tag attached to the plastic wrap on the dress. "This is strange. Did you buy this here?"

Marjorie frowned, knitting her eyebrows. I knew she didn't want to lie. I took this as my moment to be a real maid of honor. I'd fight her battles for her so the bride could stay cool, calm, collected, and honest—bridelike—to the last. "It's from David's Bridal," I said, which was itself true. "You should have it resteamed for free. It's only right." Around me, Kate and Violet pretended to shop. They wanted none of this. Marjorie smiled sweetly, and the woman started punching things into the computer in front of her. I tried to look vaguely threatening, like I was From New York and Got Things Done. "I'm sorry," said the clerk. "I can't find you listed in our store database."

"We're also here to find three bridesmaids' dresses, and a veil, too," I said, playing our only trump card.

"Oh?" She perked up a little.

"Yes. But, tell me, why should we continue to shop here if you can't fix the problem that your establishment caused in the first place?" Ooh, I had this. I had this. Below the counter, Marjorie squeezed my hand.

"Hold on for a moment, please." The woman disappeared into a small room adjacent to the checkout counter. The minutes ticked by. I hoped I hadn't pushed too far. If she came back and said tough luck or, worse, booted us from the store, we'd be up a creek without a wedding dress. She returned, a satisfied smile on her face. "We're happy to steam the dress again for you as a complimentary service," she said. "Now, what else can I help you with?"

Ha, I thought. I was the best maid of honor ever. I turned to look back at Violet and Kate, who'd discovered what might be described as the "neon princess" aisle. They were alternating between holding gowns up to themselves and doubling over in laughter.

Marjorie, in her efforts to be a laid-back, relaxed bride, had told us we could wear whatever we wanted as her attendants, but we didn't think that would look right. As much as bridesmaids complain about hideous dictated dresses that can never be worn again, or gowns that give the initial impression of comfort only to become chambers of torture at the actual event, in this case our matching wedding attire was completely our own doing. We had wanted uniformity. We'd wanted, I think, to be bridesmaids, and to be seen as such. We strolled through the aisles and aisles of racks, searching, and we found our gowns: chocolate-brown satin strapless concoctions with little rhinestone belts and tea-length skirts that would match Marjorie's. They were understated and inexpensive and, to our amazement, quite comfy. (They would, in fact, later morph into chambers of fashion torture, but not until several hours in on Marjorie's wedding day.) After we'd had the dresses fitted, we selected an array of undergarments, a pretty, simple veil for the bride, and a satin wrap she could don if it got chilly. No wedding purse, but still, the saleslady had gotten the last laugh.

We checked out with about an hour left until the three of us had to get to the airport to fly back to New York. We were in a nondescript shopping center, the natural environment for a nondescript, mammoth bridal store, and right outside there was a nondescript chain restaurant. "It's no Per Se or anything," said Violet, ironically, as our budgets were quite clearly far more beer than they were Champagne. "But I *suppose* it'll do."

We filed into a booth, ordered icy Diet Cokes all around, and were just about to place our orders for four different highly photogenic chicken salads when Kate leaned over the table. "Do I have red marks on my neck?" she asked, scratching.

We inspected. Red was the least of it. She had large welts

running from the bottom of her chin down into the V-neck of her T-shirt. "Um," I said.

"Yeah," managed Violet. Marjorie started digging around in her purse for some Benadryl.

"Holy shit!" Kate yelled, peering into her shirt. We sat looking at one another in shock as she rushed to the bathroom for a closer analysis of her skin condition. Was this what weddings could do to a person?

Minutes later she returned with a rueful expression and announced matter-of-factly that she had broken out in hives to her waist. "I need a real drink, I think," she said, and we agreed a round was in order. It all became funny.

"I think Kate is allergic to David's Bridal," Violet quipped.

"You're like the princess and the pea of weddings," I added.

"Yeah, I'm so high-end," Kate agreed, reaching toward her neck for a momentarily satisfying scratch.

Marjorie grabbed her hand. "Don't touch it," she said, the same way I could imagine her instructing her inevitable children when they were struck with inevitable chicken pox. Kate acquiesced and sighed, sipping her beer.

Back in New York she saw a dermatologist who confirmed she had a form of dermatitis that may have been brought about by the stress of wedding-dress shopping, or a sensitivity to certain fabrics at the store. It might have been a combination of both; it could have been something else entirely. She was prescribed steroids and an anti-itch cream, and the rash eventually went away. Whatever its cause, which we'd never know for sure, when Kate walked down the aisle at her own wedding several years later, she was *not* wearing a dress from David's Bridal.

Some weeks later we were flying back to Nashville, and this time Jason was with me. As he slept, I ran through what I planned to say at the rehearsal dinner and thought again about how best to fulfill my role as maid of honor. I had an anticipatory fluttering in my stomach. I'd tried on my bridesmaid dress the night before, and it fit perfectly. I couldn't wait to see my best friend again, and to be with her for this moment. I thought back to us in high school, our crushes on boys, our confessions, our dreams. I also thought about what this wedding meant for Jason and me. For years I'd been asking my mom to get my grandmother's ring—the one she'd designed herself and had a jeweler make using the diamond Hamilton Booth had given her before he died—out of the security vault at the bank. She had finally said she'd give it to me on my thirtieth birthday, which was now just a few months away. I'd imagined it being my own engagement ring. But I was no longer so sure that Jason and I would still be together for that date. We'd been a couple long enough that I should know if he was the one, I reasoned. If I still didn't know for sure, I worried that could only mean he wasn't.

We got in the Thursday night before the wedding. We'd have most of Friday to ourselves before the rehearsal dinner, for which we'd be bused to a nearby country club. Saturday would be filled with wedding preparation, from early morning (hair-call time was nine thirty a.m.) to midday (for wedding party photos and church arrival), and then the wedding itself in the early afternoon. Jason would be mostly on his own until I could reconnect with him at the reception, after my most consuming maid-of-honor duties were done.

After we checked in, we headed to the hotel restaurant for dinner, and I texted Marjorie that we'd arrived. "Let's meet at the hotel bar in an hour?" she suggested.

"Yes!" I wrote. I couldn't wait to see her and hoped Jason might feel the same way, but when I told him the plan, he said he didn't feel well. Disappointed, I went to meet her alone.

There she was at the bar, a glass of wine in hand. I suppressed my squeal of pleasure at the sight of her, and we hugged. "I have a present for you," I said, handing her my gift, a large white bowl with a tiny bride and groom etched into the bottom atop the word *Happily*. When I'd purchased it, I'd imagined her using the bowl through old age, remembering her wedding day as the years passed by.

After she oohed and aahed, the inevitable question arose. "Where's Jason?" she asked.

"He's sick," I explained, and she made worried noises, hoping it was nothing serious and that he'd recover quickly. I nodded, but I didn't understand it myself. He'd met Marjorie only once before, when she visited New York early on in my relationship with him. Couldn't he have made the effort for a brief hello in the hotel bar, a chance to again see this best friend of mine, the bride to whom I was maid of honor, before the wedding pitched into high gear? As she and I talked excitedly about what the weekend would bring, the lack of his presence hovered in the background.

"Are you feeling better?" I asked him when I got back to the room.

He was busy working at his computer. "Yeah, it was just a stomachache," he said. Well, he'd always been shy and less socially inclined than I was. I'd give him space and let him get his wedding legs, I decided. Everyone reacted to these situations differently, after all. Maybe he really *had* felt sick.

The next morning, we woke, had coffee, and planned out our day. We'd walk around town, find a place for lunch, and see some of Nashville before returning to get ready for the rehearsal dinner. It was sunny and warm enough in November that we didn't need more than light jackets. But even our relaxed plan to venture out and see things failed. That old indecision and incompatibility, which, to tell the truth, we'd never really combatted, rose up again in this new town. We couldn't find a place to eat that we agreed on, and when we did, we found that it was closed. We tried again, and finally settled on a hole-in-the-wall spot near Vanderbilt's campus. We ate bad pizza in silence, and at the end of lunch, Jason told me he had work to do. We returned to the hotel, he headed to our room, and I went to check on Marjorie. "How's he feeling?" she asked me.

"I'm not sure," I said. "He's under a lot of work stress. I think he's a little bit out of his element. I guess it's hard to be here with so many strangers."

"But he hasn't been around any yet," she said. I couldn't deny that.

It got worse. At the rehearsal dinner, surrounded by Marjorie's family and all of our friends, I gave a speech about how much my longest-sustaining friend meant to me, and how happy I was to see her with someone who was such a great match for her, who loved her so much, who wanted the same things she did. Marjorie cried, and Violet and Kate and I cried, too, and then we hugged in a big, warm friend circle and toasted with Jack Daniel's shots, which Marjorie's dad and brother delivered to us from the bar. I looked around for Jason and found him staring off into space.

Throughout dinner he continued to be distant, unapproachable, and largely silent. At one point he was offered a shot but said no, opting instead to hover in a corner and check his phone. I felt myself getting angrier. This was not just a bad mood, a stomachache, or work stress. He wasn't even trying. Marjorie's dad asked a group of us if we wanted to step outside for a cigarette, and though I didn't smoke, I went and puffed on one anyway. I'd had a lot to drink by that point, and I was somewhere between thrilled for my friend and very, very pissed at my boyfriend. I confided in Marjorie's dad, "I don't know what's wrong with him. I don't know why he can't just have a good time. What should I do?"

"Dump him," he told me, taking a drag of his cigarette. "There's plenty of fish in the sea. This is not the guy for you."

Well, I'd asked.

I wonder how many weddings take place because people have gone far enough into those relationships that it's simply too terrifying to turn back. I wonder how many of those marriages end in divorce, and how many go on to be actually pretty great. There are so many factors going into the decision to marry. Each of us can only know what we feel, and what we want to feel, and try to figure out if what we have and what we want can be compatible. Sometimes just knowing what we feel is hard enough! Trying in the course of a relationship is honorable, but there are times when the best thing a person can do is to stop trying.

At this rehearsal dinner, something in me woke up. I knew I could be happier if Jason were different, but I didn't think Jason *could* be different. He was only being himself. He would be happier if he wasn't here, I realized, and I also knew in an instant that I would be happier at this wedding by myself than I was with him. It dawned on me that this was not just true about us at this wedding. It might be time to let each other go.

"I'm going to break up with him," I told Marjorie's dad. "I just have to figure out when."

"Good for you," he said. "'Atta girl."

I put my head on his shoulder, he patted it, and we drank our Jack Daniel's.

As the guests boarded the bus to head back to the hotel, I stumbled on the stairs in my high heels but managed to keep myself from falling outright. There in the bus seat was Jason. He looked miserable. I sat down with a thud next to him. He said nothing, I said nothing. The trip back to the hotel was just the two of us sitting next to each other, waiting for the other to apologize first. Neither of us thought we'd done anything wrong. In some way of looking at it, neither of us had. We were at a standstill. When we got back to the hotel room, I threw myself on the bed without changing and fell asleep.

At some point in the early morning, I woke up and realized two things. First, he'd put the hotel wastebasket next to my side of the bed in fear I'd have to vomit in the middle of the night (I hadn't). That was his way of showing he cared as much as it was an admonishment, and it was both sweet and bitter because of that. Second, I remembered in a flash: Kate, Violet, and I had said we'd go to Marjorie's room to hang out as single girls—*one last night!*—following her rehearsal dinner. And instead of putting on my PJs and heading to her suite, I'd passed out. In one evening, I'd gone from being the best maid of honor ever to the most disliked girlfriend at the wedding to the terrible friend who left the bride alone on the night before she stepped into her newly married life. Feeling disgusted with myself and simultaneously too drunk to deal with any of it, I went back to sleep.

At nine a.m. my alarm buzzed, and my brain did the same in my skull. Oh, man. I was hungover. Hair and makeup was happening in thirty minutes. I managed to dislodge myself from bed and get in the shower, which helped a little. I left Jason still sleeping. "I have to go get ready," I whispered.

"Okay," he said from underneath a heap of blankets, and rolled over. In a way I was grateful I had a reason to get out of there.

Downstairs, Kate and Violet were waiting for Marjorie. "Did you go to her room last night?" asked Violet.

"No," I admitted. "I passed out on my bed with all my clothes on. I feel so bad."

"Me, too," said Kate.

"Me three," added Violet. "We're the worst."

"I'm unbelievably hungover," Kate said, and we nodded gingerly. Everything, inside and out, felt bruised. "Oh, there she is."

Marjorie was headed our way. I couldn't tell from the expression on her face if she was angry.

"I'm sorry!" we said, too loudly and nearly in unison, our words ringing in my ears, making me consider whether I could, in fact, vomit and feel any better, because that would be better than this. "I passed out," "I had the spins," "I totally flaked," we offered, our language itself as inelegant as our hangovers.

"Oh, God." She rolled her eyes at our antics and her own. "I went back to my room, put on my pajamas, and cried myself to sleep. It was ridiculous."

Oh, no. What had we done to the bride? "What happened? Why were you sad?"

"I was just being dramatic," she said. "I felt rejected and lonely."

"But you're getting married!" we said.

"I know, I was drunk!"

"We were all drunk, too . . ." With renewed shame, I thought again of all the ways I'd already failed at this wedding. Some maid of honor, a puke can next to her, her duties to the bride forgotten.

"What a weird night," she continued. "The night before the night you get married. What does it mean? Should it even matter? There's so much pressure that's not even real, but it also feels like you're jumping off a cliff. I think I just needed to let out some emotions. I feel way better now! Did everyone else have fun?"

"Everyone except Jason," I said, and she gave me a curious look.

"Are we ready for hair and makeup?" she asked.

I chose an updo so I didn't have to consider the state of my hair for the rest of the day—at least until the end of the evening brought the need to dig from my scalp the thousand pins that had been sprayed into my coif. Kate and Violet both wore their hair down, and Kate's blond locks, flat-ironed and sprayed and back-combed, so resembled those of the caricatured songstress who'd come to Nashville to make herself a star that she dubbed her look "big country hair." Our tresses styled and makeup applied, we sat outside the salon in the sun in our jeans and T-shirts, chugging Diet Cokes and eating sandwiches that Marjorie's mom had brought us for strength. (Wedding Tip: Always get the French fries.) None of us could look at each other without breaking into punchy giggles, what with the hair and the hangovers. Though it still felt like my brain was pulsing angrily inside my skull, the laughing helped with just about everything.

Then I was back at the hotel, slipping into my bridesmaid attire, and Jason was talking to me, though we didn't address what had happened the night before.

"You look nice," he said.

"You look nice, too," I told him.

We both did look nice, even if we didn't feel nice together. We went to the church to see Marjorie get married, Jason with his trusty camera to take pictures from the pew. I stood at the front of the room, facing the crowd after walking down the aisle carefully, a poised maid-of-honor smile on my face. I held Marjorie's bouquet for her, and we all smiled big grins when the bride and groom were married and then when they kissed. Afterward, for my final maid-of-honor duty, I witnessed the signing of the marital document, and it was over. We'd done it. We'd all done it, and no one had had to vomit even once.

There was one thing more, though. At the reception, where little girls and boys ran around tapping glasses with their silverware and shimmying on the dance floor, where a cheesecake wedding cake was served, where we toasted to the happy couple from our perch high at the top of a building with windows on all sides overlooking the city, and where Jason was quiet, again, fading into the background, there was a bouquet toss. Violet and I, still unable to stomach the thought of bourbon or even beer, were both drinking small cups of hot tea when it was announced.

"Oh, no." Violet shook her head.

"Oh, yes," I said. I was suddenly reminded of that other bouquet fiasco, the one I'd tried to banish from my mind. Those fallen flowers had signified the beginning of the end of a friendship. I could not let that happen again, not with Marjorie. "What do we do?"

"Let's stand and hold our tea," she suggested. "We'll participate. But it's not like we're going to make a dive for it holding teacups."

What we didn't know was that Marjorie had us covered, too.

We found spots at the edge of the dance floor and watched as the bride lifted her bouquet high into the air, doing her best

Statue of Liberty impression. She then turned, her back facing the crowd, before dropping her arm at the elbow and letting her cluster of bright flowers slide down her back and to the floor. The bouquet landed some six inches away from her feet. Her two little nieces, who, she told me later, she'd intended as the recipients of the toss all along, were waiting right there. Three and five, they grabbed the flowers, shouting happily. Violet and I sipped our tea, smiled, and looked at each other. Sometimes things resolved themselves, if you could only be patient and wait.

Other things you had to figure out yourself.

The next day we all flew back, into high winds in New York City. The plane stayed in the air for what seemed like hours, circling and circling, waiting for a safe opportunity to land. There was a pilot on the plane as a passenger. He'd caught a ride up to New York to see family, and he was furious that he'd made what turned out to be such a bad decision. "I should have zigged when I zagged," he kept saying. *"I should have zigged when I zagged."* Jason sat next to me with his headphones on, annoyed that we were still aloft when he should have long been home. With each passing moment I felt more about my relationship as the pilot did about his choice of plane. Like him, I was zagging when I should have been zigging. Or the opposite. In my case, though, it wasn't too late to change course.

Jason and I kept dating for a few more months. When we finally ended things, we promised we'd still be friends. It seemed an unrealistic pledge even then, but I think it gave us the courage to break up. It is very hard to lose your best friend, and sometimes you need to take the severing of those relationships in small steps.

For a while we spoke on the phone every evening, but the proof that our lives had gone on without each other in those nightly reports became too difficult to endure. We stopped talking and it felt better, and after that still, when there was distance to insulate the feelings, we'd e-mail occasionally and get together for a drink to catch up. It hurt less every day and then it didn't hurt at all, and then we stopped feeling the need to communicate with each other in any way. Humans are adaptable. What pains us deeply will eventually fade, even if it never goes away completely. Even if it doesn't seem like it will ever stop hurting when we're right in the middle of it.

On Valentine's Day 2012, after we'd been broken up for six years, I saw him on the subway. It was evening, and the 6 train was nearly empty. He was immersed in a *New Yorker*, and he didn't look up as he stepped onto the train at Union Square. I recognized him the way you do with people you once knew, and sometimes celebrities, an involuntary resonating vibration in your core: *Oh, yes, you.* He was much the same. He had a beard now, but his head was still closely shaven, his eyes were still very blue, his skin was pale, and he was as thin and tall as I remembered. I was standing down the car from him, and instinctively, I stepped toward him, thinking he might look up and see me, too, but when he didn't, I thought better of it and stepped back. He was married, I knew that, and had been for a few years. They'd had their wedding at the Bronx Zoo, he'd told me in one of our e-mail exchanges, his long-ago plan of getting married in his hometown backyard forgotten or, more likely, evolved. I surmised that he was on his way home from work, that he was going to see his wife for whatever

Valentine's Day plans they might have. I was just an old girlfriend, someone from long ago whom he didn't need to be thinking about ever, but especially not on this day. So I said nothing and got off the train one stop later to go to a bar where I was meeting some friends.

"I just saw my ex-boyfriend on the train," I announced when I got there. "On Valentine's Day. How weird is that?"

"That is weird!" they agreed. "Lady, get a drink."

It sounded more dramatic than it was, a corny plotline in a Lifetime movie: *I saw my ex on Valentine's Day.* It did mean *something*, but the something that it meant was nothing. We'd been over for years. We'd both moved on, and on again still, and what was most notable about any of this was that but for the time we'd once shared together, we might as well have been strangers. How confounding that is, the course of so many of our romantic relationships: You know each other so well, are indispensable partners to each other, love and are in love. And then a day comes and you don't know each other at all. The decision to not be together forever means, to each other, you become nothing more than a memory, a series of photographs, some stories, and, of course, whatever you've learned and will take with you to the next relationship. Those things are not nothing. Yet there was love there once, and then there's not. I wonder where it goes.

10.

Please Accept My Regrets

✦

As painful as it is when it happens, we're used to romantic relationships ending. It's par for the course that most of the affairs of love we'll have in life will, in fact, be finite. We tend to date far more people than we marry, after all. Those who come before "the one," or the two or even three, will be, if not forgotten, confined to a certain time and place in the past, and in some cases not remembered at all. And that's okay, that's the way these things work. The high school sweethearts who meet and fall in love and stay together forever are a rarity.

But friendships ending, particularly those that end not in a fade-out of geographical distance or changing interests or stages of life that no longer seem compatible, but because the friends decide they do not love each other anymore, and not only that, they don't *like* each other, either—that happens far less frequently. These friend breakups can be even more painful than uncoupling with the men and women we have loved. I've had boyfriends who have stuck around for anywhere between two months and three years. The women I consider my close friends have been so for two, five, ten, and as many as twenty-five years. I don't know what I'd do without them.

When Ginny started dating the man who would become her husband, I never suspected that what happened in her relationship, in any of our relationships with men, could so drastically change our friendship. It began so typically, and not inauspiciously: They were introduced by mutual friends; they got to know each other while watching sports at their local bar; they went on dates; they had a good time. All seemed promising, but as they grew more and more serious, there were worrisome stories she would share, the sorts of things friends tell one another, promising not to judge and to keep such things just between them—*he's my boyfriend, this might sound weird or maybe even bad, but I'm telling you because I know you'll support me.* This is where things get so complicated. Perhaps your friend is just blowing off steam, or wanting you to say, *Oh, that's not bad at all!* But you are invested in your friend's happiness, and the more stories you hear—even if they may not ultimately denote deep, intractable problems—the more you are inclined to worry. So what do you do? Do you step aside and let it be, because their relationship is their relationship? Or do you get involved?

I got involved. Hers was the bouquet I could not bear to acknowledge.

It had been two years since Ginny had married her husband. We were thirty, and we'd hung on to our friendship, but it kept being tested. At various times, her marriage would appear to be foundering and, right along with it, there we were, too, crashing headlong onto the rocks. A piece of information would be revealed that I hadn't known, and my resolve against the man she'd chosen would strengthen. At one dark point she called in tears, asking me to come over, and I rushed to her aid. We called her parents, who agreed to help pay for a divorce lawyer, if that's what she wanted. Enough was enough. They'd help her. I'd help her, too. I felt concerned, but also relieved. My friend would be okay. She could put this past her and move on.

Days later, though, when I asked, she seemed to be changing her mind, and still later, when we met for dinner, she told me she'd decided not to do anything at all. She still loved him, she said. She wanted to work things out. I couldn't see why, and several drinks in, I told her so. That's not all I said. I told her that I didn't know how I could be friends with someone who not only couldn't stand up for herself but also was so intent on continuing to pull me into her life dramas. I told her that her decision to stay with this guy made me think she was, well, not very bright. I told her I couldn't take it anymore, and I think I gave her an ultimatum: It was him or me. I said it all and was hopelessly, unreasonably cruel. I left feeling awful, knowing that I'd likely just delivered a fatal blow to our friendship, but not wanting to believe it, either.

Afterward, I reached out and tried to apologize, but it was too late. Unforgivable things had been said, and we were at an impasse. I didn't understand how she could keep doing this. She didn't understand how I could fail to support her decisions, nor how I could be so heartless when she needed my support. If I were a real friend, I'd be there for her and respect her choice. But I didn't know if I could have a real friend who kept making these sorts of decisions and looping me into them, over and over again.

How can you support someone when you believe what she's doing is not only wrong but also hurts her and you, and she continues to do it anyway? How can you respect those choices? And, on the other hand, how can you love a friend who refuses to love your choice of a husband, a man you've promised to stay with so long as you both shall live? How can you love a friend who doesn't seem to understand that *this* is the paramount thing—this is your marriage? It was awful, and it was also awkward, especially given our broader social circle, which included people who had far more patience with the relationship than I had (not to mention more inherent diplomacy), along with others who were only now being included in the drama. I felt rejected, replaced by this latter group of friends who were so willing to suddenly step in and give the support Ginny needed. They looked like the good guys, yes, but they hadn't been there the whole time, I thought bitterly. They didn't know how it felt—then or now.

For weeks after that fight Ginny and I didn't talk, but we were bound to see each other again, and as it happened, this would be at a wedding. Our friend Heather and her longtime on-again, off-again boyfriend, Rex, had decided to go on-again for good. They'd met while working as office receptionists the summer before our senior year in college, after we had all returned from our semester in Italy. Now, nine years later, they were sealing the deal with a marriage license. By the time of Heather's ceremony in Los Angeles, the aftershocks of my fight with Ginny were no longer reverberating through our group, but she and I still weren't exactly speaking, either. There was a big, raw wound that existed for both of us, hidden underneath the sheerest strip of emotional

Band-Aid. We decided silently if mutually to cope by ignoring it. We'd all stay together in a big suite in West Hollywood for this event, happy, happy. Thankfully, Ginny's husband would not be joining us.

The wedding was downtown, at the top of an old art deco building in an apartment that had once been the residence of a Hollywood billionaire, a protected old-world hideaway with turrets and secret rooms and sweeping views of the city. It was beautiful. We arrived just as the sun was setting, and in the distance, beyond the imperious modern office buildings, you could see blue skies morph to pink and red and orange, speckled with white clouds. If you squinted you could see the Hollywood Hills in the distance, or at least, that's what we said we saw. Heather and Rex were married outside on the terrace, and after the ceremony, we danced under the stars, Hollywood-adjacent to the thousands of lights still on in the buildings that surrounded us. Even closer, small palm trees decorating the patio twinkled with white lights. Everything and everyone was sparkling.

I had on a black wool minidress that I'd bought on this very trip to LA, partly because at the hotel, our friend Alice had told me the green-and-blue silk with the Marilyn Monroe–*Seven Year Itch* silhouette I'd planned to wear was "too young" for me. While I didn't love being called too old for anything, I'd wanted a new dress anyway, and the one I bought was certainly not too young. It had short sleeves and a mod structure, with buttons all the way down the back. There is a photo of me at this wedding, dancing on the terrace with my hands in the air, flapper-style, and a huge smile on my face.

The waitstaff dispensed with any propriety, and so did the guests, in the end. They'd handed us bottles of wine and Champagne and not even bothered with glasses, and in the last moments of the party, people stood in the fountain at the top of the building and drank it all in, as much as we could hold. When the bar closed down, we gathered ourselves and our belongings for the after-party at a hotel just down the street. Somehow, though, between the time we left the penthouse in the sky and our arrival at the hotel, the mood had shifted.

On the way up to the bride and groom's suite of rooms, somewhere between floors one and nine, that thing Ginny and I tacitly agreed not to discuss trickled out. And then there was a stream, a river, a flood, a tsunami. *How could she have gone back to him? Didn't she see? She was trying to make her marriage work. Didn't I see? Didn't we both see everything we'd lost in the process, and everything that still stood to be lost? Why couldn't I support her? Why couldn't she be honest with me, with us, with herself? Why couldn't I be a good friend? Why couldn't she be?* By the time we arrived at the floor where the after-party was taking place, brutal damage had been inflicted on both sides. I got out of the elevator and numbly entered the room where the wedding party was still celebrating, sort of. No one followed me.

Inside, Heather was lying on a bed, one of her bridesmaids untying the red satin bow of her white strapless gown so she could change before she vomited. "Hurry," she said, the word muffled into *"mmmmphrrr"* by the combination of Champagne imbibed and her pillow. Her husband, Rex, was casually chatting with a friend who was wearing a garter around his head and chugging a beer. Apropos of nothing, there was a large statue of a foot in the corner of the room.

"I have to go," I told no one in particular, and headed back downstairs. In the elevator, this one empty, the tears began. I found a plush couch in the lobby, sat myself down on it, and started crying in full force.

"Are you okay?" asked a male voice. I looked up to see a familiar face, a guy who was good friends with Heather. He'd been at the wedding; he had been seated at my table.

"No," I said. Though he'd been on his way upstairs, he stopped and sat next to me, and I confessed everything that had happened, as I saw it. "I don't know what to do," I told him, my words coming out haltingly among sobs. "They hate me. I'm staying with them . . . I don't . . . I'm just trying to stop Ginny from doing something she will regret. It all went wrong again . . . I hate myself . . . I hate . . . ."

"*Shhhh,*" he awkwardly soothed, patting my arm. "It will be okay. I'm sure it will all be okay in the morning."

Usually it is. Usually, after a wedding and after a blowout and even after both, you can say that with some surety. Most things are better in the morning. I knew that this wouldn't be okay tomorrow, though, and that it hadn't been okay for a long time, and that, in fact, it might never be okay.

When my tears abated, he got up. "I'm going to head upstairs," he said. "I think you should get a cab and go back and figure this stuff out. These are your friends. They love you no matter what." He led me outside, and the doorman of the hotel hailed me a taxi.

By the time I got to our room, the lights were off and it was quiet. Everyone was asleep, or pretending to be. I got in bed and stared at the ceiling, trying not to cry, until I fell asleep. The next morning I had an earlier flight than everyone else, out of Burbank. I was awake before my alarm went off, silently gathering my stuff and exiting the room. I didn't want to talk to anyone. I just wanted to get out of there, to leave it all behind. I felt like I was escaping the scene of a crime.

At the airport I called our friend Nora, who hadn't come to the wedding because she'd had to work. She'd also, she admitted on the phone, had a suspicion things might go awry. All the unaddressed issues with Ginny made for land mines in the foundation of our friendships. I told her everything. "Well, that sounds pretty awful," she said, "but I'm not totally surprised. We knew this was going to blow up sooner or later. We can't just pretend none of it ever happened."

"But what about Ginny?" I said.

"I don't know," she answered. "I just don't know. Maybe you can't be friends anymore for a while, or maybe not ever. Maybe it's time to let it go—or to give it a long, long break, at least."

Weddings don't always bring people together. Sometimes they tear people apart. When a friend makes a choice you find yourself unable to support, that can slowly but surely ruin that friendship, unless you find a way to deal with it. With Ginny, I felt that if she would not be her own advocate, I would fill the role. I tried to do what I thought was right for her, and then I couldn't stop, even when she decided she wanted something different. My struggle to set appropriate boundaries at the time, as evidenced by that fateful bouquet toss and what followed after, seems to the older me partly due to a kind of young-person immaturity. The me of today might have been able to find the distance to let the relationship do what it would while also maintaining our friendship. Then again, it's possible I would have done much the same thing even now, albeit one would hope with a bit more sensitivity, given the wisdom of years. Most of all, I wanted my friend to be happy, and, particularly as things progressed, I saw her again and again as anything but that, her complaints and concerns not one-off dissatisfactions but clear signifiers that the marriage was not working. In that case, I thought, her best bet was to get out, and my duty was to help her do that.

I also saw what seemed to me a kind of hypocrisy, I think. What was the truth? Was the truth the shiny, happy wedding day? Was it in the stories that came after? Was the truth, in fact, love and a sustainable relationship, or was it something more ominous? I wasn't privy to know more than what my friend told me and what I had seen with my own eyes. Meanwhile, hanging over both of us in this emotionally grueling time was an expectation that marriage should be seen as the supreme bond, the ins and outs of which are nobody's business but the couple's. I wasn't sure I bought into this. If friends and family are asked to come and celebrate the good times, well, I was invested in the bad times, too, but if the times were really bad, the investment was in my friend, not in her marriage. And, whether it was truly so or not, I interpreted what she was telling me as "the times were bad." So I worried about her—about how he treated her, about whether she really loved him and he loved her, if this union was indeed right, or if it was in some subconscious way the rote fulfillment of the assumption that life was about, at its most essential level, finding a partner and settling down and starting a family. And maybe I was selfish. I wanted my friend, my strong, happy, confident friend, back, too.

The tragedy, of course, is that I lost her.

As with romance, sometimes it's just too late to try to salvage what remains of a friendship. Sometimes you can't find your way to agreeing to a compromise that works for both people. And sometimes there is no compromise. It is heartbreaking, and no less heartbreaking than a breakup with a romantic partner. The loss of a friend is one of the saddest things there is. Sometimes weddings mean beginnings, and sometimes they mean endings.

I saw Heather recently while I was on a trip to LA. She and Rex had been married for six years, and she was pregnant with their second child. I asked if she had any tips for making a marriage work. "Of course: The old cliché is true—communication is key," she said. "Talking things out and not letting things fester. It's important to regularly take a step back and remember what drew you to the person in the first place. Also, accepting that people change. No one is going to be the same person you met at nineteen, or twenty-five, or thirty-five, or whatever. People grow and evolve, and accepting and allowing those changes is very important in coexisting happily."

Those felt like the very same rules for friendships.

11.

Rock-Bottom Wedding

✦

I am standing in the middle of the dark, rain-dampened Main Street of a small Connecticut town. In front of me is a bar, which I have just been dragged from, kicking and screaming, by friends, possible former friends, and the mother of the bride. I am wearing a purple dress with a ruffle down the front that I bought in Paris. It has held up surprisingly well given the circumstances. Despite the fact that muddy rivulets trace the road, which is littered with debris from the day's near-hurricane conditions, I am wearing only one shoe. The other, a black leather faux-crocodile platform pump that cost $450 as a pair, is in my recently manicured, now grimy hand. I throw it down the road with all of the strength I can muster. And then that second shoe is gone, too, discarded right along with my dignity. Those items—left pump, right pump, any remaining semblance of grace, elegance, or decorum—are now so far down the street that I couldn't see them even if it weren't pitch-black and I weren't seven sheets to the wind. The good news is, I'm so drunk I have no idea what a complete and total ass I'm being. That part comes later.

I am barefoot when I am finally coerced into the car with my friend Josh, who has been given the thankless duty of returning me to the hotel where we are staying, in separate rooms, postwedding. I drum my feet against the dashboard like a child mid-tantrum, alternating between yelling at him—*"How dare you?"*—and begging him to return me to the bar where I'd found a man—not a wedding guest, but a man who was, rumor had it, at his own bachelor party, though that wasn't in my bleary eyes a problem, not at the time. If anything, it meant we had something in common; we had both been clasped in the omnipotent embrace of so many interminable weddings. This man might be the love of my life, I reason unreasonably to Josh, a moment of false calm, a moment to breathe, before I start kicking again: *"Please-please-please-take-me-back-I-am-a-grown-woman-don't-tell-me-what-to-do!"*

I am a grown woman. Someone has seen fit to return my shoes to me for the ride, and when Josh drops me off in front of the hotel, I discard them again, aiming this time for him, or at least for his rented Lincoln Town Car, which makes him look like one of the many limo drivers waiting out their next fares in the hotel parking lot. These other drivers cluster around him and cluck over what a bitch I must be, having assumed I am a drunken passenger on the way home from a wedding. They're not far off.

I don't know this, this story about the limo drivers, or even who drove me home that night, until Josh himself tells me about it over spaghetti at an Italian restaurant in Manhattan's East

Village several years later. "I dropped you off at the front of the hotel," he said, not mad, just matter-of-fact, "because trying to wrangle you in the parking garage would have been a nightmare. You were a nightmare. You dented that car with your shoes. Thank God it was a rental."

I can't remember that, nor do I have any remnant flickerings of what must have been a slow, stumbling, barefoot course to my room, though I *do* remember what happened afterward, in bits and pieces, weirdly razor-sharp images bursting through the hazy insulating layers of white wine to sting anew each time. Much later, after the apologies had been doled out and the self-inflicted drama had lost its hardest edge, I tried not to think about it at all. But after he told me this tale, I started to have dreams of the two of us maneuvering our way through a parking garage, dreams in which I got lost or forgot my purse or somehow, inevitably, everything just went wrong. I still have those dreams every now and again.

Was this my worst wedding? Let's backtrack.

Nora and I raced to Natalie and Luke's Connecticut wedding in a rented red Mini Cooper. We'd not been invited to the rehearsal dinner the night before, but in this middle age of our wedding-going life, that came as a relief rather than a slight. We'd booked a room with two double beds at a Marriott not far from the location where the wedding would be held, on the pristine beach of an even more pristine Connecticut country club. We could stay the night and be back home at a decent time the next day, what a gift! After quiet Friday evenings in our respective East and West Villages, we met up early that Saturday, stopping for bagels and coffee, and were on our way, making great time.

The Mini was a convertible, but there was no reason to put the top down because the weather was not on our side. At first it was simply ominous and muggy, but halfway up the FDR, the rain began to come down in torrents. We could barely see the road, and our pace slowed to a crawl. By the time we reached the exit to the tony Connecticut town where we needed to check into our hotel and change for the wedding, we were both exhausted, and we were running late. We got to our room and threw our bags to the floor, ransacking them in an effort to dress as quickly as we could. I put on the sleeveless purple dress I'd bought in Paris, pairing it with black faux-crocodile platform pumps that added a little edge to the sweet silhouette and girly ruffles down the front. I did my makeup while Nora fixed her hair. We cleaned up in record time and looked at each other, doing a final check: "Are we ready?" "We're ready!" "Let's go."

We headed out to the parking lot and into the rental car. If anything, the weather had gotten worse. The trip to the country club should have taken fifteen minutes, but we took a wrong turn among the twisting neighborhood streets, which had not only their own speed bumps but also white picket fences interspersed throughout, halfway across the road, to prevent drivers from compromising the safety of children or the quaint neighborhood feel. We were lost, and the minutes were ticking past wedding go-time.

"We're late," I said to Nora.

"I know." She gripped the steering wheel tighter and tried to peer past the pounding rain.

"Do you think we should ask someone?"

"Who can we possibly ask?" she said, annoyed. "We're in the middle of a hurricane."

"That guy?" I pointed at a mailman dressed in full protective Day-Glo rain gear, sliding letters into the idyllic suburban mailboxes lining the street. We drove up, and he jerked a proprietary thumb in the direction of the country club. Nora put her pump-clad foot to the gas, plowing through a series of speed bumps. "Fuck it," she said as the little car bounced in the air.

"We're almost there!" I told her. "I can see it."

We pulled up to the front of the building, into a drop-off area protected by an awning above. A man in a tuxedo carrying an enormous umbrella bent down and looked into the car. I rolled down the window. "I'll park your car for you," he said.

"Oh, you don't have to do that," said Nora, flustered.

"It's no problem." He gallantly waved his umbrella. "Hop out, and I'll hop in."

We let him. Later we found he was the husband of one of the bridesmaids, and he'd been doing parking duty, of his own volition, for the past few hours. "He's a superstar," we told his wife. "That's why I married him," she said.

The wedding couldn't be held on the beach as originally planned because the deluge continued. Instead we'd be inside, in a lovely room more lovely because it was enclosed by four walls and a roof. We shook off the rain and replenished our lipstick, filing into seats facing an altar covered in branches and wildflowers. Beyond that, floor-to-ceiling windows overlooked the beach and the angry sky beyond. The sun had not yet set, and outside shone a strange and radiant gray. Waves of a darker hue crashed below the horizon, and from above came a crack of bright lightning that plunged straight down, seemingly right into the water. The crowd uttered a collective "Ooh!"

The aisles in front of us were full of people I knew. There was my old college friend Rob, who'd had a crush on Caitlin before she married Cash. He sat next to a willowy blond girl whom I took to be his date. They were holding hands. There was Josh, the guy I'd dated casually right after college, when I first moved to New York City. He was the one who was always falling asleep on my couch, an investment banker who worked interminable, grueling hours. He still worked those hours, and we were still friends, though I didn't see him often. When I waved at him, he responded with a small salute and a smile. There were all the ladies, too, some whom I'd gone to college with, who'd also gone to high school with the bride. Those women were the reason I'd initially met Natalie, though that was not exactly how we'd become friends.

Natalie and I had worked together, along with Lucy, in our first jobs right out of college. Prior to that, we'd both attended Jesuit schools in the Northeast similar enough that there's an acknowledged overlap in the characteristics of their student bodies. Beyond any shared values or common facts in our upbringings before, after, or during our secondary educations, though, Natalie and I knew a lot of people who knew one another. Despite that, the first time we'd met had not been auspicious. She thought

I was weird. I thought she was a snooty Connecticut stiff, a spoiled rich girl. I'd been invited to a party at some anonymous apartment in Midtown by a mutual friend, and Natalie had been there, too, and we'd exchanged words, neither of us walking away impressed. Later, when I found out we'd be working at the same ad agency, I groaned. *Not that girl from Connecticut,* I'd thought.

The truth was, when we really gave each other a chance, we found we had a lot in common. I liked her, I admitted to myself. She was hilarious, no-nonsense, and surprisingly tough, but with a kindhearted soft side. At first glance she might have seemed the sort of stereotypical girl who's bent on finding a wealthy guy and settling down with him in her hometown, where they'd live in a big house and have babies. But she was far more curious than that. She would not meekly accept things as they were or blindly go down some path because others had done it that way. Nor would she hold her tongue if she noticed something she felt needed mentioning. A credit to her courage was that she would say it to your face. I hated that job at the ad agency and was constantly consoling myself with Jack and Diet Cokes and staying out late, occasionally finding myself in the beds of strange men during the phase in our young twenties during which we were employed there. One morning, as I sat down at my cubicle, late to work again, she sniffed.

"Jen, you really need to start drinking vodka instead of Jack and Coke," she said. "I can smell you from all the way over here."

As we got to know each other better, a process that continued even when we moved on to our next jobs, we talked about dating, but it was less about the guys and dates themselves ("He bought me dinner . . . then thought he could just come upstairs!" "I'm not going to sleep with someone on a first date!" "Oh, *he's* not anyone I'd get serious with!") and more about what good relationships might look like, what we wanted, what, even, love was—how we could identify it and make sure not to pass it up if and when it landed at our feet. It might come in a different flavor for the two of us; as different as we were, it was bound to, but I knew she wouldn't criticize my brand even if it didn't match her own. "I'm not worried about you," she told me once. I took that as a high compliment, even if sometimes *I* was worried about me.

Natalie had met Luke at work. At first neither of them had considered the other, given the complications of dating someone at the office, but their boss had a matchmaker gene and smelled possibility between his two staffers. He purposely sent them on multiple trips together, they became friends, and romantic interest grew. At an event one night, "after fourteen drinks," as she put it, he got up the nerve to kiss her. The relationship began in earnest, though I recall some early wondering on her part about whether he possessed all those marriageable characteristics that needed to be checked off for her to feel ready to commit. Sometimes it takes winning someone to decide if we want more, and sometimes it takes losing them. He wanted more. She reacted by pulling away and dating other people, only to realize there was no one as good as this guy who would dedicate his life to making their life together great. She would do the same for him, she decided. They got engaged.

It was clear immediately that Luke was free from the manipu-

lative qualities we'd seen in other men. He wasn't hiding anything, and he didn't have a hidden agenda. He loved Natalie and
wanted for them to be together, and they had that wondrous syn-
ergy that made it feel they were even better together than they
were individually. The parts of her that were a little bit brittle
softened, and the parts of him that were shy and retiring found a
rock of stability and confidence. That's some marital magic there,
and when it's real, it's real. The invite came, and I was again grateful that Natalie and I had found our way into friendship and glad
I could be there to celebrate this moment in her life. What I regret
most about this wedding is that my behavior didn't represent how
happy I was for the bride and groom, and how proud of them, too.

Despite the rain, the lateness, and the shift in venue, all was
running smoothly. In our party dresses on our folding chairs
we watched and waited, and soon enough the music was playing,
Luke was walking down the aisle, serious and nervous, and there
was Natalie, with her father. She wore a stunning long white
dress, form-fitting and elegant with a cutout back, a sweetheart
neckline, and delicate lace sleeves. Her chestnut hair was tied
back from her face in a chignon covered with a sheer veil. She
held a bouquet of white flowers; Luke had a matching blossom in
the lapel of his dark suit. Her father walked her to the front of the
room, kissed her, and stepped back. The bridesmaids looked on
with rapt expressions, as did the crowd. It was all about the couple now. "She looks so Jackie O!" someone whispered. She did,
beautiful and completely poised. In front of us all, lightning

crashed through the sky again, but the bride and groom didn't flinch.

They were married.

Things happened afterward that are painful to write about. We'll start with the easiest. I drank too much. It's so easy to drink too much at a wedding. Booze is accessible. You're talking to people you don't know that well, sometimes to people you used to know better, and a drink can take the edge off that pressure. You're expected to feel things; you're expected to be on your best behavior; you're expected to act a certain way, regardless of whether those expectations have ever been directly discussed or explained, and a drink can take the edge off that pressure, too. Surely there exist people who do not have drinking problems while at weddings, but at nearly every wedding I've been to since I have been of legal age to consume, I have overimbibed to some extent or another. The repercussions are not always more than a headache the next morning, but on the occasion they have been far worse. The added insult to injury? When things go truly bad, they don't absolve you of the headache.

Usually my poison of choice is white wine, but it's also been Jack Daniel's, Champagne, prosecco, vodka soda, tequila shots, bourbon on the rocks, and ever so many signature cocktails. (A coconut filled with rum? Check.) As I was writing this book, I noted sardonically to a friend that a section of it could be titled "Jen Might Have Had Sort of a Drinking Problem for a While," and a few of my friends, and those who are no longer my friends, may well agree. At a wedding, like elsewhere in life, though, boozing can certainly add to the incipient drama, but it doesn't usually create it from nothing. The wedding and the drinking only bring these things to the surface.

Parts of this wedding—big chunks, in fact—are foggy. Some of what happened, to my great discomfort, will exist forever in photographs; more can be found in other people's memories, where I can't explain them away or offer any "I'm sorrys," and that's mortifying, too. There's what I know, what I think I know, and what knowledge I've been confronted with since.

At the reception I was seated at a table with a group of college friends, including Nora, Mattie, Rob and his date, and a guy named Gustav I'd once "accidentally" made out with back in my early years in New York—"accidentally" because I wished I hadn't. He was married now, and next to him was his much younger, pretty wife, sitting silently and looking at her plate as he made wisecracks across the table. Nora and Gustav sparred not exactly companionably as the rest of us looked on, with Mattie interjecting occasionally to try to smooth things over.

"I don't know whose idea it was to put these two together," said Rob, and everyone laughed awkwardly.

"You're just wrong, completely and totally wrong," said Gustav, who was, I think, baiting Nora for his amusement. "A woman's place is in the home. Barefoot and pregnant, the best way to be." He couldn't possibly be serious. His wife said nothing. Taking a cue from her, we all looked down at our own plates.

"You have no idea what you're talking about," said Nora. "You're being a chauvinist, and I don't care to talk to you anymore." She was still on edge from our drive, and Gustav wasn't helping. But also, Nora was a lawyer, and she was stressed about the deal she was in the midst of. A wedding didn't mean much to the partners or the clients at her firm—nor did her personal life—and she was constantly being pulled between the demands on her life from her job and the demands on her life from her life. She might have to leave early and work, she'd warned me. She poked at the food on her plate and studied her Black-Berry.

Rob, meanwhile, was walking a precarious wedding tight-rope, balancing between taking care of his date and enjoying a comfortable just-like-the-old-days reunion with his longtime friends. "This is Molly, we hit it off *instantly*," he'd told us of the woman on his arm, offering us his five-hundred-watt smile, but they hadn't been together long, and I wasn't sure they were to-gether in any serious way at all. A few years ago he'd moved from New York to Arizona, but I'd seen him more recently while on a press trip to a Scottsdale-area resort right before I was laid off from my job at *OK!* magazine. Molly hadn't been in the picture then, and he and I had had drinks at the bar, where people had assumed we were a couple. We'd play-acted that we were, imag-ining it for ourselves. We drank too much and tried to break into the pool for late-night swimming; when that failed, we went back to my room and had a water fight on the deck. Rob and I had one of those male-female friendships in which we, single, moderately attracted to each other, and maybe a little lonely, would return again and again to the question of whether there was another sort of chemistry there. I think we both knew our relationship was at heart a friendship, but we tested the boundaries of that—what were we to each other, and what did we want to be?

In college I'd asked him one late night at a party if he thought he'd ever get married, and when he said yes, I made him promise he'd invite me. (I had, as we neared graduation, asked a lot of people that question, fearing we'd all grow apart when there was little to keep us together, save the universal prospect of the wedding that was next.) He'd said okay, if I'd do the same, but now, at Natalie's wedding, I could see how far we'd drifted. I had the feeling he'd brought a date because he was afraid I wanted more from him, or he was afraid of what he wanted from me, or maybe, just maybe, he really did like this Molly person. It's entirely possible he simply wanted a date to this wedding for any of the reasons anyone wants a date to a wedding.

Still, I felt strangely displaced. Time moved so fast. If and when either of us got married, would we honor our old promise, and if we didn't, would we even care?

"Oh, guys, look, the first dance!" said Mattie.

I looked out at the dance floor, where Natalie had her head on Luke's shoulder, and then back at the tables of guests. My eyes fell on Josh, another guy from the past. We'd still talk sometimes, he'd e-mail "we should get drinks" or text "what are you up to?" in the middle of the night, but rarely could we settle on a date. We were so busy with work, and in and out of other relationships, we never really gave more time to each other than was needed to keep the relationship existing at a subsistence level. All that running around and *doing things* was a good way to feel productive, but it might be preventing something else, something that could be good and fulfilling, something that might be the most important thing of all. A person could just busy a life away, without a true human connection, without actual love, without even knowing it, I worried, until it was too late. That would be tragic.

I drank more. I'm not sure what, exactly, I ate—a roll, a bite of salad greens, a sliver of fish—but it wasn't enough.

Dinner completed, we headed for the bar, refilling our glasses and lifting them in honor of the bride and groom, who were making their way through the crowd, doling out a few words to each of us. I hugged them both. "You look gorgeous!" I said. "You're such a great couple, you really are." "We're so glad you came," they said. When they moved on, I talked to a friend I hadn't seen in a while. She and I had been close in college, but we'd fallen out of touch since, to the extent that she hadn't invited me to her wedding. Now we had such different lives, me in the city and her in the suburbs, and though we always enjoyed seeing each other, there was just never time to find our way back together in any real fashion. "How are you?" I asked her. "How are the kids?" "They're great!" she said. "How's your job? What's the latest?" Now we were people who made small talk at weddings. Perhaps everyone was destined to make small talk at weddings.

The photo I'm most embarrassed about at this wedding involves me dancing with an older man. He was a relative of a relative, or a friend of a friend, and when I say "older man," I do not mean "a cute elderly fellow like Santa Claus." This was an older man who was fit and trim and bragged about being so. Before we hit the dance floor, he'd told me he did yoga daily and had more energy than his sons, who were my age. He did lunges in front of me to prove it. Then we danced, dirty-dancing-style, in front of everyone. There is at least one snapshot in which I am making strange hand gestures while squatting to Lady Gaga's "Poker Face." It's all so unfortunate, and here is where I wish the shenanigans had stopped.

They did not.

So came the other stuff: flirting with and, rumor has it, kissing the bartender. Flirting so intently with the man who ran the country club that one of my friends had to divert me away from him. "He's really gross," she whispered in my ear. Flirting with, dancing with, and, rumor has it, kissing a coworker of the groom. Leaving the party and going to the after-party at a quaint little bar on Main Street, which was packed with non-wedding-going revelers as well.

There was a man at that town bar. He had dirty blond hair, I think, and was thin and pale and attractive, in a button-down shirt and jeans. I started talking to him. There is a flash in my mind of a dark corner, a wooden bench, an image of us sitting closely together, my legs draped over his, my mouth saying God only knows what. Then we were making out, and soon enough my friends were trying to extricate me from the situation. It was time to go. I was behaving in a way I would not want to remember in the morning. I have never enjoyed being told what to do, but when I've consumed a certain amount of drink, I become positively rage-filled in response to the perception that I'm being pushed around. That was the case here.

"You can't tell me what to do!" I might have yelled. "Go back to your own lives! I can do whatever I want! I'm an adult!" My behavior, of course, sort of stood in opposition to that last fact.

Nora pulled me aside. "Look, I know you don't want to listen to me, but I have to tell you: That guy's getting married," she said.

Through a fog, I looked at her blankly.

"He's engaged. I heard from other people here that this is his bachelor party. He's getting married," she said again.

I couldn't believe it. That guy, that guy over there, was engaged? He seemed so interested. So . . . not taken. Possibly even the love of my life. My friends were clearly against me; this was a conspiracy; this was punishment. I was directed away from the guy, who I think stared at me, mouth open, stunned and drunk and as unsure of what was actually going on as I was.

Outside, things got even worse. Nora suggested I get in the car. "Let's go," she said. "It's time to go home."

The bride's mother and brother agreed. "You should go, Jen. It's time to go home."

All these bosses of me and not a one with my interests at heart. I would have to fight for my rights here, I saw, and so I did. I would show them. This was the moment that I let my shoes fly down the road, because, in some childlike reasoning, I figured that without shoes, I couldn't be forced to leave. Hah. I win.

I lose.

(Wedding Tip: Black shoe polish is a balm to your shoes, if not your soul.)

When I finally made it back to my hotel room, the door was ajar. Nora was inside, packing. It was two in the morning.

"Why are you leaving?" I asked, my words stumbling over one another.

"I need to go back and work," she replied coolly, but I knew—

I knew—she was really leaving because of me. She was leaving because she was furious with me.

"All you do is work!" I shouted, clearly still in tantrum mode. She might have yelled back, "All you do is drink!" I can't be sure. We most definitely fought, after which she left. Alone in the hotel room, still drunk, I fell onto one of the beds and began to cry. Then I called Josh, still crying, and begged him to come and keep me company. Everything was awful. He had to come.

When he showed up moments later, he found me with mascara trails down my face, lipstick smeared, face blotchy and puffy, eyes swollen. I was a wreck, but he listened and stayed. And even when I got in bed with him later, feeling totally alone and like at least he'd be my friend in all of this, he'd be the one I could reach out to for the answer I wanted—even if I didn't clearly know what question I was asking—he didn't beat a quick path to the door, and he didn't take advantage of the situation. Josh was always a good guy.

The next morning I woke with a headache surpassed in awfulness only by the partial memories of what had happened. I was alone. I texted Lucy, who had a room downstairs with David, the two of them four-month-old newlyweds following their ceremony in Jamaica. "Are you driving back to New York?" I wrote. "I think I need a ride home."

"Oh, totally. Come with us," she answered. "We're leaving in forty-five minutes."

I got ready, putting on baggy jeans and a T-shirt and, for some reason, high-heeled pink suede shoes. I might have still been drunk. I made my wobbly way downstairs with my bag and checked out and waited for them in the lobby, not wanting to stay in that hotel room where so many feelings had been sopped up by pillows.

"Nice shoes," Lucy said when she saw me.

On the way home, we talked about what had happened, what I remembered happening, and what they knew. "You should probably apologize to Natalie's family," advised Lucy gently. She was right, I probably should. I was filled with a sense of impending dread and no small frustration at myself for having caused these problems. I didn't want people to be mad at me. I didn't want to be a disaster of a wedding guest. And yet I had succeeded on both of those counts quite fully.

That night I sent notes of apology to the bride, her mom, and her brother. I called Nora and said I was sorry; really, really sorry. No one wants a permanent stain of bad feelings upon a wedding, and the responses I received were generous, one million times more civilized than I'd been the night before. "It must have been really hard for you to write this after yesterday," read the note from the bride's mom, "but you're forgiven, and you're always welcome at our house." Nora, at first still angry, softened quickly, because there was amusing gossip to share, and it was about me.

In a comic-tragic, ripe-for-the–Three Stooges sort of moment in the middle of the reception, Rob had approached her at the bar holding his cheek. "Jen just slapped me!" he'd said in disbelief.

"Why?" she asked.

"I have no idea," he answered.

A few minutes later, Josh approached, holding his cheek, blazing with the same telltale red hand mark, and uttering the same refrain: "Jen just slapped me!" Nora repeated her "Why?" He looked at her, shrugging. "Oh, it's Jen," he said. "You know."

It would have been more hilarious if the story hadn't been about me. I didn't want to be a woman who went around at weddings slapping her own friends for reasons she couldn't remember. If one was going to slap, one should know why one is slapping!

After you rage at a wedding, you want to know why. You can parse out the blame among so many people and things: booze, the pressure of the wedding-industrial complex, the baggage we carry through life, the mixed emotions we all have about love and marriage. I could claim that my behavior was the fault of the drunk guy at the bar having his bachelor party who decided to go for one last hurrah with a girl who was equally drunk and there for another wedding. I could say it was because at thirty-three, I'd lost my job back in May and still hadn't gotten a new one. I could pin it on the end of my last relationship, with yet another guy who at first seemed great but whom I ultimately felt, once again, disappointed by, for reasons that might have been more about me than him. You can blame a rock-bottom wedding on anyone and anything you like, but in the end, you only have yourself to look at in the mirror.

A week or two later I was perusing New York City's Missed Connections on Craigslist, which was something of a procrastination technique I liked to employ. I wasn't looking for myself in them, *I wasn't*, but instead enjoyed imagining everyone else's stories (with the exception of the pervy and/or foot fetish–based ones). How people can and do meet, and the idea of an instant connection, is endlessly intriguing. I couldn't resist reading about the different ways others had felt it happen.

My eyes fell to the bottom of the page, and I clicked. "You: A little bit Amy Winehouse, there for a wedding," read the post. "Me: There for a bachelor party, a young Mickey Rourke, pre–*The Wrestler*. We talked and kissed at a bar in Connecticut. I'm not sure what happened in the end, though. Hope you're okay."

It had to be him. I told my friends. They agreed. "Did you write back?" they all asked. I wrote back. I couldn't help it. I was curious about so many things. I wanted to know if he really was engaged, and if so, what he'd been thinking. I wanted to know what I'd been thinking, what I'd told him, who I was in our conversation together. And then there's the fact that it's hard to give up on a story, and it's harder to give up on a wedding story.

He never responded.

As with life, with love, and with weddings, too, time heals wounds. In time, things pass. And in time there will be yet another opportunity, a chance to do it all better.

Next time.

12.

Maternal Instincts

✦

Honesty and friendship can often feel like a tricky balance. After what had happened with Ginny, I made a promise that I'd be more careful about what I said about my friends' significant others. I would never, ever insult a friend's choice of a boyfriend or fiancé or husband, or say outright that a relationship wasn't worth continuing. *Especially* if I'd been drinking. No matter what my friend confided in me, she might not actually want me to intervene, and she certainly didn't want me to judge her for staying with that guy. If my friends were dating people I didn't like, even if I didn't think those people treated them as well as they deserved, I needed to leave that be, lest I lose another friend. It wasn't worth it. I didn't want to be the sort of person who scolded her friends for dating the wrong men. I knew by now that if the tables had been turned, I would have reacted badly.

In retrospect, I think the key to giving advice to friends about their relationships is not to say nothing—muzzling yourself completely never works—but most of all to listen and to try to understand what your friend needs as well as what you yourself need. Of course, this is far easier said than done.

Alice was one of that group of friends that included Ginny. These were the women with whom I'd gone to college and semestered in Italy, a bonding experience we hoped would extend through the course of our lives. In our early years in New York City, I'd seen her through a relationship we can joke about now, making fun of that guy's awfulness rather than feeling trapped by it. At the time they were dating, though, I'd mostly kept my mouth shut, adhering to an "If you can't say something nice, don't say anything at all" policy. When she asked for advice, whether she should stay with him or not, I'd say I only wanted to see her happy and that she had to decide what she wanted for herself. I'd tell her, lesson learned from Ginny, that I'd support her in whatever decision she made. Surely I said a thing or two that was not perfectly diplomatic, but in this case I managed it better than I had before, and she and he eventually broke up, to everyone's relief (most of all, I think, her own).

The thing is, dating jerks—and most of us have experienced at least one—isn't all bad. Dating jerks can help you learn who the good guys are, as long as you pay attention and stop dating jerks. Alice stopped dating jerks, and soon enough there was a new guy, not a jerk at all, in the picture. Their meeting story had a twist: Xavier was her therapist's son's soccer coach, and the therapist herself had arranged the setup. Though her relationship with that therapist would end for reasons having nothing to do with matchmaking, Alice's relationship with Xavier was just getting started. A year to the month after our friend Heather's wedding, they would walk down the aisle, too. The therapist was not invited.

Xavier was from New Orleans, and that's where they would have their traditional-to-modern Louisiana wedding. Alice spoke excitedly of the plans as they came into fruition: The ceremony would be in the French Quarter at Saint Louis Cathedral. It would be followed by a second line, the guests trailing a brass band for several ecstatic blocks to the reception at the Board of Trade, a pristine white building from the 1800s that resembled something between a plantation mansion and a palazzo, with an ornate fountain in its courtyard and Corinthian columns out front. It would be in November and the weather would be pleasant, New Orleans–warm but not summer-steamy.

Alice's view of marriage itself combined aspects of the old and the new. Her own parents had divorced when she was young, and her father had remarried, bringing the complications of an extended family that inevitably ensue. In her own relationship, she wanted love and romance, of course, but tempering that was the firsthand knowledge that marriage wasn't a fantasy and it wasn't salvation, it was a form of collaborating to achieve a kind of life, a foundation for more. Even before she met Xavier— who came with his own big family and their own particular interrelationships—Alice would tell me, "Relationships are work." She was aware that she was going into something that wouldn't be perfect. It would be marriage, and it would forever be a work in progress. It was worth it not despite that, but because of it.

. . .

ora and Mattie and I stayed together in a room at one of the oldest hotels in the French Quarter. There was a seductively dim revolving bar downstairs at which we drank non-virgin Shirley Temples, and balconies above with decorative wrought-iron grating preventing those who'd throw their Mardi Gras beads onto the street from falling along with their necklaces. Alice and her wedding party had the penthouse suite. The night we arrived we went up to her set of rooms and sat with family and friends, toasting the bride, the focus of everyone's attention. The internal surge that comes from seeing a close friend take this step was running through all of us. Even when a person has grown cynical about weddings, it's hard to feel cynical about a good couple getting married, especially when it happens in New Orleans. So we didn't.

The rehearsal dinner was at a private home in the Garden District. The hosts were long-standing friends of the groom's family, and they had two sons who were about Xavier's age, Andrew and Harrison. The three boys had grown up together. It was a gorgeous old house, peach in color and patrician in feel, and behind it was a big backyard full of grass and flowers and formidable old trees, with enough space for tables at which people could sit and eat gumbo and po'boys and red beans and rice, washing it all down with Abita beer. It was chilly, so over our dresses we wore coats. There is a photo of Nora and me in the backyard that night, smiling and cuddling together for warmth; she's in red wool, and I'm wearing a black jacket with a fur collar.

Months before, Harrison had visited New York. Alice and Xavier had taken him to a Lower East Side bar that no longer exists, and I'd joined them and a few other friends. In the middle of that bar was a metal pole extending through the ceiling and down into the cement floor, a relic from some previous building purpose, or maybe a structural element. In between sipping our drinks we took turns grabbing and sliding down it, like firemen or strippers, or stripper firemen. Harrison and I started talking—it's a surefire conversation starter, a stripper pole—and later that night, on the street, he kissed me. I didn't see him again before he returned to New Orleans. The kiss was just one of those things that had happened that didn't need to lead to anything else. Still, in going to this wedding, I remembered the kiss. We had history, if kisses counted as such.

Since the party was being hosted at his house, he was kept busy, and spent the night replenishing beer and wine and food and making sure there were enough chairs and the music was at an acceptable volume for the young and old ears present. Throughout it all he was flanked by a crowd of family members and old friends, with whom he mingled comfortably. But we briefly reconnected that night, enough that it wasn't weird for either of us to look around and see in the backyard a stranger with whom we had once had a moment. He found me inside as I was waiting for the bathroom to free up. I was talking to his little cousin, who was around three or four years old. She was holding a picture book. "Is that your favorite?" I'd asked. She'd smiled enigmatically and turned pages, and I read her some lines.

"This is Neena," he said, seeing us together and picking her up. She hugged him and laughed and patted his head. "How've you been?" he asked. "It's been a while."

"Good!" I said. "Working, staying away from stripper poles. How about you?"

"Pretty good, pretty good," he answered, handing the baby to her mom, who'd just exited the bathroom. His own mother entered the room and gave him a look. "I'm supposed to help keep people out of the house," he whispered.

"Oh, I'm sorry!" I said. "I just need to use the restroom . . ."

"You better hurry," he warned, and when my face registered shock, he laughed. "Aw, I'm just kidding. She doesn't want people upstairs, is all."

"Ha," I said, heading into the bathroom and shutting the door. When I emerged, he was gone, and I only saw him again to say good-bye. He stood shaking hands with the departing guests at the door of his family manor.

"See you at the wedding," he said.

"Yep," I agreed. That was a near-guarantee.

The ceremony took place in the late afternoon. The sun was still high in the sky when we left the hotel to walk the few blocks to the church. I was wearing a purple silk dress topped with the black fur-collared jacket I'd worn the night before and was feeling very retro-chic. Saint Louis Cathedral, the oldest continuously operating cathedral in North America, is one of those incredible buildings, its architecture outshining everything that surrounds it. In the postcards and in real life, too, it looks rather like a Disney castle, but it's 100 percent Catholic, not mouse. I'll blame its awe-inspiring presence on the fact that I do not remember one iota of the ceremony, save the sight of Xavier and Alice, tiny at the front of the cavernous, beautiful church. After a priest pronounced the couple bride and groom, we headed outside and the brass band began to play. Serenaded by a tuba-forward rendition of "Just the Two of Us," Alice in her white dress and veil, a flower behind her ear, and Xavier in his khaki suit, broke into a spontaneous dance in front of the church. The guests joined in. Then the parade began, and we traveled that way, pausing to boogie in the streets when the spirit moved us, following the couple and the band to the reception. It was pretty obvious given our attire and the mood of the crowd, but strangers would stop and ask, "Is this a wedding?" When we said yes, unable to help themselves, drawn in by the music and the magic, some of those people fell in line with us and started dancing, too.

Canal Street was busy with traffic, and as we reached it, a child ran out ahead of the group. Without thinking I reached out and grabbed him, holding his hand so we could cross safely. My friends looked at me, astonished.

"Oh, my God," said Nora with a gasp of feigned horror. "*You have a nurturing side.*"

"You like kids! You like kids!" Mattie taunted. "Ha! We've found you out!"

"Everybody, calm down," I said, deadpanning. "Seeing a kid get hit by a car would have been a real downer for the reception." I turned the little boy loose and he went running back to his parents.

A few minutes later I turned to Nora and clarified. "I've never not liked kids, you know. Just because I don't talk about how I'm dying to have them, at any cost . . ."

"I know, I know," she said. "It's just funny to see you do something maternal."

If it's maternal to want to prevent a kid from getting hurt, I thought, *guilty as charged.*

The truth is, I like kids now, and I liked kids then. As a little girl, I was a loving older sister to my baby brother, even when he punched me so incessantly that my mom, fearing she was raising a bully and a wimp, told me to punch him back. (I eventually mustered the nerve to do this, and he stopped punching.) As a teenager, I babysat a family of four girls for an entire summer. I adored them, each with her own unique personality and quirky habits, and am sad that our families lost touch and I don't know what they grew up to become. I love my friends' children, and am fascinated and entertained whenever I'm around them. They do the greatest kid things, like staring into a ceramic bunny's eyes in search of the secrets of the universe; demanding a bunch of frozen mini-pancakes to be both cold and hot, *at the same time*; shouting "Wheeeee" in a deep, serious voice while being pushed on a swing; or asking for the definition of the word *transform* and then using it repeatedly throughout the night.

The decision to like kids is easy. The decision to have them is something else. I have never been someone who wanted above all else to be a mom, which could be why my friends were so amused by what they saw as unexpected and revelatory maternal antics.

Of course, parenthood, like marriage, has changed. We've

gone beyond those stock nuclear conceptions of family and into a varied field of increasingly acceptable arrangements. I have plenty of friends who've married and had children, but I also have friends who've married and never procreated. I know single women who are having babies on their own and committed couples who wish to remain unmarried as they raise their families. There are families with divorced parents; children who split their lives between two, and even more, as those parents remarry and form new units. And there's that much-discussed biological make-or-break moment that arrives for women in their late thirties or early forties, a point when marriage and children may be forced together in a rush before the proverbial curtain closes.

At Alice's wedding, I was in my early thirties. I felt like I had so much time, but I knew some of my friends didn't feel that way. That they were dubbing me maternal, I realized, might have been more about them than it was about me. At twenty-five you may not be thinking much about kids, but in your thirties, chances are they're on the horizon and even a key part of the decision to marry. While Alice wasn't rushing to the altar to have babies, the idea of creating a future family—not just her and Xavier but children as well—was part of their plan, and sooner rather than later, I wagered, they'd be embarking on that new life stage together.

We mingled in the courtyard of the Board of Trade, sitting at the fountain and sipping prosecco in the remaining sun as the second-line stragglers filed in, and when all had arrived we headed into the large banquet room where dinner and dancing would take place. I was seated at a table with Harrison and his brother, Andrew, along with a group of friends including Nora and Mattie. We found our spots, dropped off our purses and jackets, and waited for the reception to begin in earnest.

Ginny and her husband were at this wedding. We hadn't talked since LA, but I'd seen her at the church and again outside, standing near the fountain, the two of them smiling for a photo, his arm around her. I tried to put that to the back of my mind and focus instead on chatting with other guests and eating the appetizers that were being passed around. (Wedding Tip: Truffled deviled quail eggs? Yes, please!) But I couldn't stop thinking about her, about them. It was like a buzzing in my ear, this unresolved thing, and it grew louder with each prosecco. It seemed I should at least acknowledge her presence, if only so I could move on. It was weird not to, I decided. It made things worse. I broke away and walked over. I'd just say hello and that I hoped she was well, and that would be that, I could stop stewing. I tapped her on the shoulder.

"Hi, Ginny," I said. "It's good to see you."

"Hi," she answered, not smiling, but not frowning, either. She was calm, if chilly. "Nice to see you, too." She clearly did not want to talk.

Her husband was standing near her and looked at me. I thought I detected a note of censure on his face. "Well, I just wanted to say hello," I said, and made an exit. She watched me go but said nothing, and neither did he. Well, that had been a failure. Certainly I hadn't gotten what I wanted from it, even if I wasn't sure what I wanted—forgiveness? A return to the old days? An honest discussion? A hug? I didn't even know that I had the right to expect whatever it was I'd been aiming for. I had tried, and the only thing it had done was make me feel worse.

At the front of the room, there was a commotion. Alice and her mother were talking to a man who didn't appear to be a wedding guest, and as I got closer, I realized he was a cop. He was gesturing and explaining and, occasionally, writing in a little notepad. By the time I reached them, he was on his way out of the building, his walkie-talkie spitting out new information.

"What happened?" I asked Alice, who looked livid.

"This is a freaking circus," she said. "A waiter was just arrested for hitting the wedding planner's son in the head with a sheet pan."

"*What?*" I said. "Why?"

"We have no idea. *An altercation.* Also, my chocolate sheet cake has gone missing. And all the gifts that people brought with them today—all the cards with cash—are gone, too."

"That is awful! I'm so sorry," I said.

She was too angry for sorry. "It's bullshit is what it is. Utter bullshit. In even more pressing dramas: This stupid DJ we hired won't play anything from our playlist! He only wants to play salsa."

"*Salsa?* I'll fix that," I said, and walked over and cajoled this long-haired dude to please, please, please play something the bride and groom wanted to hear, something on the list of songs they'd given him. For a minute, he did. He picked "Brick House," which was at least widely recognized by the guests, who went crazy on the dance floor. Alice perked up and gave me a big smile and a mouthed *Thank you*. Soon enough the DJ went right back to playing exactly what he felt like, but by that point we would not be stopped by salsa and kept dancing anyway. Harrison joined me.

Many drinks and dances later, I found my way back to Ginny and her husband. Not surprisingly, he and I wound up in a conversation that did not go well. Out of a combination of, I think, self-protection and drunkenness, what exactly was said has been locked in the far reaches of my memory and cannot be withdrawn. I do know that it was bad, with remnants of LA and what had happened before, all that unfinished business, surfacing yet again. Maybe I was trying to explain, but more likely, I wanted to hurt him for how I felt he'd hurt my friendship with Ginny. In this too-soused wedding moment, I tried to strike back, and I failed utterly, coming across as even more unreasonable than before. Harrison came to my aid as things got heated and pulled me away. On the way to the bar designated for the after-party, I tried to explain the past years of that friendship. He listened and nodded. Morose at our destination, I had another drink, and I decided I needed to leave. This wedding had gone to a dark place for me. It was best to get home, and, in fact, I thought I might be sick.

We emerged from the bar, and Ginny and her husband were sitting outside. "Well, no surprise, Jen's drunk off her ass again," he announced loudly, and though it was absolutely true, I cursed him out with all the power I could summon on my precariously heeled legs. Harrison dragged me away again and brought me back to the hotel, where I cried and cried and vomited in the bathroom. He consoled me, holding my hair back from the toilet, nurturing and kind.

I passed out on the hotel bed, and later, Nora and Mattie came back and took an array of lurid photos of me. Semi-awake in them, I look beyond drunk, my dress wrinkled and twisted around my body, my retro-chic jacket long discarded as this new version of me, a gross replica of an American Apparel ad that would never be approved to run on billboards, emerged. I'm holding a belt, which I lashed at them because—at the very bottom of it all, one true, id-like emotion—I didn't want my photo taken. They thought these pictures were hilarious. I was embarrassed I'd lost control again despite my promises to myself that I'd be different. And I was mortified that there was photographic proof. All that stung far more than being called *maternal*.

The next day, after a shower and food had helped me pull myself together, I sat on the deck of the hotel's rooftop pool with Alice, who was now officially a married woman. It was too cold to swim, but warm enough for the sun to feel good on our skin. I was flying back to New York in a few hours.

"What happened with you and Ginny last night?" she asked.

"I don't know." I really couldn't explain, not in a way that made reasonable sense to either of us. "I messed up again. I tried to talk to her. I got drunk and ended up cursing out her husband."

"Oh, Jen. That's not good. You need to let it go," she said.

"I know. I wish I'd done that already. This only makes it worse."

"Yeah," Alice said.

I knew all this, and I'd known it, and yet the night before, I hadn't been able to help myself. I guess a part of me was still furious about having lost my friend, and angry at the man I believed had caused the rift. I didn't know where to put all that emotion. When they ignored me (the better choice, really), I got drunk and lost it. All this had affected not only my relationship with Ginny, but also, it was starting to wear on my relationships with our common friends. They hadn't given up on me, but I was testing the boundaries of what they could deal with. And it felt awful for me, too. I imagined it felt just as bad for Ginny, maybe even worse. This had to stop, for real.

"She chose him, you know," said Alice gently. "They're married. That's what it is. They're the family now."

"I know," I said. "It's just hard."

"It is hard."

None of us, married or single or engaged or boyfriended or otherwise, with kids or without, were sure we had the right answers. We were only trying to do the right thing based on what we knew, what we thought we wanted, what we hoped we wanted to be.

"Did you find out anything more about the missing cash and cake?" I asked her.

"No," she said. "Oh, well. I guess whoever took that stuff needs it more than we do." She sighed. "Wait, what happened with Harrison last night? He *likes* you."

"Oh, God." I couldn't understand why anyone would have liked me in that state, or even this one. "He took me back to the hotel room and held my hair during my puke-cryfest. I need to e-mail him thank you. I should send him a gift. A check, or one of those fruit baskets, or something."

"Oh, Harrison," she said. "I'm sure he didn't mind."

A year or so after the wedding, I was at a church in Brooklyn for the christening of Alice and Xavier's first child. There I ran into Ginny and her husband. She had their first baby with her, a little boy, sleeping in a baby carriage. The tension between us had faded. She had far more important things to deal with than me—her family, which, I'd finally realized, had always been the most important thing to her. And I had moved on, too. While we weren't friends, we didn't have to be enemies, either. Things, I think, I hope, had been forgiven on both sides, and we had both forged ahead to find the lives we'd wanted.

"He's so adorable," I said, touching the chubby, impossibly soft-skinned hand of her son.

"Thank you," she said. "He's our little angel. He's my love."

Together, we watched him sleep.

Years later still, I sat with Alice at her house in the Pacific Northwest, where she had moved with her husband and child. They had another baby, a girl, on the way. The topic of children came up, along with the topic of my birthday. I was turning thirty-seven, and while I knew that I still didn't know, wasn't completely sure, what I felt about having children, she thought she did: "You don't even want kids," she said. "You're focused on your career."

"I don't?" I asked. "I might. I don't want to say for sure I don't."

"Well, do you?" she asked. "You don't *have* to want kids. Having kids is a pain in the butt, you know. It changes everything."

"I was asking Heather if she had any tips for having a happy marriage, and she told me, 'Don't have kids, kids make everything harder,'" I said.

"Ha! And she's pregnant with her second child now, too."

"Right, so obviously they're worth it for her, and for you . . ."

"It's never the fairy tale," she said. "But, yeah." She paused. "Anyway, if you do want kids, you should probably get going on that. We're not twenty-five anymore."

"Thank goodness," I said. I knew that while I wasn't ready to get going on that, having children wasn't something I was ready to give up on, either. Sometimes things just didn't happen the traditional way, and that was fine, too.

"Oh, you know who just got married?" she asked.

"Who?"

"Harrison!"

"I saw that on Facebook," I said. "Good for him."

"They'll have the most gorgeous kids."

"They will," I agreed.

13.

Never Settle for Less

I was on the Garden State Parkway with a man I'd met less than a handful of times before. We were not dating, but we were both the bride's friends, and he'd agreed to give me a ride to Cape May, New Jersey, where the ceremony would take place and where a pre-wedding welcome party was happening within the hour. But the car had gotten a flat tire, and we were stranded on the side of the highway, inhaling tar and dirt and diesel fumes. The man, whose name was Ted, was on the phone with AAA. I was trying to remember whether you were supposed to stay in the car or not when you were broken down on the side of a highway. I was pretty sure one thing was dangerously wrong and the other was right, but I couldn't remember which.

When Elizabeth, who was getting married, had suggested I ask Ted for a ride, I'd considered it the ideal solution to my dilemma. I hadn't figured out how I'd get to her wedding otherwise. I didn't, as it turned out, know too many people who had been invited. I could rent a car and attempt to make the drive myself, but that seemed dicey considering I hadn't driven in years. Luckily, Ted had said he'd take me, no problem, I'd only have to get myself to Newark, where he was working at the time. Well, public transportation went to Newark, so that was easy enough. But now here we were. I couldn't help thinking that if I'd come to the wedding with a date, I might not be in this predicament. I shook that idea off as silly, though, and entirely regressive. I didn't need anybody. I only needed to relearn how to drive.

My driver and I looked at each other, and he tried to smile. "A guy with a tow should be here soon," he said.

"Hey, at least we'll have a story to tell everyone at the party," I offered, attempting to soothe him.

"Yeah," he said, not looking much happier. "At least we'll have that."

Elizabeth and I had met the summer of our junior year of college, when we both interned at a publishing company in Manhattan. Though we went to separate universities, we had stayed in touch, and as I plotted my return to the city from Boston in 2002, her sister was making her departure from New York and the apartment they shared in Hell's Kitchen. Elizabeth e-mailed and asked if I knew anyone who'd take her sister's spot. I answered, "Me!" An apartment at the ready, with a friend and without a broker fee? It seemed too good to be true, but there it was.

We lived together for two years in that apartment, and then came another too-good-to-be-true real estate situation: a two-bedroom apartment on the Upper West Side that Elizabeth's co-worker and his wife were vacating. It was a duplex, with one bedroom on each floor, and each bedroom had—wait for it—its own bathroom *with shower*. Despite the pain of moving, we agreed we could not pass it up. Sure, one of the bedrooms was technically in the cold, dark basement, and you could hear the elevator swinging into action with a *ker-thunk* whenever it was called from above, but so what? A two-bedroom, two-bath apartment for $2,000 a month in New York City was akin to finding a unicorn in Central Park, or a sweet, upstanding young man at a bar in the East Village. The cherry on top of the real estate sundae was that this apartment had a patio. A giant patio, for barbecues, for parties, for sunning ourselves, for a garden! Most of those dreams were crushed when we realized that the patio, surrounded as it was by the column of buildings around it, got almost no natural light. Fine. It was still a place to have parties. Even if someone in one of the apartments above us shouted rude things out the windows and threw down pornography whenever we went outside, we had that most coveted of New York City things: outdoor space.

Life on the Upper West Side was grand. We had plenty of room to spread out and live our own lives, with or without boyfriends, or men we were considering for the role. In Hell's Kitchen, we had shared a wall between bedrooms; on the Upper West Side, we had our own wings of the house and couldn't even hear each other leave for work in the morning. I was still dating Jason when we made this move, and I figured it might help improve our relationship—there was more privacy, and he loved to grill outdoors. Even though I was technically farther away from his East Village apartment, I was on an express train line where it was far more civilized to debark than, say, Times Square or, worse, Port Authority.

It seemed for a long time that if Elizabeth had a boyfriend, I would not, and vice versa. Before I'd met Jason she'd had a serious, several-years-long relationship with a slightly older man she thought she'd probably marry. They'd even gone so far as to discuss "the chip," his family's name for the heirloom diamond in the family. Then they broke up, and while she dated other guys, she was still hung up on "Chip," conflicted about why and how and what had gone wrong, exactly—was it somehow her fault? Should she have done something differently?

Jason and I ended things, and Elizabeth and I swapped relationship places again. She met a new guy, who was British and of Indian descent, while on a trip to New Orleans with her sister. She liked him and he liked her, and they had kissed and promised to stay in touch, but when she got back to New York she didn't announce, "He's the one" or "I've met my husband" or "I might have a new boyfriend." After all, he lived in London. She counted all of his potential flaws on her fingers as she told me about him. "He's nothing I'm looking for in a guy," she said. "Long distance. Not my religion. Not even American. A *vegetarian*."

"None of that might be so bad, though," I said. "You've dated plenty of guys who fit what you were 'looking for,' and it's not like they've been so great. Remember the one who pronounced calamari 'calamars'?"

"True," she said. "That guy was the worst! Anyway, he said he'd call. We'll see."

Of course he called. When they're bad on paper, they always call. But this guy, Lagan, was really only bad on paper if you looked at the paper in a certain way, squinting and with no imagination at all. He was a consultant, and after they'd been talking a while, each conversation burrowing further into the hours of the night, they started making plans for him to visit. That first trip a success, another followed, and another. He was able to transfer to a project in New York for a few months to allow their relationship to unfold in a more geographically friendly fashion. She'd told him if all went well, after that, she'd try out London for a while. Eventually the day arrived on which she flew across the ocean, all her worldly possessions packed in two suitcases, wearing the extra clothes she couldn't fit in those bags on her own body. "I hope you don't get stopped in customs," I'd said, laughing as she topped her head with a stocking cap to venture out into the eighty-degree summer day.

Well, it worked, right? This is a book about weddings. Earlier in this chapter, we left me waiting on the side of the road on my way to hers. So, yes, it happened. Time passed. He asked. She said yes.

They were still living in London at the time, and it was decided that they would be one of those modern-international-religiously-and-ethnically-intermixed-sophisticated couples who have two weddings to accommodate the family needs of each. One would be in the UK, in the summer, primarily attended by Lagan's Indian relatives, who mostly lived there. Before that, in the spring, there would be a wedding in Cape May, where Elizabeth's family had summered since her grandmother was a child. Tickets to London in June left me sticker-shocked. I'd definitely go to New Jersey, though, I promised myself, and her. Not being able to afford to go to New Jersey wasn't an option. It got close to the date, and I got the ride with Ted. And now, here we were. Side of the Garden State Parkway, on our way to a wedding. Still waiting.

"You know what?" he said. "I think I have a spare in the trunk."

"Oh!" I said. "That seems promising. I think."

We headed to the back of the car and, yes, there it was, small and precious cargo. He pulled it out of the trunk, where he had a box of tools, too, and we stared at everything for a minute. "Um," he began, and that's when AAA arrived. Quick as a wink, the driver was clambering out of his truck, assessing damage, and installing the spare. "You shouldn't go too far on this; it's only temporary," he advised. We nodded. It was a wedding. Any long-term plans beyond that, for us, at least, could be put on hold.

With renewed cheer, we took off again, heading straight to the party without stopping to check in to our hotel. We didn't want to miss everyone, and there they were, still eating and drinking and celebrating. We greeted them and told of our near-mishap. "You could have been stuck by the side of the road for days!" Elizabeth exclaimed in mock horror. She was tan and bridally radiant in a yellow silk dress she'd had made while on a trip to Vietnam with Lagan.

"You are so beautiful!" I said, hugging her. "We should get

drinks," I told Ted. "Want a beer?" He nodded, and I went in search of the cooler. It seemed the least I could do.

We went our separate ways for the rest of the party and, in fact, for the entire wedding. This was partly because Elizabeth was introducing me to every single man in attendance one by one, as a bride often does, surreptitiously or obviously attempting to set up her single friends. "Lagan's business school friends are cute," she said. "And smart, too. Have you met Cody?"

I hadn't met Cody. He was blond, with curly hair, round, ruddy cheeks, and blue eyes, a quintessential all-American boy. He was standing next to a table laden with appetizers, his hand reaching toward a bowl that contained Elizabeth's mom's trademark pickled eggs. "Oh," I said, turning to Elizabeth, that dish a reminder of another. "I brought you something!" It was her wedding present, a white, sculpted porcelain bowl embossed with a wavelike pattern. The secret was, I'd bought the bowl for myself, because I really liked it. When it arrived there was an extra bowl in the box, along with a note that explained that as thanks for my order I was getting a second, matching bowl for free. I had no idea what sort of profitable bowl business could exist with that model, but I didn't care. Two bowls for the price of one! I wouldn't look a wedding gift horse in the mouth.

"A bowl!" She inspected it. "I love it."

"Nice bowl," said Cody, observing our interchange.

"Thanks," I said. "You went to business school with Lagan?"

"Why do you assume that?" he asked. "Because I could tell it's a bowl?" Elizabeth had been waylaid by an aunt.

"Yes," I said. "You probably got a degree in Bowl Identification Processes. That's big at Harvard, right?"

"Huge," he said. "Good old B.I.P. How do you know Elizabeth?"

"We were roommates," I said. "For the last few years. Until she moved in with you-know-who." I jerked a thumb in the general direction of Lagan.

Suddenly we were surrounded by a group of fellow business school guys, all back-slapping and joke-making. "After-party at that Irish pub in town," one of them announced. "Be there, man."

Cody looked at me. "Are you going to come?"

"I don't know," I said, though it seemed a better prospect than hanging out in my room alone. "I need to find out what my ride wants to do. I haven't checked in to the hotel yet, either."

Elizabeth, who'd returned for a moment, shook her head. "I have to stick around, guys. I'm the bride."

Later that evening, after my dress options had been hung in the closet of my spacious room, which featured a queen-sized bed and even a couch—this was no Manhattan hotel, and I suspected it was bigger than my first apartment with Elizabeth had been—I went out to a local bar with some of the other wedding guests. Many of them were guys. Elizabeth was always really good at being friends with guys. A number of them had harbored their own crushes on her, and most of them had moved on, but there were holdouts, I was sure. I didn't see Cody. Instead, I started talking to another blond man, a peripheral friend from one side or the other who had, perhaps, only been invited as a formality. He seemed to know no one else there well. When I leaned over the bar at the same time he did to place an order, he bought me my drink. I figured he didn't have anyone to talk to, and understanding that state of wedding guesthood I'd experienced myself and in some ways was again experiencing now, I asked him about himself. He'd been traveling a lot over the past years, he said, and had been very busy doing whatever it was he did, something in computers or business or finance, or all of the above. We didn't talk about work much, because we quickly shifted to a real conversation, not just "What do you do?" but "Who are you?" We traded jokes and anecdotes like we'd known each other for years. I could feel my guard dropping as we spoke. And then it was last call.

"We don't have to go home yet, though, do we?" he asked. "I'm having too much fun."

"Me, too," I agreed.

"Wawa?" he suggested.

We drove to the nearest of the convenience-store locations in his car, which I remember had heated seats—I had traded up from the breakdown-mobile—and there we giddily, somewhat drunkenly, roamed the too-bright fluorescent-lit aisles before selecting giant fountain sodas, Doritos, and sub sandwiches. We went to my hotel room, as it was the bigger of the options, and we sat and talked some more as we ate. Even though I didn't know this guy, I felt safe with him, which of course is the sort of thing Lifetime movies warn you about and parents fear, no matter how old their adult children are. *Mother, May I Sleep with Danger?* is not a Tori Spelling classic for nothing. But I was trusting my instincts, even if those instincts might be said to have failed me before.

At the time of Elizabeth's wedding, it had been a few months since I'd traveled to Pennsylvania to see a sort-of ex. The confusion and vulnerability I'd felt after that trip had continued, lingering longer than it should have, partly because there'd been no one else, but also because that semi-relationship felt like a turning point. It indicated what I had chosen for myself and what I had rejected. He'd moved from the city into a two-story house in the suburbs that had all the potential of burgeoning family life, and when I visited him there, I felt nothing but trapped, freaked out, and wanting to flee. When the weekend was over, I took a bus back to New York; what a relief to be back to the city, back to normalcy. Later, though, I started to doubt myself and even wonder if I'd messed up. Here was a good guy who'd established the life he wanted and was actively looking for someone with whom to share it. People claimed it was the fault of modern women that we were single. We needed to stop being so picky and just settle and do this thing, grow up and get married and have families with the men who were decent, even if they weren't the ones who swept us off our feet, even if it felt like the supposed magic was missing. This was a case in which I had done the opposite. I had run, and now I found myself looking back.

Did my behavior make it my fault I was single? Did it mean, as well, that I was hopelessly immature and would always remain so? *Fault* seemed like the wrong word. At the base of it, I couldn't help feeling glad that my instincts would not allow me to "settle," that I'd chosen single instead of only sort-of-happily (possibly disastrously) together, forced to choose the lesser because I was afraid the greater might never appear. There was something more I wanted, and something more I could have, I knew it, or at least I really, really hoped it. I *knew* that this man in Pennsylvania wouldn't have been right, and that, regardless of what certain people professed, my only fault would have been going along with what he'd laid out because I hadn't found what *was* right.

The thing is, settling isn't settling when it's what you want to do more than anything else. But if a person settles by choosing something she doesn't want in hopes of someday wanting it, or because she only wants what accompanies it—the house, the car, the wedding—that's a far more certain recipe for ruin, not to mention less mature, than is an informed choice to be single. You can't just "go along" with a relationship. I knew I couldn't.

Back in my hotel room with my new friend Paul, I was reminded of that glorious feeling of instant connection. These are the rare moments when you can nearly see and certainly feel the magic, at least very early teeny-tiny sparks of it, flying around like just-visible dust particles in a sunny room. We kissed, and then we moved to my bed and kissed some more. We were lying in that bed, partially clothed, the covers around us, when he looked at me seriously.

"I should tell you something."

"What is it?" I asked, figuring he'd confess he hadn't slept with anyone in a while, or that he had some unusual proclivity or another.

"You sure you're ready for this?" He smiled, and I smiled back.

"C'mon, we're both adults here," I said. "Just tell me!"

"I'm married."

"*What?*" I said, finding only the words to repeat myself. "*What?*"

"Yeah," he said, putting his head on the hotel pillow and staring up at the ceiling. "I mean, I didn't mean for this to happen. I just feel like we have this *thing*, you know?"

"Where is your wife? Why isn't she here?" I demanded.

"She's traveling. She couldn't come."

"*She couldn't come?*"

At best, it was a paltry explanation for what had happened in the past few hours. I wondered who else at the wedding knew. They had to know. Unless . . . was this guy really even a legitimate wedding guest, or had I picked up a townie who'd sold me a line? At the bar, none of the other guests had seemed to notice or indicate anything awry. Had anyone seen him come back to my room? Had he been talking to anyone about me? If we *did* hook up, would anyone know? Oh, God. I could not be that girl at the wedding who was consorting with married men. I would not be that person. I shook my head.

"This is not okay," I said. "I can't believe this. I can't believe *you*. Are you really even invited to the wedding? Who do you know here?"

He chose not to answer. "We're both adults here," he said, giving my words an entirely different meaning than I'd intended. "Is it really so wrong? This has never happened to me before. I love my wife. But you and I have something; you know we do. Can't we just have one great night?"

I looked at him, his sad, serious, handsome face, and I believed him. I suspected he wasn't a routine philanderer, but that didn't mean that what had seemed so promising and special—because he was right, we had had something, for a second, for a couple of hours even—was now hopelessly tainted. "No one will know," he added, a creepy cap on how tawdry it all felt.

"No," I said. "You need to leave." Realizing it was useless to argue, he got up slowly, buttoned his shirt, put on his shoes, and left. Only later did I realize he'd forgotten his tie. Its red-and-white pinstripes pointed accusations. I put it on the table on the other side of the couch from where we'd sat and talked, behind a seashell lamp. I didn't want to look at it.

The next morning was gray and rainy. I felt that internal knot that comes of things you didn't mean to do but feel bad about nonetheless and, unfortunately, cannot change. I got out of bed and showered and dressed and was looking out the window, inspecting the gloomy conditions, when my eyes fell on his tie. I resisted the urge to toss it from the balcony. Then came a light knock at my door, followed by another, harder, and when I went to open it, there he was, smiling and full of morning pep, as if nothing had ever happened. "I think I left my tie," he announced. "How did you sleep?"

Wordlessly, I turned and grabbed the tie. I wanted that thing out of my hotel room, and fast. I prayed no other wedding guest would pass by on their way to breakfast to catch wind of this conversation. "Fine," I said, aiming for Arctic Circle–style coldness, and handed it over.

"Have you eaten yet? Want to get some food?" inquired Mr. Does Not Take a Hint.

"I better not," I said. *Is this guy for real?* "I have things I have to do. In fact, I have to go, I'm already late."

"Gotcha," he said, nodding. "Well, I had fun last night."

"Yep, okay," I said, eager to shut the door before I said what my brain was humming and I'd surely regret, something to the tune of *Dude, you're married. What the fuck is wrong with you?* I had to see this guy later. He was—I was pretty sure he was—a wedding guest. I managed a perfectly pleasant, if meaningless, "Have a good day," and then felt heavy with the knowledge that he might have just ruined mine.

By the time I was heading out onto the boardwalk, I felt a little better, though. I hadn't known. And nothing had actually happened, thankfully. But, man, people are messed up, I thought. A wedding and a marriage, was, in my opinion, supposed to indicate an ultimate kind of trust, taking that chance and putting one's confidence in the fidelity and integrity of another human. That in itself was scary enough. That the trust could be broken so easily, and so seemingly casually, shocked me. If you couldn't rely on another person, if you couldn't put your faith in that human for life, why get married at all? I knew of couples who had open marriages, and I supposed in those cases the integrity and trust was about whatever had been discussed and agreed to, but I didn't think from our interaction that Paul had an open marriage, and I knew that kind of marital arrangement wouldn't work for me. Worse, though, was lying to the person you'd promised to love and care for forever. That was a chance I supposed all committed couples took: If you let yourself believe in someone else, there's always the risk you might get hurt. That person might let you down.

I walked for a while, watching the surf, and then got ready to go to Elizabeth's shower brunch. It was at a nearby restaurant, and I arrived early, with just a few of her older relatives beating me to the location. As we waited for the bride to arrive, I reminded myself that what had happened with Paul was no more my fault than that had been the end of things with the man in Pennsylvania. I'd done the right thing, choosing single, choosing not to insert myself into someone else's idea of marriage, or their reality of one. Had I had a few more drinks, I might have been carried away and not had the wherewithal to stop things with Paul, I thought. What if I hadn't wanted to? What if he hadn't told me? That he had confessed indicated that he felt it was important. He might have wanted me to behave exactly as I had. But this was fruitless pondering. I pushed it all to the back of my mind, sat back in my chair, and put a smile on my face. The bride was opening presents.

That night we were at the bar again, and I didn't see Paul. Elizabeth and Lagan arrived late, having had the rehearsal dinner with the wedding party beforehand, and we all rushed to buy them drinks and offer our congratulations. Cody was there, and we started talking again. I don't remember what we said. It wasn't the same as what Paul and I had talked about the night before. It didn't have the same import or connective feel. But by the end of the night, he and I were clearly going to hook up, and I felt a sense of relief, because the barest minimum level of relationship acceptability had been met in this case. He and I were both single, and us being together couldn't possibly hurt anyone else.

Saturday, the wedding day, was gray and cloudy, too. The fog refused to lift, and there was a dampness to the air that made my bones feel cold. Though it was May, it had been a chilly spring, and it was barely clinging to the high fifties. It wasn't raining, exactly, but when I stepped outside onto the small hotel balcony, droplets of water seemed to come at me from every direction. I'd slept late and, waking up, I realized I was starving.

I put on a sweatshirt and jeans and headed out, past the bar we'd gone to the night before, past surf shops and souvenir stores and a place selling cotton candy and popcorn, its door hung with a *Closed* sign. Finally I reached an establishment that was both open and sold pizza. I placed my order for a couple of cheese slices and a large Diet Coke. After sprinkling my food liberally with crushed red pepper and Parmesan, I sat outside on a bench to consume my meal. There was a tall, good-looking couple headed my way, and I watched them, thinking they looked familiar. As they got closer, the woman paused. "Jen?" It was Elizabeth's friend Gillian. She gave me a hug and started in on her story: "We just got here. I couldn't take off work. Ooh, that looks good! We're starving."

"I've been here since Thursday," I said, and showed off my pizza. "I'm basically a Jersey resident now. Get some food! Where are you guys staying?"

Gillian and Elizabeth had met at work, one of those first jobs you move on from quickly, if you're lucky, retaining the coworker you've befriended who also moves on. Now she was working in real estate and doing very well. She'd married a few years ago, and she and her husband, who was quiet and a cop of some sort—I didn't want to ask again—lived in one of those prosperous, if nearly identical, suburban towns of the state. They were staying at my hotel. "How are you getting to the wedding?" asked Gillian.

"Oh, I guess I'll walk," I said. "I don't have a car. I've been walking everywhere or, sometimes, getting rides with people." I thought of Ted, Paul, Cody. Sweet fancy highway breakdown, this was shaping up to be a messy wedding. "The chapel's just around the corner, right?"

"We'll drive you," she decided. "It's too far to walk in heels. Call me when you're ready, and we'll go together." She texted me her number.

"Excellent," I said, texting her back so she had mine. Suddenly having wedding friends felt very good, and after finishing my pizza, I walked into a neighboring nail salon, where I got a manicure and pedicure in defiantly chipper crimson before I returned to the hotel to get ready. With last night's hookup with Cody separating my near-miss with Paul, my spirits lifted further. There was no reason this wedding couldn't be the great time I'd anticipated before the incident with Paul, before the car broke down, even before what had happened back in the Pennsylvania suburbs. While maybe I still wasn't entirely sure what I wanted in the long term, or how to achieve it, I could definitely say that what I wanted in the short term was to have some fun at a wedding.

I put on a magenta silk wrap dress that tied in a bow at the waist and vintage earrings that looked like little bells, and called Gillian. "Perfect timing," she said. "Meet us downstairs in the garage. We're in the blue truck."

Elizabeth had wanted to have the ceremony on the beach, but the hint of a storm brewing hadn't lifted as the day progressed, and her pastor, who was eighty-six, wasn't eager to trudge through the wet sand to marry her. The backup location was a tiny, more-than-hundred-year-old chapel. The bride arrived in a restored Ford Model T, and as we reached the church, we saw her standing next to the old-fashioned car, tall and elegant in a white dress with clean lines and a lace bodice. Clustered around her were bridesmaids in pale green, all of them carrying flowers: calla lilies, hydrangeas, and peonies. A photographer shot the scene, over and over.

Walking inside that church, with its rough-hewn wooden pews and whitewashed walls, was like being transported back in time. We took our seats, and the minister, who we'd heard had performed with John Coltrane, led the congregation in a rousing version of "He's Got the Whole World in His Hands." For the ceremony, Elizabeth and Lagan recited their vows at the front of the little room, and people laughed and cried at all the right moments. It was lovely, everyone agreed. A beautiful bride, a handsome groom, and perfect pitch throughout, musically and otherwise. It was the first church wedding for much of the groom's family.

When it was over, while more photos of the wedding party were being snapped, we got back in the truck and drove the several blocks to the Victorian hotel where the reception was being held. The clouds had cleared some by then, and rays of sun peeked through and burned off those that remained. Outside in this new warmth on the hotel patio there were beverages set out, ice-filled pink cocktails that were the signature wedding drinks, named for the bride and groom. We stood and sipped tentatively as other guests joined us. "These are pretty good," said Gillian's husband. "But I think I might want a beer."

"There's a full bar," Gillian said. "Get whatever you want." They wandered away from me, holding hands. I was alone again, and there, right in front of me, was Cody.

"Oh, hi," he said.

"Oh, hi," I repeated. "Have a signature wedding cocktail."

"I think I will."

The wedding went by like all weddings do, the white satin swirls of a bridal gown circling on the polished dance floor. Drinks and more drinks. The tables were spread with linen table-cloths in the large ballroom of that Victorian hotel and, in reference to the international nature of the couple, were named for cities they'd visited. At each place setting there was a small satin bag with flowering tea buds they'd purchased while traveling in Southeast Asia. Several tables away from me was Paul. He was a guest after all, though I never did find out whose. We sat, and we all turned in our seats to watch Elizabeth and Lagan dance to "I Got You Babe." Paul looked at me for an instant and smiled. I looked away.

At some point, Cody asked if I wanted to dance. We got out

on the floor with everyone else and moved around like fools, the best sort of wedding groove there is. As we jumped up and down and shimmied to a totally non-slow-dance sort of song, I saw Elizabeth and Lagan stop for an instant, their arms around each other, holding tight. They looked at each other and smiled. Then, the moment past, they began to jump up and down with the rest of us.

The after-party was down the street at a bar deep in the basement of another hotel. There was a band, and we danced and danced some more, and suddenly my whole body was damp with perspiration. Every part of me was exhausted. There was Cody. "Want to leave?" he said, and so we did, going back to his hotel room and collapsing on his bed. We passed out immediately, both of us still in our clothes. I woke up before it was light outside and looked over at him. He opened his eyes and looked back at me.

It wasn't so much that I wanted to sleep with Cody as it was that I wanted to wipe clean the slate. I didn't want the memory of that man in Pennsylvania still lurking. I didn't want the memory of Paul, of what might have been wonderful gone suddenly, incredibly awry. I wanted a new memory, one that I could make, one that would not let me down. A fresh start. And why not?

It was nothing special at all, just a few moments of garden-variety, morning-after-wedding sex, and even though I didn't think we'd have a relationship, didn't even think I cared about that, when I left an hour or so later I could barely suppress the grin on my face. All of that past fog had dissipated; the sun was shining. That may be a lot to attribute to a few minutes of unremarkable sex, but I'm not lying. I left that room feeling free, and when I bumped directly into the maid, I couldn't stop laughing. If there was a case for settling, it wasn't in a marriage. But sometimes, in the moments of a wedding, there could be a Mr. Good Enough. As long as he wasn't your groom—or someone else's—that was just fine.

I had lost my earrings, I realized later, and when Cody sent me a Facebook message some days afterward, I asked if he'd found them in his room. "No," he wrote. "I didn't see them. And by now I guess they're long gone." I didn't mind. Once some things are gone, they're gone forever, and there's no sense trying to get them back. You don't need them, anyway. It's nice to remember you don't need a lot of things.

14.

Appropriate Attire

✦

He showed up at my door wearing jeans. They were black, but they were definitely denim. Oh, dear. He looked so proud of himself, like, weren't black jeans pretty much exactly the same thing as a suit? Jeans could be wedding-appropriate, come on! Well, no, not exactly. But if I said they couldn't be, not for this wedding and probably not for most, I feared he'd only get angry and start railing on the bourgeois perceptions and expectations of my nouveau riche friends. He had on a jacket, at least, and a pressed button-down shirt. He'd shaved. He looked stressed, not angry yet, but on edge and ready to rage at being found fault with over something that he hadn't cared about doing in the first place. This was my deal, not his.

"You look great!" I said.

"Are you sure?" he asked, his eyebrows relaxing slightly. "Jeans are okay? They're black jeans, so they're practically black pants. I couldn't find a decent suit. I tried and I couldn't. The suits were all shitty. And expensive. I'm not going to buy a suit. Why would I buy a suit I'm not ever going to wear again?" He was very nearly talking himself into being pissed off again, and I hadn't said a word.

I didn't ask where he'd looked or what he'd seen, but I didn't really believe he'd tried all that hard. We'd been arguing about what he'd wear to this wedding since it had been determined he would go with me several weeks before. Despite feeling in my gut that it was borderline impolite, I'd asked the bride, my friend Kate—the Kate who'd once had an allergic reaction following a trip to David's Bridal—if she could squeeze him in as my date. He and I had only been together a couple of months, and this event, which would take place at a Gothic Revival synagogue on Manhattan's Lower East Side, offered a training-wheels wedding guest experience for us as a couple. It was right in our laps, all of the fun of the party with none of the trouble of coordinating a hotel stay, buying a plane ticket to get to our destination, or even, really, traveling. She said of course, there was plenty of room at the wedding. The rehearsal dinner, though, was at 100 percent capacity. I'd have to weather it on my own. There, I was seated next to the best friend of the groom, a guy the marrying couple may or may not have been trying to set me up with. Things, of course, did not go that way, what with the intervening realities of life. He is now married, and I had a date to Kate's wedding.

K ate and the man who would become her husband had met at a bar in the East Village. I had been there, too. She and I had spent the day doing charity work with New York Cares. We'd been bused out to Staten Island, where we'd painted a school, and after returning to the city, still clad in our work gear—bandannas, old running shoes, ripped jeans, and crappy, paint-stained T-shirts—we'd gone out to a bar with a bunch of co-charitable citizens. When things at one bar got a little too wild (I may have broken a glass while interpretive kung fu fight-dancing), the two of us decided to take off on our own. We walked a couple of blocks and found another spot, where we commandeered stools at the bar, all the better for buybacks.

There were two men seated at the bar, guys in their late forties or early fifties, and we noticed them noticing us. Finally, one of them spoke. It was not a predictable opener. "Are you girls lesbians?" he said, a lead-up to the explanation that our outfits were not what he expected to see on women in the East Village on a Saturday night after he'd gone to the trouble of taking a train in from Connecticut. He had a chunky class ring with a garnet stone on his pinky finger (Life Tip: *Never* trust a man with a pinky ring, especially one that's garnet) and a piggish face. We'd both known guys like this, in our hometowns, at our colleges, in our offices. He gave off such a strong vibe of generalized distaste for his surroundings that it was startling he'd spoken to us at all, and also ironic, because as it turned out, he was the distasteful one. But that form of irony was precisely his MO. "What kind of a question is that?" one of us responded, and he again looked us up and down. "What are you *wearing*?"

"We were doing charity work," I said, though there was no

need to talk to this person at all. "These are school-painting clothes."

His friend piped up. "The bandannas are a little lezzie," he said with a sneer.

"What is your *problem?*" asked Kate.

The first guy broke in again with a charming sentiment: "I don't do charity work. I just donate money. Why do it yourself when you can pay someone else to do it for you? What a waste of time. Charity work." He gave an awful, derisive laugh.

His friend spoke. "I'm a gynecologist, so that's basically charity work."

We glared at him.

"You know, being a doctor," he continued, unbelievably. "You should see what I have to pay in malpractice insurance."

Kate and I looked at each other, on the verge of departure. But instead of leaving, because we shouldn't have to leave, *they* were the assholes, we stayed. They kept talking, and we tried to finish our drinks. It wasn't until the gynecologist got up to go to the bathroom and pig-face revealed that his friend was getting a divorce and could really use some female attention to help him through this "rough patch" that the camel's back was broken.

"You are disgusting," I said, getting up from my barstool.

"You should be ashamed of yourselves," Kate added.

"Lesbians," muttered the guy, his mouth still on his drink.

"That's *not an insult*," I yelled at his back.

We'd been brought down with a thud from the high of our day, a day in which we'd felt indisputably good. If men like these were our options, we'd always prefer to be single, but that was a depressing reality to consider. Were good guys really so few and far between?

We made our way out of the bar, weaving through tables and chairs that now felt like massive obstacles in our path, trying to put as much distance between ourselves and those terrible men as possible, when suddenly it was not a chair or a table in our way but another man. We tried to get around him but there was no room, and he stood his ground. "Are you guys runners?" he asked.

Oh, not that again. We looked at our shoes.

"Yes," said Kate definitively.

"Yep," I agreed. "We run everywhere we go, actually. We don't go anywhere without running."

"We just ran here from another bar," Kate said, "and now we're about to run home."

"It's the best way to burn off beer calories," I concluded.

The guy, who had on a pair of rimless glasses, smiled and motioned toward a friend sitting at a table in the corner of the bar. "This is my buddy Mike. He's a runner, too. We all like running! Why don't you have one more beer with us before you run home?" He looked at Kate's T-shirt. "Is that Thai writing on your shirt? Have you been to Thailand?"

She had, she started to tell him. I looked at her, and she looked at me, and it seemed the night couldn't get worse than it already had, but maybe it could get better. So we sat and we had more than one beer, and the world of men and women in New York City bars was at least one iota less depressing.

The next evening, Kate texted. "OMG MY HEAD," she wrote. "Just ate a ton of greasy Chinese. Not sure it's working."

"Ordered pizza," I responded. "Considering chicken fingers as backup plan. DTW, wtf, those first dudes . . ."

"I know!" she wrote. "*Ugh.* Wait! The runner texted me! He wants to get a drink."

"Oh!" I typed back. "He seemed nice."

"Was he short and Asian?" she asked.

"I don't know, I only remember his glasses."

From that moment on, his name was Glasses. (He was neither short nor Asian.) He, like the pig-faced guy, worked in finance, but in his case it seemed okay, even a nice sort of matchy-not-too-matchy job for the possible boyfriend of a lawyer, which was what Kate was. At some point, she confessed she wasn't a professional runner, nor was she someone who insisted on wearing running shoes every Saturday to do "bar runs." They started dating. They went to bars, and they went on runs together. They managed a geographically undesirable Hoboken-to-West-Village relationship commute until he moved into her place in Manhattan. They had their friends over for dinner, serving fancy cheese and charcuterie on her matching plates. When he slipped out of the room to use the bathroom, we looked at her expectantly. "It's all going really well," she confessed, almost embarrassed that the news was so good. "And the sex is great, too!" We high-fived.

"What did I miss?" he asked, returning.

There were stylistic differences between his boyish incorrigibility and her wry smarts, and sometimes they'd fight, but they always made up, and they seemed stronger for having gone through that process. That they could argue about serious things without their couplehood being threatened seemed the signifier that this was a real relationship. Now, they were getting married. "Does this mean we have to start calling him his real name?" one of our friends had asked.

"Of course not," said Kate. Apparently, he liked that spontaneous nickname. They celebrated their engagement at the bar where they'd met, and there was no sight of pig-face or his doctor pal.

Christoph and I hadn't been dating long. I wasn't even referring to him as my boyfriend. But the truth was, I wanted a date—a boyfriend—at this wedding, not least because it seemed as though all of my friends were partnered up, married, or on their way to being so. It was exhausting going to weddings with so many solidly formed twosomes, even if the members of those couples were my friends. There are aspects of being a couple that no one else should be included in, and aspects that no one else *wants* to be included in. Still, that can make a single person feel a touch lonely, a little bit rootless and reckless, particularly at a wedding. When it's time for everyone to get up and dance, or at the end of the night, to go home, and when everyone but you has someone to do that with, well, it can feel less than fabulous, regardless of how independent-minded and self-actualized a person might be. Sometimes at a wedding you just want a teammate to fall back on, when conversation lulls, when you need a refill, when it's time for photographs. I wasn't on any sort of fast marriage track, obviously—I was thirty-three; if I'd wanted a husband more than anything else, I figured, I'd probably have one by now—but I didn't want to be the third wheel yet again, and I didn't want to be that single girl longingly waiting for her wedding setup, either. Here was someone I was already seeing, someone who could dress in the right clothes and fulfill the role. A real live date.

That what the "right clothes" were had so quickly become a matter of contention revealed much about the relationship, however. In the couple of months since we'd met, things had, on occasion, gotten weird. All would seem fine, and suddenly, there would be a dramatic turn for the worse, and I couldn't figure out why. Irritated that he couldn't open the window in my apartment, he yanked it open with all the force he could muster, and when I chastised him for breaking the lock by doing that, he became even more furious. "How dare you accuse me of breaking your window!" he'd shouted. We'd be out at a bar, having a good time, and inexplicably (to me) he would become sullen and silent and want to go home. Gradually, he revealed information that made me doubt that a relationship was the right thing for us. But there was an undeniable physical connection, which the off-kilter aspects when we were together only emphasized. When you can't rely on emotions, sometimes you rely on sex, and sometimes sexual intimacy seems like it's just as good as the emotional kind. For a while, anyway.

I had on a Diane von Furstenberg dress. The lower half of it was a slim navy pencil skirt, which led to a navy waist that tapered in and extended to midtorso. Above that, the top was an ivory bustier dotted with colorful flowers, held up by navy straps. With his jeans, I hoped, we'd look rock 'n' roll as opposed to mismatched or inappropriate. It was a Lower East Side wedding after all, and we'd be surrounded by friends I'd had for a long, long time. These were people who, fingers crossed, would still love me even if I brought a date who did not meet the dress code to their wedding.

I grabbed my purse and we left my apartment, which was just blocks away from the synagogue. Being able to walk there was a luxury, and on the way, our clothing decisions final, we perked up, a happy couple en route to a wedding. We arrived, checked our coats, and entered the cavernous multilevel room where the ceremony would take place. There we found seats in the rows of folding wooden chairs positioned facing the altar, which was flanked on either side by large vases of cherry blossom branches. The backdrop to the altar was a set of doors decorated with wrought-iron vines. White petals decorated the aisle that the bride and groom would walk down, and white flowers were everywhere, picking up the subtle pink, purple, and red hues of the stained glass throughout the synagogue. It was all eerie and gothic and beautiful, as if we were in an enchanted castle, or a Guillermo del Toro movie.

Marjorie, who'd flown in from Nashville for the event, was a bridesmaid. She was behind the scenes preparing for her walk down the aisle, but a few seats away, there was her husband, Brian, next to our old roommate Violet and her boyfriend, Ashok. I waved. We'd be sitting at a table together for dinner. I noticed

Kate's mom, with the man she was dating, on one side of the aisle. Kate's dad, with his girlfriend, had been seated on the other. The bride's parents had been divorced for a while, but they hadn't met each other's new significant others yet. The plan was to keep them away from each other as much as possible. We all bring our own backstories to a wedding. Some are far more significant than black jeans.

The music began, and we fell into a hush. A trio of tiny flower girls traipsed down the aisle, carrying baskets full of more petals to add to those already decorating the floor. *"Awwww,"* murmured the crowd, and we got ready to stand up for the bride.

Following the ceremony, we went upstairs for Champagne and hors d'oeuvres, passed around by waiters clad in neat bow ties and suits. I felt a wave of embarrassment over my date's attire. When I introduced Christoph to the bride's mother, I thought I noticed a barely perceptible double take over his jeans, but I convinced myself this was a figment of my paranoid imagination. It was only clothes. Why was I getting hung up on something so stupid, or, as Christoph might say, so bourgeois? We drank and sat with my friends and their dates in a row of bleacherlike seats overlooking the area below, where shortly thereafter we'd eat tomato soup and filet mignon and dance and party out the rest of the night. Glasses and Kate arrived upstairs after photos, giddy from their vows, flushed from the excitement, and we toasted and congratulated them. Everything was fine, but something was off. I leaned in to Christoph. "Are you having fun?" I asked.

"Sure," he said, but I couldn't tell if he meant it. I went to get us another round of drinks from the bar, and when I came back, he was quiet, staring off into the distance. Ashok and Violet and Marjorie and Brian were talking and laughing around him.

"You know who you look like?" Marjorie asked him, leaning in and smiling.

"Who?" he responded.

"Jimmy Fallon!" she said. He looked back at her. "I think he's handsome," she added.

"I don't really watch TV," he said.

It was at some point around then I figured that if we were kissing, we weren't talking, and I didn't have to worry about whether he was happy or sad or what anyone else thought. I didn't have to think about those jeans. So that's what we did, over and over again, to the exclusion of most, if not all, else. This wedding goes down in history as the one in which I out-PDAed everyone else in the room. When my friends mention it today, Ashok can be relied on to make a lapping sound, as if soup were being eaten, to signify my extensive levels of makeoutery. On the upside, my date and I didn't subject the other guests to our behavior for long. We left the wedding early, skipping the after-party, but we'd checked out long before that.

When I woke up the morning after the wedding, he was asleep next to me. My eyes fell on those black jeans thrown over the arm of the white chair across from my bed, and I felt a mixture of confusion and sadness. Regret. I should have stayed later. I should have been a better friend. What was I doing, trading the people I knew and loved for this? For what? A wedding date? I wondered what I'd missed.

. . .

I 've forgotten a lot of the details about that relationship. I can't, for example, remember how we met. I remember our first date, how he offered to come and pick me up in his car. "Look for the Mercedes," he'd said, and I'd thought, *Oh, he's that kind of guy,* but then it wasn't what I'd assumed at all. The car was barely chugging along, with the passenger-side window taped up so it wouldn't fall back into the door. I got in anyway, and we went and ate tapas in Williamsburg, and it was a good date. I remember staying at his apartment but refusing to take a shower there; the stall was coated in a layered grunge that made me fear it had never been cleaned. I remember him later using that against me, accusing me of not liking him enough because I wouldn't shower at his house. It wasn't about liking him, I tried to explain. It was about not liking *fungus.*

One night, several weeks after the wedding, we got into a screaming match. I can't remember what set it off. Afterward, I took a cab to Nora's, where I stayed for the night while he texted me incessantly, so much that Nora and I both became concerned and even a little fearful. I turned off my phone. I knew later he would say he was sorry, and he'd mean it, but it was clear we'd reached the breaking point. I was done.

I did agree to meet him for coffee once after we ended things. We took our drinks to Tompkins Square Park, in the East Village, and we sat in the grass, in the sun, and talked. It was early spring, but unseasonably warm. He had on cutoff jean shorts. In fits and starts, he tried to explain why we should keep dating, but with every compliment he would say something to undermine it, his grand-gesture plea chock-full of inherent negs. I don't think he really wanted to get back together with me any more than I wanted to reunite with him. But ending things, letting go and saying good-bye, is hard—even when it's something you've decided you want to do, and even when you know your friends all have your back. Even when it's only been three months, or two, or fewer. I remember that day in the park, realizing I could sleep with him one last time if I wanted to. There was a strange feeling in my stomach at that thought, the power of the option. It was very clearly not the right thing to do. I did it, anyway.

Mostly, though, I remember the wedding, because you can't forget a wedding, and you can't forget someone who's been your wedding date. Even beyond the photos, there's something about the event itself that locks in perpetuity in your mind: *I was there*, or, if you were with another, *we were there*. Weddings get their own special place in history. There are, of course, pictures of the two of us at Kate's reception. Many are too embarrassing to consider. (Wedding Tip: You know what's not photogenic? PDA.) The dedicated photographer did manage to snap at least one in which we're not lip-locked. We're sitting at our table surrounded by multiple glasses of wine. My date is looking at me with an intense expression, his mouth open in midconversation, and my head is turned toward him. I am listening, and I am not smiling, exactly. I recall that throughout the dinner, Marjorie, across from us, tried to interrupt and engage me in conversation. I hadn't seen her in a while, and she and Brian were in from out of town. My preoccupation with this new guy seemed to hurt her feelings, and

I could feel her disapproval, too. This was not a man I could hope my friends might someday not only be proud of me for dating, but also would want to be friends with themselves.

Later, I thought back to Ginny. I'd been so harsh in my judgment of her for continuing to work at her relationship in the face of what had seemed to me clear indications that her choice in a husband was wrong. We'd been twenty-eight then. I'd had five years to think about it, to miss her, to try to make sense of it all. If letting go of Christoph was complicated and emotionally wrenching in its own way for me, how had it been for her, after getting married in the sand in front of all of those people that day, after taking vows and promising to stick with it regardless of how hard it got? Things seemed good for her now, but I felt a renewed pang for my behavior, for how things had ended between us, and for how bewildered and conflicted she must have felt back then. I hadn't helped matters, and, of course, there were all the external social pressures, too.

Even before they married, by our late twenties there had appeared this looming sense that a relationship had to be something important, and that the end goal of all of this was a wedding. If any of us went down one road with a guy for long enough, and it was okay enough, it would be real, we would be on our way. That's what we wanted, or thought we wanted, and at that point the investment in time and energy would have accrued to such a degree that it would be nearly impossible, and ever so painful, to turn back and have to start all over again. But sometimes in those relationships we were still simply trying to figure out if we wanted to be together at all, not making plans for the future.

Despite the need to take it day by day, hanging over our heads was this impossible pressure-cooker question of whether what we'd put in would pay off in the end. It felt unfair, an impossible conundrum. If you're always pushing for the next thing, the next step, the ring, the marriage, how can you ever consider fully whether the person you're fighting so hard to get to the next level with is the right person for you at all?

In the aftermath of a relationship that ends, we tend to think, *I should have known*, and ask ourselves, *Did I just waste all that time?* But each person dated and each relationship experienced leads to the next. I dislike the idea of "wasted time" and the term "failed relationship" because these attitudes define success as getting married and staying together forever. Sure, a relationship may be a success if it lasts forever, but there are ways for it to be successful if it doesn't: if you learn something; if there are moments of enjoyment; if you come out of it more able to move on to something rewarding. If I hadn't dated Jason and taken him to Emily's and Marjorie's weddings, if I hadn't dated Christoph and taken him to Kate's, I would have known much less about myself and what I wanted. Of course, it's not always so easy to appreciate our exes.

It's clear to everyone, I think, that a marriage certificate does not a successful relationship make. Even in marriage you can still turn back. In any relationship that doesn't feel like it's working, you may well decide you have to. Other times you hang in there and keep going. It's time in the market, not timing the market. Or that's the old cliché, but pig-face could probably explain it better.

Save the Date

. . .

Four years after their wedding, Kate and Glasses bought a big house in Westchester and moved there from Brooklyn, where they might have stayed forever but for the complexities of having children in the city. "I just want to say, go outside, and for them to actually be able to do it," Glasses had told me one day when I ran into him pushing the older of his two little girls in a stroller near the park. "Having kids changes everything."

Recently, Kate threw him a fortieth birthday party at a winery in Manhattan. She invited their closest friends and flew in his sisters from San Francisco to surprise him. Violet and I took a car in from Brooklyn to attend, complaining about having to go into the city on a weekend, having to drink on a night when we both hoped to wake up sober the next day and get some work done, because that's what crotchety Brooklynite thirtysomethings with otherwise pretty burden-free lives do. Poor us, the saddest trombone plays on. Curmudgeons or not, we had a great time. When we sat down to eat, Glasses thanked us all for being there, but most of all, he thanked Kate. "To the person who made all of this happen, to the love of my life, my wife," he said with a grin as big, goofy, and pure as the one I remembered from his wedding day.

We lifted our glasses and drank.

15.

Real

✦

When you reach a certain age, a certain real age and also a certain wedding age (five of them? Fewer?), an invitation to attend a wedding that doesn't require you to rent a hotel room, to cross state lines or time zones, or to immerse yourself in a life that's any different from your own for more than a few hours begins to come as something of a relief. This is a stark change from the thrills, chills, and excitement—not only am I going somewhere, I'm going somewhere *to a wedding!*—brought about by the destination wedding you attended in your early twenties. At one point, having only gone to a few, I wanted them all to be destinations. It seemed to make a weird kind of sense that the sacrifice I'd made to be there would in some way match what the bride and groom put into planning their wedding and marrying. Later, the joy I once felt when an invitation arrived announcing a far-off wedding locale (*What's Iceland like this time of year, anyway?*) was surpassed by my pleasure at a wedding taking place so close to home I could practically walk, and could certainly cab. That's not to say I'd lost all appreciation for romance in going to weddings. I'd just gotten a little more *practical* about them.

I got my wish for a local wedding in the spring of 2011, when my good friend and former boss invited me to hers. It would be a quintessentially New York event, but more than New York, it would be *Brooklyn*, with all the appropriate hipster bells and artisanal whistles, plus views of the Brooklyn Bridge. Shifting to the borough in our midthirties was an adult move with regard to both weddings and real estate, and Annabel, who was a few years older than me, represented a new kind of bride. Despite her younger-year pronouncements that she'd never do the marriage thing, times and her feelings had changed, and it was happening.

Annabel and I had worked at a magazine called *Radar* together from 2006 to 2008. When I first met her, in the large reception area of the temporary office space the company was renting for the third go-round of the publication—it had launched and folded twice already, but there were new backers to be had—we liked each other instantly. We had both grown up in the South, it turned out. We had similar taste in clothes. We had charted eerily resonant courses in love, though we didn't know that right away. And we were both copy editors by training, but the kind that liked people as much as we liked grammar, punctuation, and red pens. We especially liked socializing with people when we, and they, had a glass of wine in hand. At our initial encounter, though, as employees at a neighboring Internet startup played foosball in the background, it was the clothes that stood out.

"I love your dress," she said.

"I love yours!" I told her. "I just bought mine in LA."

"Oh my God, did you get it at Fred Segal?"

"Yes! I couldn't help myself. I just wore it to a wedding."

"I love that store; I buy something I shouldn't every time I go there," she confided. "I was just in LA, too. I bought this." She gestured to her outfit.

"I love it," I repeated. I didn't even have to lie.

Though she gave me a take-home copy test in which I had to correct errors in a story about pubic-hair dye (I had dreamed of this edgy gig!), an integral part of the interview had been done in the first five minutes. Could we work together? Resounding affirmative. When she called me to offer the job, I didn't pause before saying yes.

As it turned out, not only had it been a job interview, but also, at least informally, it was a kind of friend interview. She was older and wiser and stylish and cool, and her role at the magazine was something I hoped I might do someday, too. And I just liked her. We had a lot to talk about, much in common, and our differences were not such that they prevented us from seeing eye to eye. I felt I could learn from her, and maybe she could learn from me.

We would both work late during the madness that was producing an issue, and often we'd get a drink after work, and always that drink would turn into several. In those years we probably kept a handful of East Village wine bars in business. Early in our friendship she was casually seeing a guy who was over twenty-one, but still young enough that she and her friends had jokingly dubbed him "the teenager." We found this hilarious, but there was some deeper stuff going on, I think. When you date someone you call a teenager, you can hardly ask him to be an adult, and in a way, choosing someone so clearly more immature, not just in age but with regard to his life, means you never have to be surprised when that relationship ends. You could have predicted it all along, so you're protected from feeling hurt. The problem is, those endings can't help hurting, no matter how we try to protect ourselves. I was beginning to recognize in myself the tendency to try to avoid rejection by choosing unsuitable or unavailable men, because that way any rejection was already a done deal. I knew it all before it even started, and well before it ended. I had orchestrated it myself.

Before we met, Annabel had had a serious boyfriend, a relationship that paralleled what I'd had with Jason. We'd often share stories about those men and, more important, what we felt we'd learned by dating them. While we worked together, though, we were both for the most part single, seeing someone here or there, hooking up with guys and then not calling them back, or waiting for their calls, which sometimes came and sometimes didn't. We were the embodiment of a certain kind of New York City woman: independent, committed to our careers, with enough money to buy ourselves nice clothes and drinks and a generally good time. We had productive lives full of fun and friends, but we were rather unfulfilled by what we were finding out there in the world romantically. So we relied on each other, and we filled any emotional voids with work, of which there was plenty—you could fill emotional voids with work all day and all night if you wanted to. Though it might not sound it, I knew then and I still feel now that this time was one of the most enjoyable periods of my life. But it couldn't last forever.

Sometimes the right people are right there in front of you and you don't even know it. Years before Annabel and Ryan started dating, they'd met, but she hadn't been interested in a serious relationship. At that point, too, he'd been engaged, but part of him had been intrigued by this sophisticated, smart, pretty person. When they met again, his engagement had been broken off. For her, I think, the realization had come that there was more out there to be had than unreturned phone calls, bar make-out sessions, or hookup texts in the wee hours of the night. Our thirties brought a certain understanding that if we wanted families, we also probably wanted husbands, or at least loving, supportive companions with whom we could foster good lives. Annabel had said she didn't think marriage was for her, but that didn't mean she didn't want to find love. She and I both knew we were ultimately after people we cared about deeply who felt that way about us in return. It just took some time—and the right timing—to get there.

In 2008, I was going to Paris with some friends and invited her to go along. She meticulously weighed the pros and cons until it was too late—the price of the ticket had become outrageously high. She decided to see friends in LA instead. That happened to be where Ryan lived, and a mutual friend dragged him along to drinks. Their second meeting sparked a connection compelling enough that they decided to date, even though they lived on separate sides of the country. They took trips together, and eventually she moved to Los Angeles to give the relationship a real try. I inherited her job and went on in New York without her, coping with the now struggling magazine and mourning the loss of my best work friend.

A few months after that, *Radar* folded, leaving me jobless. Around that time, I went out to LA for a few days to see her. It was just like old times, but sunnier, and with Ryan. We ate at good restaurants and drank loads of wine and talked and talked and talked. While I was there, I reunited with a wedding guest from the past. Cody, from Elizabeth's wedding, had flown into LA on his way back from a business trip, and since he was there, and so was I, we decided to meet. We all hung out in Annabel's backyard, sitting on a blanket, eating chips, and drinking beer as we watched a rat work its way across an electrical wire above. Unexpectedly, Cody announced he had to leave. "Traffic is only going to get worse," he said, and drove away, home to Orange County, never to be heard from again. That was fine, really, I told Annabel and a suddenly protective Ryan when they asked what his problem had been. What happens at a wedding doesn't always translate to real life.

They'd moved back to New York by the time they got engaged, and the magazine industry had recovered enough that she quickly found a job at a reputable publication. I'd transitioned to writing at that point, and we'd never again enjoy the luxury of being able to Gchat from a nearby cubicle, "What are you doing tonight after work? Wine?" or pause at each other's desks to have the conversation in real life, but we made efforts outside of that, and her relationship with Ryan continued to seem enviable.

Honest. Adult. I was proud to be the friend she hadn't gone to Paris with those years ago, because instead she'd found him. It was like I was forever a little piece of their lives, even if only by omission.

In 2011, the wedding invite came. This would be an utterly Brooklyn affair, complete with a photo booth; tattooed, bearded waiters; and green-market-esque food, with Momofuku Milk Bar cookies as party favors. It was all just a cab ride away from my East Village apartment. I RSVP'd and, though I was given the option of a plus-one, decided to go alone rather than convince some friend or passing fling to accompany me. I was sure to know lots of people: former magazine staffers and friends of Annabel's I'd met over the years. Plus, it was in Brooklyn! I could leave early and responsibly. I might even wake up without a hangover the next day.

We met for celebratory wine, and there, Annabel informed me that there was but one single guy invited to her wedding. He was, it seemed, the only single guy they knew. My, the tides had shifted.

"I don't know that you'll like him much," she said by way of warning.

"Why?" I asked.

"Well, he's kind of opinionated. He seems like someone you'd fight with. Because, you know, you might not like *his* opinions."

"Or maybe not fight, but *debate*," I suggested, remembering Boyd and Jamaica. "Am *I* really that opinionated?"

"Yes," she said. "I'll probably put him at your table."

That sounded about right. I couldn't wait.

Save the Date

. . .

At home in the East Village on the Saturday afternoon of the wedding, I showered and put on a flowy lavender dress with cutouts at the shoulders and an uneven, bias-cut hem, cinching it with a large black belt I'd bought on a shopping excursion with Annabel. I slipped on black patent stiletto-heeled Mary Janes I'd purchased back in my days at the magazine, when I could afford such items, and transferred my necessities to a tiny gold clutch. I grabbed a cab and was, of all things, early to the ceremony. The restaurant had not yet opened, so I stood outside with a former coworker named Amy, who'd arrived just moments after me. We watched a couple walk their two giant dalmatians, the dogs taking surprisingly mincing steps on the cobbled Brooklyn streets before us. I felt a little nervous, that pre-wedding anxiety that comes before the first glass of Champagne when you contemplate what will happen in the hours to come. The moments before a wedding can feel like anticipating a spaceship launch, and then, if all goes well, the evening is steeped in the euphoria of *We have liftoff.* The opposite is too terrible to contemplate. *It will be great,* I reassured myself. I was over the wedding ridiculousness of immature times past, puking and fighting and crying.

"Your shoes are awesome," I said. Amy's bright blue pumps were covered in steel spikes. She'd been telling me about a new guy she liked; he was Swedish and only in town through the end of the summer. They'd met at a bar in Williamsburg several nights ago and had been hanging out nonstop ever since, until she had to break away for the wedding, of course.

"Aren't they great?" she said, turning her shoe to the side and looking at it. "I love them." She peered inside the windows of the restaurant. "Jen, the waiters are sexy. Only Annabel would have tattooed hottie waiters!"

Within minutes we were being let inside and handed drinks from trays, then ushered into the large space where the wedding ceremony would take place. Lining one wall was the bar. In the middle of the room, chairs were set up around a spiraling staircase. Floor-to-ceiling windows let us look out at the street and beyond, allowing the sun to join us inside. As other guests arrived there came the standard kissing crush of weddings, one cheek or two, sometimes even three, and hugs for people I hadn't seen in weeks or months or years. We traded compliments over outfits or accomplishments or both, not always because we meant what we said but because compliments are a good way to break the ice, and everyone is cheery and bright and fresh and on their best behavior at the start of a wedding, so people *do* look better, too. The beginning of a wedding is when anything can happen; the ending is when everything did.

We settled into our seats in the middle of the room, facing the spot where the bride and groom would be wed. As we waited we gazed outside and admired the nearer views, too—white cloth-covered tables with arrangements of white roses on each; tall, flowering branches positioned throughout the room; candles adding a warm glow to everything. The expectant hush was interrupted by the sound of a crying baby. It was Ryan's sister's child. She'd decided, Annabel had told me, that she wanted to be a mom, if not a wife. She'd considered the options, arranged for the necessary procedures, and gotten pregnant. With the help of her parents, she was now raising her child on her own. I admired and also feared her choice. For me, the partner came before the child, if I didn't marry or commit to someone in a serious way, someone who also wanted kids, I wasn't sure I'd go down the road of motherhood at all. But I was impressed that she'd known what she wanted and had been brave enough to go after it in a nontraditional way.

The ceremony was fast and full of love, with touching, funny speeches delivered by family and friends, including one about a girl dinosaur and a boy dinosaur who despite the odds manage to find each other. Annabel wore a long, slim ivory dress with one architecturally jutting sleeve that passed both of our fashion muster but which she did not purchase at Fred Segal in Los Angeles. She had on a delicate veil made of French netting that covered just a smidge of her face, coquettishly. When the ceremony ended we headed upstairs to another spacious, windowed room. There we snacked on bacon-wrapped shrimp speared by toothpicks and sipped colorful cocktails. We admired the wonder that is the Brooklyn Bridge at sunset and waited to admire the bride and groom, who joined us shortly. I ran into our former editor in chief, who was there with his boyfriend. "She looks gorgeous, doesn't she?" he said. "This wedding is just so *Annabel*." I knew what he meant.

As the bride had told me ahead of time, I would share a table with the only single guy at the wedding, who in the world of the orchestrated wedding ecosystem might as well have been the only single guy in New York City. He was seated right next to me. Tom was bald, or had shaved his head to be bald, but either way, the effect was the same, and maybe, just maybe, he reminded me of my old boyfriend, Jason, though with a stockier, athletic build. He had on a crisp suit, paired with an expensive-looking tie. Though he was the only single guy at the wedding, there were more than a handful of single women present—next to me was Ingrid, a novelist and friend I'd met through Annabel, and down at the next table there was Amy, to name just a few. Amy would not be interested in Tom, though. She was already captivated by the bartenders, not to mention her Swedish love, and Tom had no visible tattoos. Worse, he appeared to work in *business*.

I was already at the table when he sat down and offered his hand and his name. "I'm Tom," he said. "And you are?"

I took his hand and shook it. "I'm . . . well, let's see. Who am I?" I picked up the place card inscribed with my name that sat in front of my plate and studied it. "Today I am Jen Doll."

"You need a card to tell you that?"

I leaned toward him and dropped my voice. "I'm a wedding crasher. I do this nearly professionally, or at the very least, competitively amateurly."

"Fascinating," he said. "How did you get in?"

I pointed toward the windows behind us. One of them happened to be a glass door, which I'd noticed earlier. "Fire exit. The alarm is disabled. It's so easy, it's almost embarrassing. No one ever suspects. You'd think they'd have better security at these things."

"But what if the *real* Jen Doll shows up?" he asked.

I looked at him sadly. "I've taken care of that. Sometimes un-
fortunates get in the way. Wrong place at the wrong time, you
know. I'm not proud of it, but I've got to eat."

"That's right, food. What are you going to order?"

I'd already decided. "I'm having the chicken. It comes with
mac and cheese."

"And I'll have the steak," he said. "We can share, Jen Doll."

There is something that occurs at weddings when you are single and you happen upon another who's single and you find
each other moderately attractive and tolerably pleasant. Two
such people might decide they are better together than alone at
this fair, if temporary, juncture, and they might abandon all
pretense and just be together, as if they're a real couple, for that
night. There's love in the air, who can resist? We've all heard the
great wedding legend, the tale of Someone who knows Someone
who totally met his or her Someone at just such an event. If it
happened to Someone, it could happen to you, too.

Let us call this pairing the Wedding Insta-Couple. The force is
powerful. Always in the moment it feels like the right thing to
do. We are vulnerable at weddings. They're not comfortable
like old shoes or our own couches in our own homes, or even
like the grimy barstools at our favorite bars. They are big, important events at which we need to be on our best behavior, or at
least, we'll do our best to try. But the bride and groom, who may
be our closest friends there, are busy. Many of the other wedding
guests may already be coupled. If there is only one single guy, or

one single girl, at a wedding, chances are they'll have the opportunity to go home with someone else who's single, too, if they play their cards even remotely right. That's not to say that weddings make us easy, or anything else you might pick up from a shallow reading of the movie *Wedding Crashers*. It is to say that almost every human on the planet wants love and companionship in some form or another, and inserted into an environment in which such things are the stock in trade, we may be inspired to take a chance and try to find them for ourselves, too, even if only temporarily.

Being alone at a wedding can be terrifying, but the promise of love found at a wedding is the opposite. Think of how many movies depict a female character who hires or bribes or convinces some guy to be her date to a wedding, because she can't stand to go alone, for fear of humiliation, or perhaps because her ex will be there. These plots are silly and sometimes belittling, too, but there's a kernel of truth there: Sometimes we *don't* feel like being by ourselves, and a wedding is likely to be one of those times. In the movies, the couple that connects at a wedding frequently falls in love and goes on to get married themselves. This is a real kind of American fantasy, even if the majority of its examples live in Hollywood, not reality.

My insta-coupling with Tom had in my mind been a done deal, probably from the time that Annabel had told me he and I would not get along. I love a wedding challenge, as we've previously determined. And so that evening, after he gave me bites of his steak and I cut up portions of my chicken and moved them to his plate, we walked around together as if we had come to this event as each other's dates, as if we'd been dating for years, as if we, soon, might head down an aisle of our own. He had his arm around me, and we introduced each other to the friends and family members (mine the bride's side, his the groom's) that we saw. "How did you meet?" they'd ask, taking us for more than side-by-side assigned dining companions, and we'd say, "At the dinner table!" and everyone would laugh at our adorable couple antics. I thought, *Hey, this is sort of fun. I could get used to this.*

When the restaurant closed, we walked down the street to the bar where everyone had agreed to converge for the after-party. In contrast to the white petal–strewn airy brightness of the previous venue, it was dark there, even a little ominous, with crimson-hued lighting and a pool table surrounded by men in concert tees. By that time I was pretty drunk, as were most of us. But as I'd promised myself, there would be no puking, no crying at this wedding. Instead, I became ever so slightly confused about the status of my fake relationship. Was this guy with me or not with me? Was he now, suddenly, flirting with a waitress? I looked. It appeared that he was. Was he spending time talking to that other woman, *another* single woman at the wedding? I looked again. Yes. *Had this all been just a game to him?*

In an instant, my wedding insta-relationship, the one that I had never even cared about, not for real, began to crumble, and I to crumble along with it. The unit of two that had seemed so protective and nice and safe, a fake relationship that felt even better in this moment than one that was genuine, was gone. I was alone again, on my own, having to fend for myself. I didn't even want another drink. I wanted to go home, climb into bed with my dress on, and pull up the covers, shut my eyes, and go to sleep, only to wake to the brightness of morning. That was the moment in which I should have gone home. Instead, I confronted him, interrupting the conversation he was having with a girl who did not look familiar.

"I think I want to leave," I said.

"Well, silly, then you should go," he told me. "It's late." Wrong answer.

The girl yawned, looked at her phone, and she herself left. Smart girl. I persisted. "You should come *with* me."

He glanced at his watch. "I have to be up for this thing really early in the morning." (Wedding Tip: This is a death knell that means precisely what you think it means! Do not proceed!) I proceeded. I gave him what I felt was a charming come-hither sort of look. It may have only served to convince him that I needed an escort to get home without injury for which he would later be blamed. "Well, all right, I guess," he finally said, finishing his drink, and we were in a cab back to the East Village.

What I wanted, I think, was to end the night in a way that felt compatible with how we'd experienced the wedding itself, him cutting me pieces of steak from his plate and taking some of my chicken; us walking around the venue together, arm in arm. That is to say, together. I wasn't ready for our newly constructed twosome, which had felt surprisingly good, to be over just yet. Maybe our insta-coupling had legs. And, yes, probably I wanted to make out with him a little.

We got back to my studio apartment. There were not many places to sit. I took off my shoes and found a spot on the bed, and he joined me. We kissed for a while, until he again looked at his watch. "I better go," he said.

"Really?"

"Yeah, I have to be up early in the morning," he reminded me. "I have that thing."

"Oh, yeah," I said. "That thing. What thing is that again?"

"It's just some stuff I have to do," he said.

Well, if he was going to be that way. "Fine." I pouted.

He was going to be that way. "It was great to meet you, Jen Doll," he told me, getting up. "Or whoever you are."

"You, too," I said.

And he left.

It was funny, though. After the door had shut and I was again my onesome in my little apartment, I wasn't angry he had gone at all. So much can change in the matter of a few minutes, outside of the grasp of the wedding. Now I could go to sleep, happily single, comfortably on my own. The next morning I could wake up alone in my own bed, which I could sprawl across if I felt like it, hogging the blankets and sheets and pillows with abandon. I did not have to be concerned about a stranger next to me and what he wanted and how I might need to care about what he wanted, too. I did not have to worry about brunch. I felt relieved. He hadn't been the one. He was just one.

Before I fell asleep, I ate my Momofuku Milk Bar wedding cookie, the favor from the bride and groom. It was delicious.

. . .

Several weeks after that, I sent Tom a Facebook message saying I'd had fun meeting him and thanks for helping me get home. I felt the need to counter any behavior that might have been interpreted the wrong way, and I was curious, too. Had there really been something there after all, or was it only Wedding Insta-Couple Haze? I figured I could be an adult about this and told him, if he ever wanted a drink, I owed him one.

He never wrote back.

The word was that he'd just gotten out of a relationship and he'd tentatively gotten back in it. I don't know what happened for sure, and it certainly doesn't matter now, if it mattered even then. He wasn't really the only single guy in New York, much less the world. He was merely the only single guy at that wedding. But he did me a favor. I could thank him for helping me realize that the only true relationship shame was in not being real, in not being honest with myself, and honest with those I dated, too. There is a not insignificant amount of fear associated with saying, *Yes, this is what I want: a partnership that looks and feels like this,* because on the other side of that lies the paralyzing possibility of rejection, of failure, of choosing wrong. But it's not very fulfilling to go through life passively, guarded and not taking chances, trying not to let things hurt you. And if you don't at least try to say what you want, it's very unlikely that it will suddenly appear on your doorstep with a shiny red bow on top. Sure, you can fake who you are in an effort to keep your heart safe, but that will never make your heart feel that other thing most of us truly crave. If I wanted a relationship, really and truly, it was time to admit it.

Before Annabel met Ryan, she'd explained her lack of interest in marriage by saying, "I want to make that choice to be with someone every day, not have it be a foregone conclusion." Now that she'd done the thing she never thought she'd do, she took a different view. "It feels really good," she told me almost two years after her wedding day, as we shopped at a tiny Brooklyn boutique, her baby sleeping peacefully in a stroller in the corner. "But to tell the truth, I don't even think about it, being married versus not being married. I'm just living it."

16.

At Last

✦

In 2011, I was a full-time staffer at the *Village Voice*. Though I wrote a few cover stories for the paper in my time at the alt-weekly, my duties were primarily confined to Runnin' Scared, the news blog, which had a focus on New York City but incorporated a range of global and viral topics as well, all the better for page views. At first I wrote eight to ten posts a day. They could be short, riffy things, because, for goodness' sakes, it was eight to ten posts a day. We were told as bloggers that we should always try to make the phone call, always try to get more information. We did try, but I had the feeling a lot of the veteran staffers, those who'd been around as reporters during the heyday of the paper, thought we largely just produced a bunch of garbage as the bottom-feeders of journalism. They weren't all wrong. I very much looked up to those reporters and did not want it to be that way, but I didn't know how to do everything I was required to do and leave my desk, too. In some ways, my background in print journalism had prepared me little for creating online content, and most days I felt like I was flailing. I kept writing and got faster, and I slowly got better, too. Our post quota was downsized to a more reasonable five or six daily, which seems insane to me now but was a relief then, and reporting (the kind you could do without leaving your desk, mostly) was encouraged.

Occasionally there would arise an opportunity for which I might be present someplace real news was happening. I relished those moments to see and report back, to write about an event I'd witnessed myself instead of simply picking it up from another outlet and appropriating it for our site, tapping the story with my own stamp of "personality" or "an angle." In June, the New York State Legislature had passed the bill making same-sex marriage legal in the state. When the news was announced, I'd been at dinner with a friend. We emerged from the restaurant to an atmosphere of no-holds-barred joy in the streets. We'd tearily hugged, so proud of our state and suddenly filled with optimism for the future. In the weeks that followed, one of my coworkers at the paper suggested I try to get a press pass to the wedding that New York City mayor Mike Bloomberg would be officiating at for two of his staffers—the city's commissioner of consumer affairs, Jonathan Mintz, and the mayor's chief policy adviser, John Feinblatt—at Gracie Mansion on July 24, the day the law went into effect. I sent an e-mail with my request to cover the ceremony, and to my surprise and pleasure, it was granted. *This* was something to write about.

I wasn't sure what to wear, it being the first wedding I'd attended as a reporter, not a guest. It was hot, and the July morning had been thick and humid, but the weather cleared up by the time

I was leaving my apartment in the late afternoon. I settled on clothes I might well wear to a casual summer wedding: a long tank dress with alternating dark and light blue horizontal stripes, the waist cinched with a matching belt. I'd bought it at a boutique on my block, won over by the fact that somehow, despite what you hear about horizontal stripes, it managed to be slimming. I'd worn it on a date earlier that month, and it had gotten a "Great dress." More than that, it was practical. Sleeveless, it would allow me room to maneuver and stay relatively cool, and it was pretty but not too showy. With the blue and bluer stripes, it even felt vaguely governmental. I had on flat sandals, and I carried a notepad and a pen, as well as my phone, from which I planned to tweet and also take photos. At the last minute I threw a couple of *Village Voice* business cards into my tote. The *Voice* was pretty laid-back about formal procedures, and I had yet to be issued an actual press pass. I hoped these would do the trick if need be.

On the uptown street corner where my cab dropped me off, across from the barricaded Gracie Mansion, a small group of Orthodox Jewish men were protesting. Along with various placards expressing their distaste for gay marriage, they had a grotesque-looking stuffed dog hanging on a pole and a sign declaring that a man marrying a man was akin to a man marrying a mongrel. There were cops stationed about in case anything got out of hand, but no one seemed to be paying the protesters much mind. Wedding guests dressed in festive clothing streamed blithely across the street, heading through the barricades and onto the grounds of Gracie Mansion. I followed them. There was a press line stretching into the distance, and I filed in behind two other women, reporters with their own notepads and a no-nonsense brusqueness that I lacked. I was feeling those wedding jitters I always got before a ceremony. It was funny that they happened whether I knew the couple or not, I thought.

At the front of the line, I showed off my business card to an approving nod from security and was pointed to a set of risers upon which reporters could stand and take notes and photos during the ceremony. I claimed a spot in the back, where I figured I'd be out of the way and also up high enough to see over the heads in front of me. The media was gated off from the rest of the crowd, contained in our little area, but that only added to the experience. Around me, people who looked like bona fide professionals—slightly disheveled attire, pens tucked behind ears, cell phones in hand—were setting up cameras on tripods, taking photos and shooting video and jockeying for positions. A woman who worked for a city tabloid got into a screaming match with another writer, and I watched, overjoyed. News! It was happening everywhere around us. The crowd pushed in tighter. Scribbling details onto my notepad, I tried to make myself small and unnoticeable, fearing I'd be forced to relinquish my space to someone from a bigger venue.

From my riser, I saw Matthew Broderick walk into the wedding tent. He had on khaki pants, and there was a pastel pocket square tucked into his navy jacket. I began to notice other people I knew from writing and reading about New York City, and I felt a little ping of satisfaction as I checked them off, one by one: Christine Quinn. New York City Schools Chancellor Dennis Walcott. Police Commissioner Ray Kelly. There was Broadway legend

Joel Grey, who would serenade the grooms after the ceremony. And of course Mayor Bloomberg was in attendance. He'd brought along his two yellow Labs. The dogs lolled happily on the lawn. At the very front of the cluster of white folding chairs set up for invited guests, not nosy reporters, there was a group of little girls in party dresses. I guessed they must be friends of the school-aged daughters of the grooms. A quartet in front of them, facing all of us, performed charming renditions of romantic classics like "Our Love Is Here to Stay," but as with any wedding the crowd began to grow restless, shifting in their seats. Helicopters droned above as the sun slowly set. Everyone was ready to get this thing going, no matter why we were here.

Suddenly, movement appeared in the windows on the second floor of the mansion. A little girl in white peered out, guests and working stiffs alike straightened up and paid attention, and the wedding began.

It was a short ceremony. After a brief introduction and some marital guidance from the mayor—"Never stop listening, and never stop laughing," he advised—the two men were pronounced married. Each groom broke a glass under his heel, Grey performed, eco-fetti was thrown, and the press began to depart en masse as quickly as they'd set up, while the actual guests headed into the tent for the reception. I saw a woman take her shoes off, digging her bare feet into the green grass and looking out into the horizon. Pink punch was being poured into glasses and passed around to waiting partiers, and there was an ice-cream truck pulling up into the parking lot adjacent to the mansion.

Save the Date

I felt a twinge of sadness that I was missing out on the fun part of the wedding, but I knew it wasn't for me. I had no role in this event beyond getting the story, telling it as well as I could, and being a part of history in whatever small way a writer can be. It was the most fully adult ceremony I'd ever been to, or at least, the one at which I'd behaved in the way most becoming of an adult. There was no need for drama, there were no friendships or relationships ripped wide open again. I walked away completely sober. As I headed toward the exit, I found myself trapped behind Mayor Bloomberg and Christine Quinn. I have an excellent shot of the back of Bloomberg's neck from this moment. I showed it proudly to the political reporter at the paper the next day, and though he sweetly tried to match my enthusiasm, I think he mostly thought I was nuts.

Walking west to find a cab, I texted Nora. "Dinner downtown? Just covered my first wedding!" (Wedding Tip: It's not a wedding without wine.) She met me at our regular East Village Italian spot, and we ordered all of our favorite items, the kale salad and tomato bruschetta and fresh-made pastas, and a bottle of Verdicchio, which we drank leisurely as we caught up. Conversation ranged from meaningful—what this new era of New York history, and, we hoped, beyond, could mean for the world at large—to mundane—had that guy I'd seen the concert with asked me on a second date yet? What was happening with the man she'd recently met? Everywhere we looked it seemed happiness and love were entirely possible, and even present.

That evening, home with my feet up, sated on wine, spaghetti, the emotional food of the wedding, and the conversation with a good friend that had followed, I opened my computer and began to type. "This blogger has been to a lot of weddings," I began, which was true then and is only more true now. "This blogger, however, was keenly excited to see (1) Mayor Bloomberg marry someone, someone not his daughter or a former mayor (the two types of people he had once vowed he would only marry), and (2) to partake, even in a small way, in the first same-sex marriage of two people who work for our city and, despite not being able to legally wed, had loved and created and sustained a beautiful family for themselves—all the happier to make it 'official.'"

It had been everything I'd hoped it would be. It felt sort of like the world was growing up, and maybe I was, too. It had only taken me thirty-five years, but who's counting?

17.

Now Serving C661

✦

One sunny August morning I rolled out of bed, showered, put on a cream-and-blue-printed silk shift dress and my most comfortable walking-around summer wedges, the ones with rust-colored leather uppers and cork soles, and grabbed my going-out bag—orange vintage Louis Vuitton, purchased at a secondhand store—instead of the large bookstore tote I usually stuffed with gym clothes and an array of books and papers before heading to work. Though a Friday, this was not a workday. I was going to a wedding.

I checked my clock. The plan had been that I'd grab a cab with the bride and groom, who lived so close to my new apartment in Brooklyn that we'd decided to ride-share to the Manhattan courthouse together. We'd heard the wait became longer as morning turned to afternoon, and though the bride was one of those people for whom you always gave a ten- or fifteen-minute time window, at which she'd inevitably arrive at the end, the groom was adamant that they be at the front of the line. I left my apartment and walked to Flatbush, where I got a text: "We already left! He hailed a cab and didn't want to wait. Sorry!!!!" Oh, well, that was fine, I could get there on my own, I thought, and motioned for my own taxi, following my friends across the Brooklyn Bridge and into Lower Manhattan. Sans date, I took a photo of myself, or, well, my legs and my purse next to me, on the way.

Violet and Ashok had met at an ad agency where they had both worked. He was a producer and she was an art director. She was one of my oldest friends from Alabama. He had been married before and had a little boy with his ex-wife. In New York, Violet and Ashok hadn't paid much attention to each other, but after a two-week shoot together in Vancouver, she told me she "could never imagine not talking to him again." To us, he became known as her boyfriend, though she failed to tell her family in Alabama about him—that he existed, that he was divorced, that he had a son who was in elementary school. She worked slowly with that information, doling it out on a need-to-know basis, and in fairness, he was not incredibly forthcoming about her to his family in India, either. At one point after the two of them had been dating for a while, before a visit from her father, Violet pulled me aside and whispered, "Hey, um, don't mention that Ashok has a kid, okay?"

"Your dad doesn't know yet?" I'd asked.

"One bombshell at a time," she said. "First I need to tell him Ashok's been married."

The Christmas came when she finally took him home and introduced him to her entire extended family. Though he was horribly allergic to her stepmother's cats, everyone loved him, and soon everyone knew everything, and it was all fine. He was a producer; charming people was his business. "I guess I shouldn't have worried," she said.

Technically, on the way to this wedding, they were already married. Early on in their engagement they'd asked if I wanted to be their officiant. I'd eagerly said yes, but the pressure of doing something that would suit the couple's diverse, geographically spread Alabama and Indian families was too great, and I got an e-mail from her several months later telling me the plans had changed. "We have decided to elope to India with family," she wrote. "Going to get married in Agra at the Oberoi Amarvilas hotel, by the pool probably. You are more than welcome to marry us there! But it's a twenty-hour journey." She added, "Just can't do the wedding thing!" She felt it wasn't her, and more important, wasn't *them*, so they created something that was. One of the benefits to having a wedding in your midthirties or beyond is that a lot of the rules and traditional expectations cease to matter in the slightest. You have the confidence and the financial standing to do it your own way, and that makes it all the better.

After the wedding they'd travel through India, to Delhi and Jaipur and wherever else the whim and time and money took them. As the plans became more concrete, they again urged me to go with them. Violet's older sister and I were friends, too, and she was going; we could share a room to save on costs. They were one of the few couples for whom I *would* travel to India to see get married. But I'd just bought an apartment and started a new job, too. I didn't think I could spare the $10,000 the trip would cost, or the time off work, or the energy to deal with all the planning, even though I also knew it would be the trip of a lifetime. Just not my lifetime, not right now. I said no. I couldn't do it. In the photos I jealously perused later, it all looked amazing.

Just because you don't go to a wedding doesn't mean that wedding, or that coupling, ceases to exist for you. Sometimes it becomes a bigger deal than if you'd attended in the first place, following through with all the ritualistic processes involved, buying a gift from the registry, wearing a dress, wishing your love and congratulations. These are the "ghost weddings"—the missed ones that haunt you in some form or another for long after the wedding actually occurs. They may be weddings you're not invited to and which go on without you despite what you would have hoped, jabs that indicate you're not as close to the bride and groom as you thought you were, or that they no longer want you to be close. When you don't make the cut, that can change your relationship with the marrying couple forever. Other times, you're invited but must send your regrets: You live too far away, the associated expenses are too much, you can't take time off work, you're busy with your own life, you choose to go to an-other friend's wedding, you don't approve, or you don't want to bother. This, too, may end your friendship, unless you have a very good reason for saying no. A save the date is not just a piece of paper. It is a piece of paper that means something. It can change relationships in ways the invited, the uninvited, and the bride and groom may never expect.

Luckily, with Violet and Ashok's wedding, my "no" did not

make for an end to our friendship, nor did they take my refusal the wrong way. But when Violet told me they were having a second wedding, this time at the city clerk's office in Manhattan, I knew I had to be there. I'd gotten a second chance. I took the day off. This would be an event.

I arrived at the courthouse a few minutes after they had, and they were already in line, a handful of people in front of them. She had on a long white sundress with short sleeves, a deep V-neck, and a nipped-in bodice. He was wearing a black suit with a purple-and-white-striped tie. They waved at me from behind the velvet rope separating the guests from the couples. "The line's moving fast!" said Violet. "Smile, I'll take a picture," I told her. Soon Pandora, Violet's sister, arrived and we both shot rapid-fire candids of the couple like we were their personal paparazzi until they reached the second stage of the process. Getting married at the city clerk's office in Manhattan is a *process*. There are multiple phases, each with its own bureaucratic hurdles to hop. Prior to this trip to the courthouse there had been other steps necessary to get here, and now there were more: paying the fees, showing the proper forms of identification, signing the papers, and finally, finally, finally—the ceremony.

Ashok's witnesses, his boss, Bob, and Bob's wife, Phyllis, arrived, and we sat on the benches lining the room and waited for the process that involved us. As one might at a crowded deli counter, Ashok took a number, the sign that would indicate their ceremony time had arrived. I took a picture of him proudly holding that auspicious paper tag, which read "C661." Sharing the narrow, airportlike waiting area with us were other couples of all sorts. Men and women, women and women, men and men. They were young and old and middle-aged, and in all varieties of races, ethnicities, and religions. At this UN of weddings, everyone was united by the societal tradition, regardless of the societies from which they might have descended. I studied the couples there waiting for their turns, standing in clumps, sitting on stools in front of the various service windows, perching on the benches like we were and watching for their own numbers to appear on the light boards positioned throughout the room. "Now serving number ____," we would hear as that number flashed on the screen, and whichever couple it applied to would look at each other and rise and smile and head to the appointed station, because they were getting married.

A group of four people came running through the room, two women in dresses and two men in suits, and it was hard to tell who was marrying whom as they rushed to the clerk to file their papers. Elsewhere, a young Asian couple stood with flowers purchased at a nearby kiosk and smiled as an older family member took their picture. There were children waiting to see parents marry; there were parents waiting to watch children wed. A twentysomething girl with long blond hair and pillowy lips strode through the room in white pumps, her model-like giraffe legs bare but for a pair of small white cutoffs. She had on a blousy, ivory-colored shirt and held a giant bouquet of white flowers in her arms. Her hair and makeup were impeccable, the only color she was wearing a bright red lip. The man she was marrying was dark and handsome, with black hair and tanned skin, a narrow, tall build, and lips as pillowy as his bride's. Their friends, all rangy and slim in carefully planned formally informal outfits—shorts and T-shirts but expensive pumps; ties and diamonds and tuxedo jackets with tank tops and thousand-dollar handbags—clustered around them and giggled and looked as much like a photo shoot for the hippest of wedding magazines as possible.

We were called forward so that Violet and Ashok could sign another set of papers, and then we were ushered into a smaller, round waiting room, just outside the chapel, for the final and most important part of the process. We stood around on wedding pins and needles, anticipating the big event. The model-couple emerged from one of the chapels, which was really just a room— there was one on each side, identified as West and East—and Phyllis glanced at them and said, "I'll give that six months."

I felt suddenly protective of the pretty young things, though I'd been thinking along the same lines. "Oh, I don't know. Maybe they're in love."

"Ha!" Phyllis scoffed.

"You never know," I said.

"C661?" asked a man in a dark suit, peering out of the chapel on the left, and Ashok raised his hand.

"That's us!" he said.

"Come on in," said the man. "I'm going to get you two married."

It could have been a room in any administrative building, with drab, colorless carpet and gray-green walls, but it was a chapel, because inside people were being married, a couple at a time. Marriage record books from the 1800s and 1900s were displayed on a glass-paned shelf, some of them opened to pages that reflected a specific time in the city's wedding history. Each entry outlined a story, charting the basics and leaving the reader to fill in the blanks. In October 1943, on one day in New York City, a navy man from Wisconsin married a waitress from Seattle; a thirty-three-year-old soldier who'd come from Ireland married a twenty-two-year-old domestic, also from Ireland; and a merchant marine from Los Angeles wed a telegraph operator from the Bronx. There were furriers and newsdealers and ball players and students and chauffeurs, from the Upper East and Upper West and Lower East sides, from Alphabet City, from Woonsocket, Rhode Island, from Germany. They were in their thirties and their twenties and sometimes older, too, marrying for the first and second and third times, their ceremonies conducted by Catholic priests and clergymen and rabbis and deputy city clerks, like the one about to marry my friends. This was the history of New York City as much as it was the story of these couples. Someday Violet and Ashok would be in the book, I thought.

"Ready?" asked the clerk. "Ready!" we answered, and he began. A person could pack in a lot of ten-minute ceremonies a day, but regardless of how many he was doing in his shift, this guy was not phoning it in. He delivered his lines with gusto. Violet and Ashok looked at him with serious faces, repeating their lines, cracking smiles occasionally when he made a joke. "Okay, now for the kissing part," he announced. "Cameras on? Go!" They kissed, we clapped and cheered and hugged, and they were married. On the way out we stopped for a few photos in front of a trompe l'oeil painting of the courthouse, lit by studio lights so there was no need for a flash, and we briefly perused mementos in the gift shop: coffee mugs, T-shirts, and mouse pads all bearing the phrase "Just married." But there was no need for a mug when what they had was each other. "Brunch?" said the bride.

We taxied to a restaurant in TriBeCa where, years before, during the height of the *Matrix* frenzy, I'd caught a glimpse of Laurence Fishburne. It was fairly empty this summer Friday, the celebrity diners confined to the couple who'd just gotten married. We drank Champagne and talked about advertising and weddings and the way things had been done in the old days and how they were done now. The conversation was full of non sequiturs, but somehow the themes connected: "I recently went to a wedding down South," Pandora told us. "The day before the ceremony, the ladies went antiquing, and the men went hunting. I couldn't bear to antique, so I went out hunting with the boys." "In the old days of advertising there was so much more care for product, so much more craft to it," said Bob. "Now everything's online; everything's done faster and faster. That doesn't make it better." "There's so little thought to some of it," added Phyllis.

I thought about my own writing, from print to blogs, and I thought about the old books I'd seen in the chapel. Did progress make things less valuable, less valued? In some ways marriage had become so much *better*, as demonstrated by the range of gender and ethnic mixes I'd seen at the clerk's office. On the other hand, divorce was immeasurably easier, a common reality for many, including people at this very table. But it was oversimplifying and not entirely correct to say that time had devalued the institution, or that people who decided not to marry, or who divorced, had made marriage itself as flimsy as a dashed-off banner ad. People were still getting married, and though we did it differently, it still mattered very much to the people who were doing it—maybe it mattered more than ever. It mattered to Violet and Ashok as much as it mattered to Bob and Phyllis. And though I hadn't done it, it mattered to me, too.

Our Champagne brunch done by ten thirty, it was time for the reception. Outside it was sunny and growing hotter, but within the little dive bar the bride and groom had selected as their celebration location, it was cool and dark, offering that disconcerting but cozy feeling of going to a movie in the middle of the day. It was like a vacation, and it was a vacation, I suppose: We didn't have to go back to work, there'd been a wedding, and it was whatever time we wanted it to be. The drinking hour was now. We settled in at a round table at the back of the bar, and Ashok asked the bartender to keep the beverages coming. "We just got married!" he announced proudly. The bartender grinned big. "Congratulations, man," he said, slapping him on the back. "That's awesome."

Violet and Ashok and I were the first there; Bob and Phyllis had departed to go back to work like responsible adults. Beers were ordered. I got a white wine, happily noticing the bar also offered sandwiches for lunch, though, as it happened, I never ended up eating one. Ashok's friends from work started to show up, and the table grew crowded. Pandora had gone to pick up a wedding cake, a small white fondant-covered creation shaped like a wrapped gift, complete with fondant bow. We cut into it and started to eat, washing it down with pinot grigio and Brooklyn Lager. It had a raspberry filling. It couldn't have been more perfect, this pairing.

The hours went by, and as it grew later we began to reminisce about the ceremony, putting distance between it and ourselves, turning it into a permanent history in our minds. "Remember when?" we'd say, though it had only been that morning. Ashok would introduce Violet to people she already knew, just to get to say "This is my wife" again. Everyone at this party except Pandora and me seemed to be married, I suddenly noticed, whether their spouses were there or not. Everyone had taken this plunge. I went up to the bar to get another drink and casually flirted with the bartender, who was impressed with not only the wedding but also our longevity and was giving us wildly discounted drinks.

Then the people with families at home began to leave, and the party evolved again. The bar got more crowded with strangers, less crowded with us. The cake was depleted to just a few remaining slices on a plate. It seemed to grow dimmer in the bar, though outside the sun was still shining. I got a text from my boss letting me know that my coworkers were all heading out for work drinks. I'd told him the day before that if the wedding party ended early, I might join them. It was five p.m., headed toward six, and I'd been drinking for hours. There was no way I was joining them.

A friend from high school who was in town visiting came in with her husband and daughter. The little girl was just starting kindergarten, and I watched her interact with her dad, whom she clearly adored. She kept going over to him to try to sip his beer or get his attention, which reminded me of myself as a child, of my relationship with my own father, and beyond that, of the endless cycle of weddings. She was a little younger than I'd been at that first one I remembered. I wasn't sure this was any more than a party to her, or maybe just some old people hanging out and being silly. Did she know where she was, what this was? "Are you having fun?" I asked her, and she laughed before running away and burying her face in her mom's skirt.

It was time to leave. Things were getting fuzzy around the edges, and I didn't want them to get fuzzier. I hugged Violet and Ashok and steadied myself to get home. As I made my way out of the bar, I ran into one of Ashok's friends, a guy with whom I'd chatted pleasantly earlier that day about things like work and real estate and the various weddings we'd attended. He was just coming back inside.

"Are you leaving?" he asked. "It was great to meet you." He reached out to hug me, but deep in my subconscious I felt that if I stopped for even a hug it would be over. I was focused, focused, trying to stay focused while washing ashore on the waves of a bottle or more of pinot grigio.

"I don't hug," I said abruptly, and rushed out, or so he told me a few months later when we all gathered again to celebrate Ashok's birthday, an event at which I made up for my gaffe and gave this man a proper good-bye embrace. But that night, I left him aghast, standing in the doorway of the bar. A girl who didn't hug. That was like a woman who didn't get married.

At the time, I thought nothing of what I'd said, my eyes on the yellow cab that was rounding the corner and heading down the street, right outside the bar. I waved, and the driver stopped. My ride to the courthouse that morning had been full of eager anticipation, curiosity as to what the day would bring and what a courthouse wedding would involve. My trip home was the counter to that. It was still sunny outside, and my eyes, used to the dim surroundings of the wood-paneled bar for so many hours, had to adjust. I squinted, and my pupils returned to the appropriate size as we crossed the bridge on the way back to Brooklyn. I felt that sleepy satisfaction that comes from going home again after a positive and productive day, though the productivity was not my own to claim. Inside my apartment it was quiet and peaceful. I lay down on my bed for a quick moment, just to rest my eyes.

I woke up several hours later when it truly was dark outside. I was ravenously hungry. I got up and ordered pizza, throwing in an order of chicken fingers, which came with French fries, for good measure. I'd have leftovers, but I could eat them the next day, I reasoned. Of course, I ate nearly everything once it got there, sitting on my couch by myself with my feet on my coffee table, watching old episodes of *Veronica Mars*, so comfortable in my solitary state. Being with people I loved was great, but being by myself could be pretty amazing, too, I thought, just before I nodded off.

18.

Did That Just Happen?

✦

People say you never find love when you're looking for that special someone, and it's true, I was not looking. I'd gotten out of a relationship months before—that is, if "getting out" meant the guy you'd dated for a couple of months one day shut down all contact and never spoke to you again. Mere weeks before that, he'd gazed at me with a searching expression and, when asked why, uttered to my discomfort, "I'm trying to imagine the rest of my life with you." Well, if that was the page he was on, I could give it a try, too, I thought, and opened up enough to leave travel-sized packets of fancy face wash at his apartment. Things had not gone smoothly after that, and then it had been plainly and abundantly clear that it was over. But his silence stung more than the end of the relationship. *Just tell me it's over,* I thought, *don't simply cut things off and refuse to acknowledge that I continue to exist.* I wasn't perfect, but wasn't I, or anyone, due that respect? Also, dammit, that was good face wash.

It had been long enough that I knew this guy was doing me a favor by ending it so definitively. No longer was I fantasy-plotting to have hired goons (i.e., my friends) kidnap him and put a bag over his head and take him to an old abandoned warehouse where they'd not kill him, of course, never *kill* him, but instead scare him until he pooped himself, a part scatological, part Scooby-Doo humiliation I imagined they'd document and disseminate across the Internet, per my bidding. While I was over the guy, over the thing that had happened and how small and inconsequential being ignored had made me feel, I certainly wasn't looking for anyone new. I was keeping my head down, I was working hard, I was channeling my energy for revenge scenarios into work and, at night, drinks with friends. Living well is the best revenge, or so they say.

One Wednesday night in August I had planned to go to a birthday party but instead went out drinking with a coworker when our day at the office ended. One drink turned to several, as it does with the very best sorts of coworkers. We sat in our favorite booth at our favorite smelly bar—disinfectant with undertones of feet and a hint of old mop—and gossiped and plotted our hoped-for great futures. He looked at his phone and it was ten p.m. A TV writer, he had shows to watch. "And you have that birthday party to go to," he reminded me. I'd nearly forgotten. "It's right around the corner," he said. "You should just stop by. You'll feel good about doing it."

I agreed, and headed the few blocks to the bar where the party was being held. Inside, the birthday girl was surrounded by a group of people who were all getting ready to leave. I'd made it by the skin of my teeth. "Happy birthday!" I yelled, trying to hide my lateness with enthusiasm.

"I'm so glad you came," she said. "Some of us are going back to my place. Join us!"

There were six of us in all: a single guy I was always running into at parties; a couple I hadn't met and their friend, who was in from out of town; the birthday girl; and me. We gathered around a small table in her apartment and drank beer and white wine. The couple's friend was a man with dark hair and glasses. He was seated in a chair next to the fridge, slightly outside the cluster the rest of us had formed, a perch from which he delivered the occasional bon mot. I liked his demeanor—he was acerbic but somehow sweet, too—and we started talking. I don't remember what was said, exactly, but I know I was several drinks in before this leg of the evening had begun, and that sauciness and pinot grigio are historically directly proportional to each other when they meet in my bloodstream. In addition, I had my guard up, all too aware of what I had so recently been reminded of yet again: Guys might charm you, but they'd just as soon never speak to you again, if the whim struck. While I wasn't being rude, exactly, I wasn't being particularly nice, either. The most decent way to say it would be that I was giving this bearded, bespectacled man, whose name was Will, though I didn't know it until the next day, a hard time, being deliberately challenging and sarcastic while also hoping to keep him intrigued enough to continue talking to me, at least as long as I liked.

Then he mentioned his eleven-year-old stepsister, and the

words he used and the expression on his face when he talked about this little girl whom he clearly loved melted all my steely resolve. This guy was not like the rest, I just knew it. I started to listen to him, and suddenly, as in the corniest of corny movies, it was just the two of us in the room, in the world, and suddenly we were getting up and leaving because we really did want it just to be the two of us in the room, in the world. We left so abruptly that I forgot my phone, and we gave no explanation for our departure to our friends, because to us, none was needed. When I went back to pick up my phone the next day, my friend told me those who'd remained—including the couple Will had been staying with; he was just in town for one night and lived in Seattle—had looked at one another, perplexed but amused, and said, "Wait. Did that just happen?"

Apparently, it had.

He stayed at my apartment that night. We went to sleep at some so-late-it-was-way-too-early hour after talking and talking and talking, the way people do when they've found each other and can't believe they've managed to exist for so long on their own *without* that having happened. There is so much to know, so much to catch up on. Sometimes that feeling lasts, and sometimes it fades over time, but the initial pull of it is one of the most magnetic experiences in human existence. You can't ignore those moments, and you certainly don't want to end them by doing something as ridiculous and totally unnecessary as going to sleep. So you stay up as late as you can, damning work the next day, defying reality. You let yourself fall in love a little, and you kiss and cuddle and maybe you have sex or maybe you don't, and you hope it will all still be there in the morning.

I woke at the requisite early hour to blog, because the Internet was always up even if I didn't want to be, and he slept for a while and then got up and read while I worked. It was oddly comfortable getting to know each other in this incredibly irregular way, but soon I had to go into the office and he had to catch his plane back to the West Coast. "Do you want to get lunch?" he asked me, but I couldn't.

"I don't really get lunch," I explained, and he nodded, *She doesn't get lunch*, a nugget of information about this person he barely knew. "I wish I could," I said, not wanting him to think this was rejection. At the time my days were so scripted from wake up to blog to blog to blog to blog to home to sleep and repeat that I barely had time to make a doctor's appointment, to do an errand, to drop off or pick up laundry, to go to the gym. This was my own pressure on myself, but I felt it, and it was real, so even a half hour for a sit-down, talk-about-things kind of midday meal was an impossible dream. I could barely pick up an iced coffee at the bodega below the office without feeling like a slouch. Lunch was a thing that happened at my desk.

Before we left my apartment he'd pulled me to him and kissed me, and we stood that way for a few minutes, as long as I'd let myself. We looked at each other, acknowledging: Something was here. But he didn't take my phone number or my e-mail, and I figured if he wanted such details about me, he could find them easily enough, so I didn't offer. There was another matter, or two, of no small concern. He was twenty-six. He lived in Seattle. I was thirty-six. I lived in New York. Maybe something was here here, but would it be there and here, or here and there? He found my e-mail, and later that day, I received a message from him. His flight had been canceled due to electrical storms. He would be in town for another night. Did I want—did I have the inclination, or the energy, if I wasn't too tired—to hang out again? I did, thankful for these magical electrical storms that seemed fated to be, meaning perhaps everything about this new person in my life was fated, too. I wrote back with faux casualness, for some god-awful reason, "Let's totally hang." To prove (ironically) that I was really someone worth his time, I included a link to an article that quoted something I'd written about Boo, the so-called World's Cutest Dog, who, it was being Internet-alleged, might only have achieved his fame because his owner worked for Facebook. In a cuckoo-crazy world, good things were afoot.

That night was a strange kind of second date, our conversations extending further into what-if and how-could territory than any regular second date with two locally based participants would ever demand, yet with the understanding that we had no idea what, exactly, we were going to do about all this, or if we even should. We said that if we lived in the same town, of course we would date. We talked about how there was clearly a connection between us, something that people don't find every day. If nothing else, we should be "friends forever," we decided. But I didn't really want to be his friend, not just his friend, if what I could be was something more. I think—I guess—he felt the same way. When he left the next day to catch his flight to Los Angeles, and then Seattle, he had both my e-mail *and* my phone number. And unlike the guy who'd never contacted me again, he did call, over and over again, in the beginning texting first, a gesture that endeared him to me still further. "Is this a good time to talk?" he'd ask, and I'd write, "Yes," or "Sure!" or "Of course," or even "☺☺☺."

Each night we talked, and every morning I'd wake to an e-mail from him that was the closest thing to a love letter I'd ever received. He'd tell me about his life up to that point and things that mattered to him, large and small, explaining who he was and the kind of person he wanted to be. I would write back, attempting to do the same, inspired by his openness and intelligence and heart. Some part of me still conflicted about our age difference, I described him to friends as a "Seattle twenty-six," as opposed to a "New York twenty-six," which meant, in my mind, more mature, more commitment-ready, just a better guy than a lot of the New Yorkers I'd dated. I mean, he had a dog. Guys with dogs were inherently better and more grown-up than those without, and I was more of a "Seattle twenty-six" than a "Seattle thirty-six," anyway, I reasoned—whatever that meant. A close friend who's known me through many a relationship and had previously categorized me as only dating "Option A: reliable, good on paper, utterly boring" or "Option B: batshit crazy" shouted with glee, "You've found Option C!"

The relationship, because that's what it was, we admitted, that's what it was going to be, and that's what we wanted it to be, took root and started to grow. Despite the geographical and age-related odds, it felt natural, even easy, in need of watering by way of phone calls, texts, and plane tickets, all of which seemed doable and an investment well worth what we got in return. I felt calm instead of panicky, peaceful instead of nervously waiting for the other shoe to drop, or for those shoes to end up, against my rational will, halfway down the street. I had not forgotten that things can be destroyed faster than they can be built. On weekend mornings I'd lie in bed after I'd woken, letting myself luxuriate in how much I liked this person, how it seemed he liked me back, and how it felt like I might finally know enough to do things right this time. I hoped we weren't fooling ourselves, but I didn't want to know if we were. It felt too good, this Option C.

The day came that I ran into that other guy, the one I'd dated briefly who had surely thrown out my face wash long ago. I knew I'd see him again. New York can be as provincially small as it is an impenetrable monolith. I was heading to a bar for after-work drinks with my boss, and the two of us were deep in conversation. When Face Wash got so close he had to say something, he did, waving at the both of us: "Hey guys," I think it was, along with a shrug of acknowledged awkwardness. My boss knew the whole tale and had told me, over previous drinks, that it was for the best that this relationship had ended. There'd be someone far better, he had predicted optimistically. "Oh, hi," we responded in unison to my erstwhile man-friend, and without pausing, returned to each other. We walked for several blocks as if nothing had happened until my boss finally interrupted: "I feel I should say something. Was that okay? That was okay, right? Because it felt okay."

"Totally," I said. And it *was* totally okay, it was better than okay. Sometimes feeling nothing about someone else is the best feeling of all. The only better feeling is standing on the precipice of infinite possibility with someone new.

Right after Will and I had first met, I had drinks with a friend who was visiting from out of town. We were talking about dating and love and marriage, and she said, "You know, I never understood why we're supposed to wait for the wedding to have the honeymoon. We should have the honeymoon first, get to know each other and relax and have a good time. Later, get married and, whatever, take a trip after that if you want. But have the honeymoon first! We should all get the honeymoon, regardless of the wedding." I'd told her about Will, and she leaned in and commanded with intensity, "Go on a honeymoon with him. *Take the honeymoon.*"

I laughed. "I probably won't pitch it that way," I said, "but you're right. We should go on a trip." I texted him from the bar, bold with Grüner Veltliners, "I have a great idea! But I'll have to tell you on the phone." Later, when we did talk, I was nervous. Would it seem too forward to suggest we travel together, to assume that he'd want to spend money to go somewhere with me? I was definitely not going to say the word *honeymoon*, a promise I felt I could rely on myself to keep even after many glasses of wine. Still, wedding locales did pop up in my mind for our trip. Jamaica, where Lucy and David had gotten married, but that was a long, expensive flight from Seattle. The Dominican wouldn't work, either, though an inn like the one I'd stayed at in Vermont with Jason would be cozy. Surely there was a location in the nearly three thousand miles between our two homes that would be ideal—a resort in Arizona, or we could try Austin, Texas. Something that would be right for *us*. I had butterflies, fearing that I'd take this risk, confess how I felt, and be rejected; worried I might push too hard and lose him entirely. I thought I knew him well enough that this would not be the case, but it had been absolutely no time at all for it to feel like, already, so much had changed.

"What's your idea?" he asked.

"Oh . . . I . . . I don't know. I'm embarrassed to say," I stuttered, losing my nerve completely.

"Tell me!" he said, encouraging.

"Maybe we should go somewhere together," I managed.

"Yes," he agreed, without hesitating. "I'm in."

Then it was logistics. We talked midpoints. Neither of us had unlimited funds or time. We started to scale back, deciding he should come to New York, and I should go to Seattle. They weren't "honeymoon" spots, per se, only the humdrum places where we actually lived, but it made more sense, seemed less upending to our lives, and it would certainly be cheaper, with fewer concerns about bedbug infestations sustained from hotel stays or the availability of functional Wi-Fi if we had to work. And if we were ever to have a life together, someday, we should know how each other lived, like, *really* lived.

"You know what," he said, once we'd agreed he'd come to New York in early September, and I'd travel to Seattle after that.

JEN DOLL

"I have a wedding in October, on the Olympic Peninsula." He'd
gone to college with the bride, who was an actress; the groom
was a puppeteer. "It might be intense," he warned me. "This is as
close to a family wedding as I can have without family actually
being involved . . . but if you do want to come, I would be very
happy."

How could I say no?

Much of the year it's gray and drizzly in the Pacific Northwest. That, of course, is the weather it's traditionally known
for, all the better for habitual coffee-drinking and stocking cap–
wearing and the Seattle Freeze, which, as Will's friends explained
to me on my first visit, is the local habit of being more coolly
distant than anything else. After all, there's no sense going to the
trouble of actively befriending folks who aren't going to stick
around past the first spate of rain.

But in early October, there is no freeze. It can be as beautiful
then as it ever is, and this early October was the most beautiful of
all. The sky was clear and brilliant blue with fluffy white clouds,
a skillful child's rendering of an atmospheric condition that rarely
exists in nature. You could see to the mountains and beyond, and
even beyond that, you could see the tip of snow-capped Mount
Rainier. Unlike in New York, you could just *see*. We set off on a
Friday into the horizon, to Max and Ava's wedding. Getting to
our destination involved a car ride, a boat ride, and more hours in
the car, but even that seemed something to look forward to, all

this alone time in which we were finally again together. Weeks ago he had, as promised, visited me in New York. We'd had as great a time as our first meeting, and I saw no reason this trip would not be more of the same.

We made a stop for lunch, a shared salad and burgers in the sun, after we got off the ferry, and took a detour through winding roads to see Will's childhood home. It was at the end of a dirt path on the edge of town, a place with its own barn that his mom and dad had built before they'd separated and moved to different houses in Los Angeles, before Will's life became intrinsically divided. We parked there in the gravel driveway, and a sweet old brindled dog came to investigate, walking around the car, paying us only a fleeting sort of benign canine interest. "That looks like the same dog that lived nearby when I was growing up," said Will. We were quiet for a minute and then were again on our way, leaving a cloud of dust and memories in our wake.

It took a couple more hours to reach the former army base turned state park overlooking Puget Sound where the wedding would take place. We got the key to our quarters, a sprawling space with multiple rooms that used to be military housing and now, as wedding guest lodgings, would be shared with several of Will's friends. We explored, claimed our bedroom, and waited for more people to arrive. The sun was just starting to set, and there were big-eyed gentle deer lingering around outside. We could hear the barking of seals echoing out above the water. It seemed we were in another world, to which we'd arrived via a fully enjoyable and borderline magical journey.

Still, I was a bit nervous about this wedding. It was the only one I'd ever attended at which I'd known no one beyond my date, and he was a man I was just getting to know. I was hopeful about this relationship, and I wanted no repeats of disasters from weddings past: no thrown shoes, no thrown friendships, no clandestine cliff pukes, no nights ended in tears. I wanted this one to be, yes, perfect. It could be . . . couldn't it?

Will had tried to prepare me for what to expect. He'd gone to college with most of the people I'd meet. They were not only good friends but also many of them worked together as part of the theater company they'd founded in Seattle after college. This collective was, as he'd explained, the closest thing he had to family without actual blood ties, and because of that relationship, he was expected to do some things that wouldn't be required of the typical wedding-goer. Some guests were performing at the rehearsal dinner, and others would contribute to the ceremony itself, but the main duty assigned to Will and a handful of his friends was on the morning of the wedding. They'd been asked to help set up the hall where the ceremony would be held later that afternoon. I said I'd help, too. I wanted to, not only for the brownie points, but, well, what else was I going to do? Hang out in the room and eat bonbons? I figured it couldn't be that bad. It would be fast, and we'd be on our way to do more interesting things, and then to the wedding. Weddings were *fun*.

The rehearsal dinner was held at a nearby VFW hall. It was a potluck with food prepared and brought in by friends and family. The event provided the expected wedding convergence of people and the ensuing confusion as well: meeting, hearing a name and forgetting it as soon as you hear the next, despite how diligently you try to come up with mnemonic devices. Will would occasionally disappear, talking to friends he hadn't seen in years, while I spoke to strangers I was meeting for the first time. It felt natural, though. We were together but able to be apart as needed, and then we'd come back together again. I felt no pressure to be anything I was not among these other guests, who seemed pretty much exactly who they were, too, and who welcomed me. It probably helped that they all liked Will. (Wedding Tip: Choose your date wisely.)

That night, there was a talent show. A married couple in a band played a song. A puppeteer friend did a routine. There were light shows about love and commitment and togetherness. Another group of friends and family sang a cappella. When the evening was over, a bunch of us went back to our big rented apartment and stayed up and drank for a while. A group of people ventured out on an exploratory mission to the lighthouse nearby, but Will and I went to bed, tired from the drive, knowing we had to get up early the next day. (Wedding Tip: Don't ruin yourself on the first night.)

The next morning we roused ourselves by nine, threw on clothes, and walked the short distance to the building where the ceremony and reception would be held that afternoon. Not stopping for coffee or food was a rookie mistake. It was cold in that room, and dark, the sun still too low in the sky to deliver much warmth or light to us inside. A handful of other guests were already there, standing around, waiting for direction. We jumped up and down and rubbed our hands together to take off the chill as we waited for someone to tell us what to do, idly chatting with the other helpers, wishing we were still in bed.

There was a woman there who I later found out was the wedding planner. I also later found out she'd just had surgery and was on a lot of pain medication, which made me feel particularly bad about what happened next. She started giving orders, and everyone seemed to come to attention. She said, "Who wants to volunteer to stand on ladders and hang up these paper lanterns?" Someone volunteered, and another someone offered to help. "Who wants to put tablecloths and centerpieces on tables?" Two girls said they'd do it. Chore after chore was given out, but I didn't volunteer. I figured I'd just help whoever needed help, that my status as date didn't entitle me to jump in and claim an entire job all for myself. At the end of her delegation, the woman looked at me. "Are you here to help?" she asked, and, true or not, I detected accusation in her tone, a sniffiness to her demeanor. "Who *are* you?"

There were many things I could have said to that, but what came out of my mouth was this: "Nah, I'm just here to watch." It was one of those quips a person might later wish they'd thought of to say in the moment, but in my case, I wished I hadn't. *So much for brownie points*, I thought, envisioning my upcoming memoir, *Getting Off on the Wrong Foot: The Jen Doll Story*. The wedding guests surrounding me burst out laughing, but the woman narrowed her eyes at me.

"This is Jen," said Will finally, and I said, brightly, "I'll do tablecloths!" That seemed easy and not terribly dangerous, something at which I should be able to easily succeed and accomplish fairly quickly. Will started to help with another project, and the room buzzed with the activity of purposeful people.

Within a half hour the tablecloths were laid out with nary a wrinkle, clusters of candles positioned across the white spreads, and we'd placed small decorative bags of battery-operated lights in the windowsills on both sides of the room for an appealing cross-twinkle later that evening. The matter of hanging the lanterns turned out to be a far more arduous one. The ladders available for stringing the paper globes to the ceiling were too short, and the string was not strong enough to hold them; despite being paper, they were unexpectedly weighty. The plan that the bride and groom had laid out optimistically did not seem feasible in any form of reality. Gravity was a bitch. We tried, though, we really tried—or at least, the members of the theater company tried. They were used to technical difficulties, and, one by one, each person threw out a new plan to solve the problem. Though these solutions, one after another, failed, no one seemed frustrated. They just kept trying. I stayed busy and attempted to be helpful by doing odd jobs, menial things necessary to the completion of bigger tasks that I had no idea how to tackle. I strung lanterns together, or replaced batteries for the light sources within them. I laughed when people made jokes. The thing is, when you're someone's date to a wedding, to the wedding of his friends, surrounded by others of his friends you're meeting for the first time—and when this person is someone who it seems may be important to you for a long time—you are a good sport. I wanted to be a good sport, and I could be, I would be, but I was getting crankier. And crankier. One more crank. We hadn't had coffee,

I reminded myself. We could have coffee later. Just a little bit longer, and this would be done.

Several hours later, we were still working, and there was one string of lanterns that had been successfully attached to the ceiling. The plan called for seven strings, or possibly eight. A lot, was all I knew. There were deliberations about whether that first string needed to be taken down, because the lantern in the center was in the guests' sight line and was likely to prevent them from seeing the bride's face. A couple of people hoisted a ladder on top of a table, and a guy started to climb up onto it. This seemed to me a very bad idea.

"Are you sure you should be doing that?" I said, my voice coming out quavery and meek. "It seems kind of, er . . . dangerous."

"It's fine," he said.

"I . . . I just think no one should break his neck here today," I said, louder, and then even louder, "That would make for a terrible wedding!"

He rolled his eyes and muttered as he kept climbing, and the people holding the feet of the ladder steady atop the table gritted their teeth and held tighter. I had a vision that this would end horribly, so I took that moment to hide in the bathroom. *Oh, God, I've become a mom*, I thought. I had been totally lame, a nagging worrywart, and in front of all of Will's friends. Still, I really didn't think a person should climb onto a ladder that sat on top of a table. Feeling sure I'd seen warnings about such things somewhere, say, in seventh-grade shop class, or perhaps on ladders themselves, I held fast to that resolve.

When I emerged a few minutes later, everything was fine. There had been no disaster, the ladder was no longer on top of the table, and people were singing and talking and diligently hanging up lanterns. Progress was being made. *I can do this,* I told myself.

Will walked over to me. "Hi."

"Hey," I said. "I just got kind of weirded out about the table . . . I'm good now."

"Let's go," he said definitively. "We've done enough. We need to eat."

I was not inclined to argue with that. We left and went to a tiny cafe in town where we sat outside in the now-warm sun and ate egg dishes and drank coffee after coffee. Suddenly, life was wonderful again. We meandered through a little street fair that was also an organic market, featuring brightly colored fruits and vegetables and hemp soaps and fresh-baked breads, and we tasted local cheeses and bought one to take back with us. All of the stress of the earlier morning gone, we returned to our apartment to get ready for the evening. Two of Will's friends were in the kitchen making pies and cakes to be served at the wedding. They'd appropriated the kitchen next door for this purpose, too, and for the past hour or more had been going from one oven to the next checking on their baked goods. All seemed well, so they decided to go ahead and take their showers. This is often precisely when all hell breaks loose.

We were standing in the kitchen next door talking with some other guests when it became clear that something had gone wrong in the oven. There was smoke pouring out of the top burner, and having little knowledge of what one should do in case of an oven fire (Wedding Tip: Don't open the oven!), we opened the oven. Flames danced inside, red and gold tendrils reaching out at us. Oh, that was not good. We slammed the oven door shut and ran around the apartment opening windows. Though we'd turned off the stove, smoke kept pouring out of it, abating briefly and then billowing up again. In the distance, smoke alarms were going off. We feared the arrival of a cadre of firefighters, or worse, management, who might kick us out and would probably, definitely, charge us for a new oven and any other damage incurred. "Where are Heidi and Natasha? Get Heidi and Natasha!" someone said, but the girls in charge of the pies and cakes remained blissfully ignorant as they showered. This was our problem to handle; you can't wait for someone else to handle fire.

You can, however, delegate. Having done all we knew to do, Will and I returned to our parlor area, away from the smoke, leaving the people who were staying in the apartment with the compromised oven to Google "What to do in case of oven fire." Yep, should have kept the oven door closed in the first place. Oops. The fire died down, and soon after, Heidi and Natasha appeared, their hair damp and in towels, and pronounced the burned cakes inedible. "I don't know what she put in that cake!" said Natasha, blaming Heidi's laissez-faire recipe interpretation for the inferno. Fortunately, the baked goods in the other oven were fine, and very nearly but not quite burning down your lodgings at a wedding is the kind of story the bride loves to hear about after the fact.

We never were charged for any damage, either.

Save the Date

. . .

I didn't know much about Max and Ava, the groom and bride, but I knew from Will that Max had asked Ava to marry him previously, and she'd said no the first time. She hadn't been ready, but after some time had passed, he asked again and she was. I liked the idea that love could grow even from a form of rejection (that wasn't, in the end, a rejection at all), and I liked that this couple seemed so thoughtful about marriage. They wanted to be sure. They were both tall and slim, attractive and creative. They seemed, simply enough, a good match, people who looked right together and people who had decided they *were* right together, too.

Getting ready that evening, I put on a silky red dress, wrapping myself in a black belt that tapered the waist and made the skirt flare. I had brought the patent leather stiletto Mary Janes with four-inch heels that I'd worn to Annabel's wedding. They were gorgeous and made my feet hurt so badly that one night out in Brooklyn I'd had to take them off and walk home barefoot. I also had with me a pair of brown and gold suede heels that I loved but that a friend of mine had once dubbed "sensible." Fuck it, I wanted to be able to stand. I wore the sensible shoes, went without tights, and applied red-coral lipstick. I emerged from our room, and Will saw me and smiled. "You look great," he said. He did, too, all dressed up in a jacket and tie, formal clothes I hadn't yet had the occasion to see him in. He'd made himself a drink of ginger ale and some shady bourbon that had been hanging out in the backseat of his cluttered car for the past few months, sopping up the occasional Seattle sun and more frequent cloudy skies. I took a sip of it. Not bad. It was wedding time.

Like us, the hall we'd spent the morning in had been transformed. Lights were hanging from the ceiling's beams in a flattering way that would not block the bride's head. Candles flickered throughout the room, which was filled with color and prettiness and interesting things: art installations from friends who'd crafted them as gifts, photographs of the couple displayed about, and fresh-scrubbed, happy people in their party clothes. Everyone was milling around in front of the bar, and there was that special about-to-get-started energy in the room, all of us in our best, and in the best moods, too. I saw the wedding planner and approached her. "Everything looks so good," I said, motioning around the room. "Thanks so much for helping," she responded. Not a hint of sarcasm passed between us. It was a wedding miracle.

The bride and groom appeared. She had on a sparkling, pale gold gown with long, flowing sleeves and a low back; it looked like a long column from top to bottom and was cinched with a jeweled belt. The effect was very old Hollywood in Washington State, her hair coiffed and a jeweled brooch tucked above her ear, her lips crimson. The groom wore a gray-blue pinstriped suit over a pale yellow shirt that brought out the gold in the bride's dress, and a blue and gold tie. Beyond their collaborative styling everything seemed to just go, and the whole room appeared itself alight with jewels. I could feel proud of my candle placement, if not my fearlessness around ladders.

At this wedding, especially once my initial nervousness dissipated, I took a more anthropological view than I ever had before. It was fascinating to sit back and watch as the event transpired, to see how things played out among these friends—many of whom had known one another since college and how this couple had envisioned their wedding. There were five or six long tables lined up across the room, and a buffet set up in the front, those wedding-omnipresent Sterno burners blazing underneath to keep things hot. There were vegetarian options, grains and beans, stuff that was filling and earthy and also tasted good, and plenty of pans along the buffet line to choose from. Instead of a separate cere-mony and reception, everything seemed to happen at once, al-most like dinner theater. People got drinks and found places at the tables, and the speeches and toasts began from friends and family.

The bride and groom were married onstage by one of their close friends, another graduate of their college and member of the theater company. She stood between the couple, who held hands in front of her, and addressed the room. "I asked my mom, who has been married to my dad for more than thirty years, what the biggest surprise of their marriage had been, what she knew now that she could not possibly have known then," she said. "Her response: 'I didn't know how long it would be.'" There was a pause for laughter, and we heartily obliged. After a moment, she continued with her mom's words: "'I didn't know there would be so many trials we'd have to go through together. I also didn't know how much Dad and I would grow together, how much our values would stay the same, how important it was that our values were the same.'" There was another pause, this one for some wiping of tears.

Then it was vows time. We watched, rapt, as the bride and groom delivered the marital promises they'd written to each other. "I will always listen," "I will have your back," "I will accept you as you change," and so on, back and forth, words that weren't about obeying one's husband or looking after one's wife, but which signified a more modern promise to always try to care and communicate in equal measure, because without that, where are you? Blind, enforced obedience is so very *yesteryear.* "I will eat your young," said the bride, or it may have been the groom. At least that's what I thought I heard, and across the table one of Will's friends caught my eye. He was suppressing his own outburst of laughter. I tried to keep from spitting out my wine, and I mostly succeeded. "I will be your *home,*" that's what had been said, a lovely sentiment, I thought, feeling involuntary giggles rise up in me again and semi-successfully quashing them.

The vows over, we ate, drank, and mingled. "There's someone I want you to meet," said Will, pulling me aside so he could introduce me to one of his former professors. She and I sat and talked. "Isn't he wonderful?" she said. "He is so wonderful," I agreed, getting a little misty over how wonderful he, and all of it, was.

Later we climbed onto the stage where the bride and groom had been married, the same spot that earlier that day had been a staging ground for lantern assembly and hanging. In its latest iteration it was a room for shadow dancing, sheets hung across the stage and pulsing pink and green and blue lights everywhere. If you stood on the other side of the curtain and looked up from the floor where guests had been seated for dinner, you'd have seen dark moving forms on the sheet. This was where we now danced and jumped up and down, pretending to talk on an old plastic rotary phone that had been part of an art installation decorating the room. It was making its way across the dance floor, passed from friend to friend, a live, literal version of telephone. "Hello!" we shouted into it. "Hello?" someone would respond. "How are you?" "I'm great—I'm at a wedding!" *Riiiiinnngggg.* "Oh, hi!" And so on, until the reception was over.

The apartment where the cakes had burned to a crisp had been designated as the official after-party location. We arrived and others began to show up, too, more and more of them, everyone wedding-weary and sweaty and sufficiently boozed, but not tired enough for bed. Hours of fun remained to be had. In the room adjacent to the kitchen, which still bore a greasy, palpable sheen from the oven fire, a large table was being set up for beer pong. Will stationed himself at the head of that table, his tie flung over his shoulder rakishly, and began to play, surrounded by his former college buddies. I found a spot on a couch next to a few women, each of us clutching a plastic cup of wine in hand, and we kicked off our shoes and traded stories and laughed, oh, how we laughed. As the dawn broke, we stumbled, sleepy but satisfied, back to our rooms with our dates, and we fell asleep in their arms, the perfect ending to a perfect wedding.

Well, not exactly. Because it just doesn't happen that way, no matter how we try.

. . .

What really happened was this: Everything was fine and dandy, until it wasn't. Suddenly I was drunk, tired, and most of all, tired of being a good sport. I'd tried, I'd really tried! And now he was playing this dumb college game with his college friends, and just expecting me to be okay with that. He was clueless that something might be brewing dangerously on the couch, in his wedding date, and that was because he was not paying attention to me at all. I felt ignored and neglected. I felt . . . *the need to make my feelings known.*

Here is where it all goes wrong at a wedding. In a moment, something that is really quite small and maybe not an issue at all, if you were being reasonable, blows up in your mind, and all at once it's so big, you can't stand it. It's encroaching on the sides of your cranium. It's struggling for release. It's making your body and heart and soul and most of all your mouth want to scream, and you have to let it out. This is the Wedding Tantrum, a buildup of everything sustained throughout the day—the excitement and anxiety, the happiness and sadness, the expectation and disappointment, and whatever else might have seeped into your deepest, darkest emotional caverns. It is inherently unreasonable. These feelings desperately want to go somewhere, and because you're a little bit (or a lot) drunk, and a little bit (or a lot) tired, they will frequently be laid upon whatever person in the immediate vicinity cares about you the most: whoever is there and will not stop loving you because you're about to have a shit fit. Whoever will take it. It's a dangerous game, however, because you never know if this person might not take it at all and will instead say screw it, you're not worth all this trouble, and walk away. Sometimes that happens.

That's not what I was thinking about right then, though. I wasn't really thinking, or if I was thinking, it was in Neanderthalic utterances rather than in rational human sentences—far more Tarzan beating chest than, say, even Andie MacDowell delivering stilted but at least cogent lines in *Four Weddings and a Funeral*. My mind was full of impulse-driven thoughts: *Me Feel Bad. Me Mad. Me Want Attention. Me Gonna Get It.*

I paused in my conversation, stood up, and walked over to Will. He didn't stop playing his game, and this burned me up further. *Me Want ATTENTION.* "Wanna try?" he asked, one eye still on the competition. I made a halfhearted attempt to get the ball in the cup and missed by a mile. *I hate games*, I thought, *and I especially hate games I lose. HE KNOWS I HATE GAMES I LOSE.* And I am about to lose it entirely. All of the weddings, all of the relationships, all of the times I felt I'd tried and hadn't gotten what I wanted, whether I knew what that was or not, were right back with me again. I thought I'd matured. I thought I was finally an adult. But the truth was, inside, I was just a little girl in a party dress with jaggedy, badly cut bangs, who was about to yell and kick and scream and cry to try to make herself feel better, because the wedding had stopped being fun. "That's okay," he said, handing me another ball. "Go again."

I am not entirely sure I did not throw the ball across the table, across the room, away, in any case, from me. I am sure that something terrible came out of my mouth, something that might have been along the lines of "I HATE BEER PONG, AND I HATE

YOU!" And I'm definitely sure that, like an eighties antiheroine in a movie about prom, I turned on my sensible heels and ran out of there, down the hall until I reached our bedroom, where I threw myself across the bed and started to cry. Well, I'd gotten attention. Everyone had seen *that*. It just hadn't gone quite as planned. Yelling at someone else to make yourself feel better almost never works, unless you're on the phone with your cell service provider.

As I began to calm down, I was struck with a horrifying thought: *Is this how every date I've ever taken to a wedding felt? Alone, as if I wasn't paying them enough attention, as if I wasn't doing enough to take care of them? Alone, and maybe even taken for granted?* I felt for Jason, for Christoph, for the men I'd brought with me who knew no one, and who had struggled, gamely or less so, to be a part of my event. These were the guys I'd criticized for not being better, and yet here I was. It wasn't always easy to be a date at a wedding, even in the best of circumstances.

A few minutes later, Will was in the room with me. "What just happened?" he asked. "You can't do that. You can't just get mad and freak out and storm off like that." He was right, of course. Or I could, but if I did, it didn't bode well for us or for me and anyone I ever wanted to be with. Still, he'd followed me to tell me that. He'd cared enough to choose me. I apologized, and inwardly I vowed to be better, to listen, to have his back, to try to communicate without resorting to toddler tactics, and to never eat anyone's young. If this relationship was going to go anywhere—and where it might go, I didn't know, but I wanted the option to see what might unfold—I would need to do all of that, and I'd need to work on it every day. And we weren't even married.

The next morning, I woke with the ache of regret. It had all felt like it was going so right, and then out of the blue, it had taken a turn I hadn't predicted. In hindsight in these situations, you know you should have done your best to shore up the course for just such a thing, because it wasn't out of the blue at all. Then you beat yourself up doubly, because you didn't. It wasn't a mistake that I'd felt neglected or even that I'd gotten angry. It was a mistake that I hadn't been mature enough to talk about it in a reasonable way. It was a mistake that I'd been such a baby. Growing up is hard. Being a grown-up at a wedding can be even harder.

Weddings. They are fraught with emotion. They can be powder kegs. They are full of love, but they also can be tinged with anger, resentment, insecurity, doubt, and all the baggage we come with as adult humans. At a wedding, the habits we've adopted to cope with and get by in daily life confront these weighty traditions we may or may not even believe in, and that is a recipe that may lead to oven fires. That's why it's important at a wedding to check the cakes, to breathe and think twice before you storm out of a room or head down a path you don't actually want to go. It's important to be patient and kind and attentive to your dates, whomever they may be. And, if you're me, it's important to try to stop somewhere around the sixth glass of wine. Or, fine, the seventh. Hey, it's a wedding.

We packed up and checked out and said good-bye to all his friends, the people I'd just gotten to know. I felt a pang of embarrassment about how I'd behaved the night before, but no one appeared to be holding it against me. The occasional Wedding Tantrum is inevitable. Surely something like it had happened to more guests than me. Despite or because of that ubiquitous wedding phraseology of the "perfect day," it is ever so difficult to be perfect at a wedding.

This wedding wasn't like Jamaica, or the Dominican Republic, or even like that long-ago wedding in Alabama or the more recent one on the Jersey Shore. There were no grand vows to keep in touch or efforts at further friendship, because Will and I had gone as our own little team, a unit of two, in the first place. He'd visit me in New York, and we'd see his friends, and he'd see mine, and the same thing would happen in Seattle, but there was no need to make promises other than to each other. If we continued to see each other, the rest of them would be in our life, too.

On the boat back to Seattle, I took a picture of him, his hat cocked askew on his head, dazed and comedic in his wedding hangover state, wearing wrinkled pants and an untucked shirt. I threatened to post it to Facebook. "That will only make *you* look bad," he said, and I found that very funny. It didn't matter if he looked bad in that photo because he didn't look bad to me, and, I realized, I didn't mind if I looked bad to anyone else so long as he didn't feel that way. The good was enough to outweigh the bad.

I stayed in Seattle a few more days before going back to New York, and it didn't rain once.

19.

Thank You for Having Me

I took a plane trip recently, one of those flights during which the attendants are bent on making that glorified bus ride in the sky feel fun. After they introduced themselves, they announced to the cabin that we should all get to know one another better. "Does anyone have any news?" they asked. No one came forward to confess anything, so they prompted: "Anybody gotten engaged recently?" Nothing. "Married?" Still nothing. "Divorced?" A tentative hand was raised, to some obligatory laughs. "Really, no one's gotten married?" the flight attendant leading the charge asked incredulously. She couldn't believe it. I couldn't, either.

Engagements, weddings, and divorces, but especially weddings: These are the main events of our lives, punctuating our twenties, our thirties, and on and ever on. Yet sometimes they appear to stop, and you look around, and you feel their absence. It feels, oddly enough, like a loss. What, no weddings this year? No built-in party, no joyous event to both look forward to and resent in equal, diametrically opposed measure? No request for your time and energy and money that's a gift itself from the bride and groom, who want you to experience this moment with them, and who are, in inviting you, placing you forever in a common history of you and them? If they didn't ask, you would be so hurt—not that that means you won't complain about their asking. The weddings never stop, and then they do. Just when they were getting good.

Not to worry; the weddings never *really* stop. There will always be more weddings. My boss's wife's best friend. A guy I used to work with. A guy I still work with. My friend who met her fiancé in a cheese shop. The woman whose birthday it was the night I met Will. Surely you've been invited to your own set of parties for someone's impending nuptials, and maybe you've attended one or several ceremonies in the time it's taken you to read this book. Maybe there is one, maybe there are many on the horizon. "I'm moving in with my boyfriend," a coworker confesses, and you know where that's headed. A photo of a ring on a finger appears on Facebook; you don't need anyone to interpret that. "Guess what!" your best friend gasps in a late-night phone call, and you know, you already know.

There will be gaps between wedding seasons, times when there are droughts and times when the floods rage high, but the second it seems everyone's paired off or settled, another invite shows up in the mail. It might be from that middle-aged guy you used to date ten years ago and have remained on good terms with. He's finally decided to tie the knot. Maybe it's the friend who'd been married in her early twenties, gotten a divorce in her thirties, embraced her new singlehood, and then, in her forties, met someone new worth going down the aisle with. Maybe it's a parent or a grandparent who, having lost a first love, has found another. It could be your little brother. He and his fiancée have finally decided to have their ceremony. No, it won't be in any of the places that have been discussed over the years—Saint Lucia or Jamaica or in a Brooklyn park or Tucson or your parents' Florida backyard. It will be somewhere else entirely, somewhere you never would have suspected. Just because people get married doesn't mean they won't keep you guessing, when and how and why and where and even, sometimes, who.

If there's one thing you can count on, regardless of how you yourself feel about marriage, it's that there will always be weddings. They will be as different from one another as can be, while sharing that key aspect at their core that, I think, has a lot to do with why we keep getting married at all. A *New York Times* Vows article shed light on this notion when, in January 2013, Margaux Laskey wrote of ninety-seven-year-old Ada Bryant, a widow, who was marrying eighty-six-year-old Robert Haire, a widower. The first time he asked her, as with my own grandmother and her boyfriend, Henry, she said no. "There's a great difference in our ages, as you can see," she told Laskey. Yet her mind was changed for reasons that combined the romantic and the practical: "I didn't think it was the thing to do because I don't have that many years ahead of me," but he said, 'That's all the more reason,'" Bryant explained, concluding, "I like him very much. I love him. So we're going to be married."

Perhaps there is no better reason than that.

. . .

Years ago, while I was still in a relationship with Jason, and several of my friends were dating the men they would go on to marry, there was one evening, several drinks in, at which one of us proposed a contest. "We should all place bets on who will be the last to marry," she suggested. "We'll pool the money, and the last single person standing will get to keep it. Then she can throw a big party or something!" I don't know why, exactly, but this idea infuriated me. Was it because even though I had a boyfriend at the time, I thought I'd be last, that I knew that relationship would end? Or was it something else, indignation over the sense that marriage was a kind of game-based achievement, with winners and losers—the ultimate loser of which would have to be soothed with cold, hard cash? I'm not sure if my instinct was selfish or something broader-minded, but I said, in no uncertain terms, that I did not want to play along. "Lame," said my friend. She might have been right. I could well be the one holding the bag of money if I'd joined in. But for what? Marriage as a game seems a thankless pursuit. If I'm going to choose to do it, it won't be for a bag of money, nor will it be to avoid the dubious win of a bag of money, either.

Then there was a cab ride I took far more recently. It was a weekday evening, and I was on my way from Brooklyn to the downtown Manhattan apartment of a man I'd been seeing. He was cooking me dinner, but instead of thrilled, I felt panicked. Our relationship seemed to have shifted so quickly from romancing in candlelit bars to spaghetti and meatballs (to use up the beef, which would soon go bad, he said; that's a metaphor if ever there was one) and practical conversations in the fluorescent light of a kitchen, then bed with his Breathe Right strip positioned just so by ten p.m. I could feel my world getting smaller before I'd had time to consider what I even wanted, what size, exactly, I wanted my world to be, and more important, what size it needed to be. I worried that I was just dating this man because he seemed to offer what I, somewhere in the back of my mind, thought I was supposed to want. At the same time, I worried that it would be stupid for me to give up that something, even if the signs pointed to me not wanting it at all, not that, not with him. The creeping fear, of course, is that we won't get another chance. That we won't know we knew until it's too late. That this is as good as it gets. That we're running out of time, and that if we don't do this thing, there must be something wrong with us. So sometimes we hang on, even when we know in our guts we shouldn't.

"You must be going to the apartment of a man," said my cab driver.

"Why do you say that?" I asked.

He turned in his seat and looked at me. "It's a Wednesday. You're . . . how should I say this? . . . not a *party girl*. You look like you worked all day."

I was wearing sneakers with jeans and a T-shirt. I had, in fact, worked all day. "Are you saying I look tired?" I asked.

"Yes," said Mr. Charming. "You look a little tired."

I don't know why I told him—to compensate for the insult, to prove that I was not just a *tired, non-party girl*?—but I did. "Yes,

I'm going to the apartment of a guy who's going to cook me dinner."

"He must be very nice," said the cab driver, who spun into a speech about how he had so many passengers, ever so many, women in their late thirties and forties and fifties, who complained about being alone. "Their families die," he said, snapping his fingers, knocking off humans like flies, "and then they have no one, because they never married."

Somehow, I had hailed the cab from hell. "Mmm," I said, hoping he'd just stop talking if I appeared disinterested. No cigar.

"I had one woman passenger who was on the phone, crying and crying, talking to someone, and she got off the phone and told me her father had died. She had no one; she didn't want to go on. I convinced her not to do anything crazy. I told her, it's okay, you could still find a husband," he said. He dropped his voice as if he were confessing a horrible secret. "She was probably too old, but I told her that anyway."

I doubted this brave-cabbie-prevents-suicide tale (more likely she was crying because he kept lecturing her about marriage), but I nodded. "You're a real lifesaver."

"I know," he said. "It happens all the time, these women crying, women alone. You ladies wait too long. You wait too long and then you don't have anyone. I have been married for forty years!"

"I'm sure your wife is very happy. Oh, you can let me out here," I said, still several blocks from my destination. As a small gesture in defense of single women, I did not tip him.

A week or so later, my relationship with Spaghetti and Meatballs ended.

I am not married, and most of the time I do not feel alone, and even better than that . . . I'm, dare I say it, pretty happy. But I haven't decided I don't want to get married, either. I know that if I do get married, I don't want it to be because of fear of aloneness, or because I think I've waited too long and won't have any options left, or because I might end up a girl in the back of a cab having to justify to a judgmental driver why I'm still single, and why I'm okay with that. I don't want it to be so that I "win." I want it to be for the right reasons, and with the right person, for *me*. I have quite a few married friends who have given me an example to live up to. Whether or not their reasons for marrying would be the same as mine isn't important. What is important is that we all figure out our own reasons and find our own paths, knowing that those paths can, but don't have to, involve marriage.

More than ever in contemporary society, deciding to marry is a choice. No one should settle, I'd never recommend that, but settling is not about whether you get married or not, it's about not wanting the choice you've made as much as you really should. It's about picking the wrong thing. It's also a judgment that tends not to come from a bride or groom, but instead from someone looking on, who may not be privy to the full details of that choice. If we're being honest with ourselves, we don't settle. But it can be very difficult to be honest with ourselves when it comes to addressing a defining life choice like marriage, which carries both so many expectations and so many unknowns.

It goes back to all of those confusing messages about finding love and "the one." Do you set a goal and then work at making it come true (and if so, how best to do this)? Do you passively sit back and cross your fingers and wait and hope for it to happen, for the knight in shining armor (or skinny jeans and a T-shirt proclaiming your favorite band) to arrive? It's hard to know how much to actively choose, particularly when you're someone who's spent her life working to make dreams come true that don't relate to love or marriage. Sometimes, not choosing at all becomes a point of stasis. If you don't choose, you don't lose, or at least that's how it can feel. And yet marriage, like anything else in life, *requires* choosing, picking one thing (married life) over another (single life) and sticking with that decision, day in and day out, even on the bad days. It's not something that just happens. It's not magic. Nor should it be forced, done as a rote performance piece or to adhere to some one-size-fits-all ideology.

I don't have the absolute answers because I don't think there are any. But I do know this: When we try to be what we're not, forcing square wedding pegs into round wedding holes, or when we don't think and instead simply do because that's what's always been done before, that's when things tend to go wrong. When we cease to see the forest for the trees, or the marriage for the "perfect" wedding day, whether we are brides, grooms, or wedding guests, that's when friendships are ruined, shoes are lost, hearts are broken, and someday much, much later we wake up to realize we've made a mistake. But of course, we all make mistakes—

the real mistake is not admitting that. Whether we've too harshly judged a friend for the person she's chosen to marry, or we've gotten drunk and done something we later deeply regret, or we've, perhaps, mistaken a person who was only good for us for the moment for our "forever person," none of us is perfect, just as there is no "perfect day." All of our choices have consequences, but we need not be so plagued with shame or feel like failures when we realize we've chosen the wrong thing. The best we can do is to try to learn and keep moving forward, to know ourselves better and be a little bit better every day, every wedding. And, if necessary, sometimes to say we're sorry.

When as a small child I was asked by family members and friends of family for a kiss, the story goes that I would run from them in hysterical laughter, find a mirror, and kiss myself in it exuberantly, so whoever had asked could see *exactly* what they were missing. Eventually I grew up, I stopped wearing diapers, and I stopped preferring to kiss myself. I think at some point we all realize that not only do we want but also that we *need* others whom we love, and who love us back, in our lives. It gets boring to keep running away and kissing ourselves for laughs. But also, just because someone asks for a kiss doesn't make another person obliged to deliver it. Just because someone assumes we all want to grow up and get married doesn't mean that's the reality for everyone. There are choices to make, and with luck and thought and trying, we will tackle them in the most informed, beneficial, world-opening way for ourselves.

You know, what's funny is that in order to get married, you don't even have to love the idea of a wedding. You just have to decide to do this thing. You find another; you do or you don't say "I do." And then you take it from there.

In some ways, that's not all that different from what a single person does with a wedding invitation.

I opened my mailbox, and there it was.

Acknowledgments

✦

It is the exceedingly rare couple who expects, in offering an invite to their wedding, that the guest will go on to write a book about it. For the openness and generosity with which I have been allowed to witness—and, later, discuss, clarify remembrances, and write about—my friends' pairings, I offer each of them the deepest, bottom-of-my-heart thanks. You have all taught me much about love, and this book truly would not be possible without you.

This book would also not be possible without two amazing people. To my agent, Ryan Harbage, who got in touch one fateful summer day and asked, "Do you want to write a book?" (Um, yes!), who listened to my ideas and supported them wholeheartedly, who listened to my concerns and told me it would all work out, who most of all listened (and keeps listening), thank you. To the lovely Ali Cardia, my editor-soul mate: You are a wonder—you really are. Every day I'm more impressed with your poise and intelligence and how you just get it. I can't believe how lucky I am to have found myself working with you. Thank you. Thank you, too, Emma

Acknowledgments

Straub and Julie Klam and Meg Wolitzer, who enlightened me early on as to the many and substantial merits of my publisher, Riverhead, where special thanks are due to Elizabeth Hohenadel, Glory Plata, Megan Lynch, Geoffrey Kloske, Jynne Dilling Martin, Margaret Delaney, Lydia Hirt, and Mary Stone. To all of you at Riverhead Books, I can't believe how lucky I am to have found myself a member of your publishing family.

There are a host of friends who offered thoughts on early versions of the book. One of them, Paige Clancy, read it more than once, offering keen insights and sensitive, considered edits each time. So much love to you, always, my dearest BFF. Sara Barron, Kathleen Baxter, Abby Gardner, Sarah Griffin, Drew Magary, Wendy Mc-Clure, Maureen O'Connor, Lizzie O'Leary, Francesca Stabile, Courtney Sullivan, and Jeff Wilser: Your readings, comments, and support have been invaluable and are deeply appreciated. The intrepid trio of Jennifer Perry, Courtney Perry, and Tamal Mannan listened to chapters read aloud into the wee hours of the night and offered critiques and wine (T., you're an asshole, but I love you!). Over the months I spent working on this book, there have been many others who have read snippets, sometimes in bars on my iPhone. I thank all of them. I realize this party trick may have grown old.

Nick Greene, you are my one-man Gchat support system; drinks are on me. Joe Coscarelli, will I ever forget what you told me about rhetorical questions? Katie Drummond, you were right about opening the document. Spike Friedman, Caitlin Sullivan, Kirsten Magen, Camille Dodero, Richard Lawson, Philip Bump, Maris Kreizman, Michele Filgate, Jason Diamond (and Vol.1 Brooklyn), Jessanne

Acknowledgments

Collins, Jami Attenberg, Laura McMurchie, Myles Tanzer, Esther Zuckerman, and, oh, so many others who've bestowed upon me friendship and kindnesses great and small . . . thank you for being you. I'd also like to extend my appreciation to Gabriel Snyder, Kate Julian, Nicole Allan, and *The Atlantic*, and to the folks at the many media organizations that have kept me in a close relationship with words throughout the years. (Extra-special love goes to The Hairpin, where an essay containing seeds for this book first appeared . . . <3 you, Edith and Emma!). To Alexandra Shelley and the Jane Street Workshop: You were there in the beginning, I haven't forgotten. Stephanie Coontz, I'm honored you took time out of your busy schedule to discuss your excellent research on marriage with me. Maureen Corrigan and Beth Kephart, consider me ever grateful for your wisdom and kindness—you are both such inspirations.

There are many friends, and a few exes and former friends, who appear in this book in some form or fashion. To them: Please know that I have tried to treat you all with fairness, and that no matter the state of our relationship today, I have cared for you deeply and wish for you the best.

Brad and Scarlett, your just-the-way-it-works-for-you partnership is beautiful, and Mom and Dad, thank you for telling me I could be whatever I wanted to be, but never making me feel I had to be anything different from what I am. I love you.

JEN DOLL has written for *The Atlantic, The Atlantic Wire, Cosmopolitan, The Hairpin, Mental Floss, New York* magazine, *The New York Times Book Review, The Toast, Vice, The Village Voice,* and other publications. She has attended dozens of weddings and had pretty much every possible feeling about them. She lives in Brooklyn.